The LAST WORDS
of ROWAN DU PREEZ

The **LAST WORDS** of **ROWAN DU PREEZ**

SIMONE HAYSOM

JONATHAN BALL PUBLISHERS
JOHANNESBURG & CAPE TOWN

Some material from this book was published as the chapter "The Life and Death of Rowan du Preez" in the anthology Safe House: Explorations in Creative Nonfiction, *edited by Ellah Wakatama Allfrey, 2016, Toronto: Dundurn Press.*

Originally published in South Africa in 2018 by
JONATHAN BALL PUBLISHERS
A division of Media24 (Pty) Ltd
PO Box 33977
Jeppestown
2043

ISBN 9781868428687
ebook ISBN 9781868428694

Every effort has been made to trace the copyright holders and to obtain their permission for the use of copyrighted material. The publishers apologise for any errors or omissions and would be grateful to be notified of any corrections that should be incorporated in future editions of this book.

Twitter: www.twitter.com/JonathanBallPub
Facebook: www.facebook.com/JonathanBallPublishers
Blog: http://jonathanball.bookslive.co.za/

Cover by publicide
Design and typesetting by Martine Barker
Set in Baskerville/Optima

Printed by **novus print**, a Novus Holdings company

CONTENTS

Author's note

This book concerns a trial which ran for over nine months and generated almost 5 000 pages of transcript. In order to make the events recorded here more intelligible to readers I have edited dialogue for concision and sense. I have sometimes substituted a proper name for 'this witness' or 'Accused No X', for the sake of clarity. I have omitted the repetition, tautology, and redundant phrases which inevitable crop up in spoken speech, as well as some M'Lords and other nods to protocol, where these impeded understanding. I have also translated testimony from Afrikaans into English, and also relied on the translators' versions of any Xhosa testimony.

In regard to the changing of names, I must also mention that Kock was once Von Sitters, her maiden name. Likewise, Wilhelm was once Heyns. They are referred to by their previous names in their statements and other documentation from that time, and in court proceedings were referred to by both names. This was confusing within the trial and in the interests of clarity for the reader I have changed all instances to their married names, at times altering reported speech in order to do so. The same homogenisation has taken place for Blue Downs/Mfuleni station.

The spelling has not been corrected in quoted affidavits, WhatsApps, SMSes or diary entries.

CAST OF CHARACTERS

The Peter-Mbadus

Angy Peter (Accused 1)
Isaac Mbadu (Accused 2)
Their children, in order of age:
   Reitumetsi (aka Thumi) Peter
   Ntobokeng (aka Boontjies) Peter
   Hope Bokamoso Mbadu
   Tukelo Alexander Mbadu

The other accused

Azola Dayimani (Accused 3)
Christopher Dina (Accused 4)

The Ndevus

John Ndevu, Rowan's grandfather
Desiree Jack, Rowan's aunt
Veronica Ndevu, Rowan's aunt
Nathaniel Ndevu, Rowan's younger brother

Rowan's friends

Ntsikelo (aka Rara) Dlabantu
Asavela Zici
Roger
Simphiwe 'Caras' Mdedi and Abongile 'Cheese' Khabiqueya, co-accused in Rowan's armed-robbery case

Other Bardale residents

Nomawethu Mbewu, neighbour
Malwandi Yentu, son of the crèche owner
Ta Topz

Vuyisile, the owner of the Pink House

Police officers

Captain Lorraine Kock, officer at Blue Downs Police Station

Constable Raul Vince Barnardo, officer at Blue Downs Police Station

Constable Chandré Nadia Wilhelm, officer at Kleinvlei Police Station

Lieutenant-Colonel Riaan Redelinghuys, Head of Detectives at Blue Downs Police Station

Constable Stanley Muthien, the investigating officer, Blue Downs Police Station

Sergeant Lesley Freeman, arresting officer, Blue Downs Police Station

Captain Tchangani, officer at Blue Downs Police Station

Colonel Luyanda Damoyi, Station Commander at Blue Downs Police Station

Captain Jonker and Captain Coetzee, senior officers at Blue Downs Police Station

Anele (aka Andile) Patrick Tshicila, aka Ta Ager, Crime Intelligence officer

Riah Phiyega, SAPS National Commissioner

Lieutenant-General Arno Lamoer, SAPS Western Cape Provincial Commissioner

Lawyers

Judge Robert Henney

Advocate Phistus Palesa, National Prosecuting Authority

Attorney Joshua Greeff and Advocate William King, representing Accused 1 and 2

Advocate Israel Ndlovu, representing Accused 3 and 4

Medical witnesses

Mohammed Abdullah, paramedic

Andrew Swarts, ambulance driver

Martha Pieterse, ambulance assistant

Dr Jessica Bernon, ER doctor

Dr Izelle Moller, pathologist

Expert witnesses

Dr Elmin Steyn, trauma medicine expert

Dr David Klatzow, pyroforensic expert

Dr Estie Meyer, ear, nose and throat (ENT) specialist

Social Justice Coalition / Treatment Action Campaign:

Mandla Majola, co-founder of the TAC and SJC

Abdurrazack 'Zackie' Achmat, co-founder TAC and SJC

Phumeza Mlungwana, General Secretary of the SJC 2013–2017

Gavin Silber, Deputy General Secretary of the SJC 2010–2013

Dustin Kramer, Deputy General Secretary of the SJC 2013– 2017

Joel Bregman, Head of Policy, Communication and Research until 2016

Liat Davis, former SJC staff member, and friend to Angy Peter

Pollsmoor Prison

Phumeza, Portia, Ncumisa: Angy's cellmates

Gerald, Kuwela, Bong, the Brick Gang: Isaac's cellmates

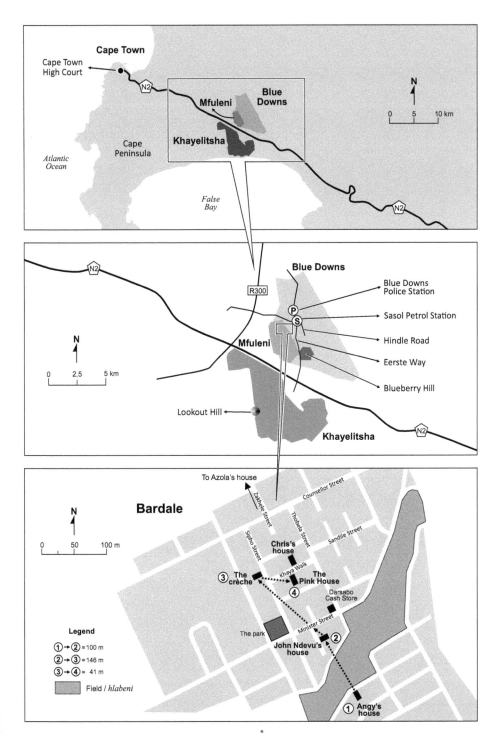

Important locations in Bardale, Mfuleni, Khayelitsha and Cape Town

Only crime and the criminal, it is true, confront us with the perplexity of radical evil; but only the hypocrite is really rotten to the core.

— Hannah Arendt

Prologue

In the middle of an October night in 2012, alongside a road that ran through bush on the outskirts of Mfuleni township on the Cape Flats, a 22-year-old albino man called Rowan du Preez lay on the sand with his face to the sky, naked, burnt, and crying out for help. The remains of a tyre smouldered nearby, the only light in the dark verge of the dunes. He was eventually found by two police officers from Blue Downs station.

Some 18 months later these police officers gave testimony in the Cape Town High Court about that night.

'We then stopped the vehicle, M'Lord,' Constable Raul Barnardo said, 'as we heard screaming coming from the bushes outside.' He and his colleague Captain Lorraine Kock left their police car and walked in the direction of the man's screams. They found an 'unknown albino male' who was 'completely naked and severely burnt'. Barnardo also noted bruises on his body, and dark burn marks around his groin and on his feet. 'What's your name?' he asked.

'The victim replied to me wildly that "My name…" that "I am Rowan du Preez".'

He then gave Barnardo his address.

'M'Lord, then I asked the victim what has happened to him. The victim replied to me saying: "I was taken from my house by Angy and her husband, who stays nearby me."' Rowan told him that 'Angy and her husband' had thrown him into a white Toyota

Quantum. "'They drove me to Blueberry Hill. They then assaulted me and they put a tyre and tube around my body. They then set it alight and then they left me.'"

I had been introduced to Angy Peter's story a few months before. While intrigued, I was unsure of the wisdom of trying to make sense of it. In the months leading up to the trial, Angy told me she had little idea what argument the state was intending to prosecute.

It was only when I first heard Raoul Barnardo tell this story that I knew that I had to write about the death of Rowan du Preez, and the trial of Angy Peter. When Barnardo took the stand, I realised what it meant for three police officers to testify, and, if Angy was telling the truth, each tell a blatant, elaborate lie.

PART ONE: DISCOVERY

Chapter One

If there was one reason, above all others, that made it hard to believe Angy Peter, it was that I could not reconcile all the ways the world reacted to her. Full-figured and short, with a face that was heart-shaped and apple-cheeked, she was most famous for her sharp tongue. Upset, she looked at the world imperiously from high cheekbones; relaxed, she would often break into a low, laid-back chuckle. Angy was not short for 'Angela', was never spelled with an 'ie', and scanned on a page it easily read 'Angry'. Often I would be asked, 'How's that Angry Peter story coming along?' Or, 'So did that Angry woman go to jail?' She was self-possessed until the moment she lost her temper, understood morality in black and white, and believed this was a good thing. Some people soon looked up to her, and others instantly disliked her. The people she was most likely to rile – and do not doubt the reaction was immediately mutual – are those we call 'figures of authority'.

Friends – colleagues, comrades – recounted how she had once won a month's free gym membership in a weightlifting competition, had started a crèche when she saw how the women in her neighbourhood struggled for childcare, and adopted abandoned children and raised them as her own. Her husband would tell you they could never be on time. On the streets of their neighbourhood Angy couldn't take more than a few steps without someone greeting her, waylaying her with jokes or parrying a jibe. He would tell you people were always knocking on their door, in the hope that she could help.

But then there were other neighbours who said they wouldn't put it past her to commit a crime. She was a stubborn person. She wouldn't 'mind your face' to tell you what she thought. She was a *wayene nkani*, reckless with words, like someone straight out of Pollsmoor Prison. And when it came to Rowan du Preez – well, she'd held a snake in her lap, and it had bitten her, and then she'd become angry.

I met Angy in December 2013. It was four months before her trial would start, and three before the commission of inquiry into policing in Khayelitsha began, a commission she had been closely involved in instigating. It was the hottest month of a hot and dry summer. I was living in Johannesburg but I had come down to visit my family for Christmas and tagged on an interview with Angy while I was in Cape Town. I took the N2 to Khayelitsha and, not having driven that route in many years, I was constantly checking my phone to make sure I had not missed the Spine Road turn-off; I seemed to have travelled so far.

Rowan du Preez, the man she was accused of murdering, had known her well. Over two years he had regularly joined activist meetings that Angy and Isaac, her husband, held in their own home. They had become, in the parlance of Cape Town's activist NGOs, comrades. But in 2012 they had fallen out badly, and in view of the whole neighbourhood. Then, on a Sunday morning in October, Angy Peter and Isaac Mbadu were arrested in the adjacent township of Khayelitsha for Rowan's kidnapping, assault and murder. The state would claim at the bail hearing that they had gone to Khayelitsha to flee justice after committing an act of vengeance. In turn, Angy Peter's not-guilty plea stated, 'Killing or hurting [Rowan] was the last thing I wanted. The very real probability exists that the charges against me have been fabricated by policemen.'

I was looking for a story to tell, a stitch that gathered all the dilemmas, contradictions and conflicts of my society together – which

I could then unpick, and neatly explain. Angy and I had a mutual friend who had introduced us. They were once comrades, and a few weeks earlier he'd said to me: 'I just came back from Cape Town and the craziest things have been happening to a friend of mine.'

Angy had been involved in activist work that took the rise of vigilante attacks in the townships of Cape Town as the symptom of systemic problems with the justice system, problems which could, her organisation argued, be addressed. Then she was accused of committing a vigilante murder herself, and arrested and charged by the same system she was trying to reform.

At the safe house where Angy and Isaac were living, I felt embarrassed when Angy answered the door. She was made up with rouged cheeks as if, reasonably, expecting me to have brought a photographer. But I was not yet sure I even wanted to write about her case. I was wary about wading into something where the lead characters were activists, where the pull to exonerate 'the good guys' would be strong.

During that interview, Angy and I talked mostly about her activist work. It was obviously what she was most proud of, and, she argued, what had led to her arrest. We sat on a cracked pink leatherette sofa, while Angy's infant son, Alex, crawled around our feet and over her lap. On the TV display case were photographs of her three daughters. Angy's phone rang several times. 'It's the mother of a thug,' she explained. Angy had been taken off the criminal justice work by her NGO, but these mothers still had her number and called her when their sons were in trouble. She used the word 'thug' as if it were a neutral term, the way you'd say someone had brown eyes or green.

When it got to Rowan's murder she could tell me little about the case against her. I pressed. She looked at me confused, almost hurt. She wasn't involved. Her body language said, How would I know exactly what had happened to him?

Yet she said that at her bail hearing the state had mentioned something about eyewitnesses to the assault, and some kind of statement

5

that Rowan himself had made. A few months later, in the gallery at Angy's trial, it soon became clear this wasn't a case where a conviction might turn on a detail remembered falsely, or a false identification of someone who looked vaguely similar to the true culprit, or the biased interpretation of forensic evidence. This was a case where both sides were accusing the other of wholescale fabrication. Someone was lying. In fact, in either scenario, several people were lying but it was not clear who, or what their motives could be.

Almost everyone I talked to about the case found one side instantly believable. In lefty, liberal circles people hardly bothered to hear the details before declaring that Angy had surely been framed. But anyone who'd worked with the police or the courts, or who lived in places where vigilante violence was rife, didn't blink at the thought she was guilty. 'All my clients say they're innocent,' said one advocate who specialised in criminal law. 'And how would the police even have done it?'

She was clearly guilty, she was clearly innocent. A mother of four had committed a brutal murder for the sake of a television set; an innocent woman had been framed by the police because she had campaigned for better policing. The paradox of these two certainties entrapped me, soon obsessed me, and I spent years trying to arrive at the same state of conviction.

Chapter Two

Mfuleni was a township of about 50 000 people laid out on the east bank of the Kuils River. To get there you drove some 25 kilometres from the centre of Cape Town, took the turn-off for Blue Downs, drove past razor wire discarded in vast twirls by the side of the road and a river overgrown by reeds. You swept past an electricity substation and turned in by a line of blue gums, swaying and scattering husky leaves. It was the very periphery of the city, where you were somewhere between the furious highway and the quiet slopes of vineyards. A wrong turn might take you through wild dunes along perfect roads glittering with shards of glass, then down potholed tracks beside hundreds of shacks, until you popped up suddenly, staring at newly-built townhouses and a billboard declaring, 'You can be a homeowner too!' It was a scrambled place, a land in disarray.

For most of the 20th century, Mfuleni was a small settlement isolated by distance from both Cape Town and the town of Somerset West. It grew in bursts when people were evicted and exiled by forced removals, or when political violence displaced people in other townships. At the advent of democracy it was a model apartheid town, complete with workers' hostels and a beerhall, and home to a small population of mostly Afrikaans-speaking black families. These families watched a steady stream of poor rural migrants arrive in Mfuleni, creating vast informal settlements in the area. Much of the township was built in the late 1990s and early 2000s when the city's new democratic government slowly bulldozed sand dunes, and shuffled shacks into vast serviced agglomerations called 'extensions'. When I started researching Angy's story, Mfuleni was one of the city's most contested and divided townships, and one of its fastest densifying areas[1].

Bardale was one of the last neighbourhoods of Mfuleni to be laid out by the city, which distributed small serviced plots there in 2010. They serviced each resident's patch of land with piped water, an outside toilet and sink, and brought in electricity in low-hanging wires, like geometric webs above the neighbourhood. But they did not build houses. These were built by their owners with plywood, cardboard and zinc.

Most of Bardale's first residents had been squatters living in informal settlements in Khayelitsha or the Strand. They were prioritised in their bid for public housing because they had been evicted to make way for a power plant, or to reclaim a buffer area near the railway line, or because of some man-made or natural disaster. The settlements they moved from were fluid communities marked mostly by the precariousness of anyone's life in the city. In the middle of Bardale was a sandy field, which was referred to as the *hlabeni*, meaning simply earth or ground. In the minds of the residents this ground marked a division between the people from the Strand and the people from Khayelitsha. And on a bad day this might mean a division between an honest person and a dishonest one, a selfish person and a generous one. If you stepped out of the shacks where Rowan du Preez lived in 2012 you could peer through a gap between the houses at the end of the cul-de-sac and see, across that field, Angy Peter's and Isaac Mbadu's house.

❖ ❖ ❖

Angy and Isaac were not living together when they moved to Mfuleni. They had been staying in different informal settlements in Khayelitsha that were demolished for infrastructure projects and the inhabitants were compensated with sites in Mfuleni.

Isaac was drinking at a shebeen near his shack in Phase One on the first night they ran into each other in their new township. He recognised Angy from Khayelitsha. She'd stayed in the shack behind a friend of his in RR Section, and they'd struck up a friendship in the course of his visits. His friend had been impressed. 'She's not really easy to get along with,' she'd said about Angy, surprised that Isaac was able to banter with her difficult neighbour.

That night in Mfuleni, Isaac invited Angy to join him for a drink but she declined. She wasn't there to socialise, she told him, but rather to root out underage drinkers, a regular activity of hers. If she found one, she would pour the person's drink into the street, while giving the tavern management an earful. Isaac quipped that he hadn't seen any teenagers there that night and tried to steer the conversation to more personal topics but Angy wasn't interested in sticking around. She said goodbye and disappeared into the night.

In many ways, Isaac was the opposite of Angy: a man who moved through life with a warmth that did not draw attention to itself, seemingly always patient in conversation, and generous in his judgements of others. Even Rowan's grandfather, asked, in court, for his first memory of Isaac, recalled that he spoke politely. Such was the impression of manners Isaac left in his wake. Isaac usually wore the regular guy's unofficial uniform of chino shorts and polo shirts, and with his broad build and shaven head, looked youthful and approachable. To me he admitted that Angy was nothing like the women he'd dated before he met her, who were far less independent.

The couple's backgrounds, however, had striking similarities, even though they grew up hundreds of kilometres apart. Both had fathers who were miners. Isaac's father had left the mines before Isaac was born and moved to Cape Town. On his father's ankle was a single scar, like an acid burn, the only testament to the time he had spent 'down there'. Isaac's mother was a housewife. Angy's father, Tlokotse Peter, spent his life working for Anglo Gold in the Western Deep Number 11 shaft near Carletonville. Her mother, Matseleng, was a policewoman. Both sets of parents were deeply religious: Isaac's Jehovah's Witnesses, and Angy's Catholic. Neither Angy nor Isaac shared the faith.

In fact, Angy's earliest memories were of arguing with her father about Christianity. Their church infuriated her. She couldn't understand why the leadership was all male, even though women made up most of the congregants. Nor why God and Jesus had to be male, or why Jesus's disciples were all male. In her eyes, Jesus had taken all the credit for being the son of God, and Mary too little for delivering and raising him. She wanted to know why God was a man and was told by her father that such questions would get her punished.

Both families forbade their children from taking part in political protests. Isaac's first memory was of crawling into his father's bed to whisper to him news of the outside world, on days when protests shut down the roads from Khayelitsha and his father couldn't get to the construction sites where he worked. Tlokotse Peter's family lived in Khutsong, and in Khutsong in the 1980s and early 1990s political protest was daily bread. Marches passed in the street outside Angy's house – a stream of people toyi-toying, advancing to the rhythm of protest songs, caught up in a unitary purpose. Without even knowing what the march was about, she'd felt compelled to join them. 'You cannot participate in illegal things!' her parents told her, ostensibly because it was 'un-Christian' to do so, but also because Matseleng worked for the police.

During those years Khayelitsha was also wracked with protests, marches, and boycotts. Isaac, several years Angy's junior, was a young child yet he, too, had been caught up in the energy and excitement of a protest march. This took him clear across Khayelitsha, until he ended up lost in the dark. A stranger helped him find his way back. Returning home late he thought it wiser to tell his parents that he'd been picked up by a man asking for directions who had then inexplicably refused to let him out of his car, yet who had just as suddenly released him. Any excuse – even a kidnapping – was better than admitting he'd been on a march. Like Angy's, his parents believed that Christians shouldn't be involved in 'worldly things' as such activity led you away from God.[2]

When Isaac approached Angy at the shebeen that night, she'd seemed unimpressed, but he thought there was something interesting about her and, undeterred, began to visit her regularly. His first attempt at asking her out ended in disaster. She told him she was not interested and he should never mention it again. For weeks, ashamed, he avoided her, then plucked up the courage to make a second attempt. Isaac knew if it backfired, there would be no recovery. This time, she accepted. 'I don't know if you are stupid or brave,' she told him. 'And I'm not promising anything. But we can try it.'

Angy was six years older than Isaac, the mother to several children, and HIV positive. She had received the diagnosis in the back room of a pharmacy in the basement concourse of the Golden Acre shopping centre, after submitting a blood sample because she thought she might be anaemic. The first doctor she saw informed her she was also pregnant, and that the child might be born with HIV, in which case it would die, painfully, in infancy or adolescence. She was told her only option was an abortion. At the time, the South African government had embargoed antiretroviral medications believing them to be ineffective and toxic. Luckily, another doctor was able to get Angy into a study for a drug which was supposed to prevent mother-to-child transmission of HIV. Thumi, Angy's second-eldest daughter, fathered by Steve, was born HIV negative. (Later, Angy left Steve because he had a drinking problem.)

When Isaac and Angy's relationship became more serious they

went together to a clinic to have a sexual health test. Angy was adamant that she had already told Isaac that she was HIV positive but she couldn't get him to believe her. Isaac was equally adamant that at their visit to the clinic Angy reacted as if she were finding out for the first time. When I told Isaac that Angy claimed he knew already and had definitely known her status for years before they began dating, he said, 'Well, maybe that was her way of telling me.'

After the test results came back – Isaac's negative, Angy's positive – they both said that the mood between them was sombre. They both agreed that Isaac took a long nap when they got home, and then Angy went to bed early. He slept late the next morning and when he awoke Angy said to him, 'You can go now, this isn't serious yet. You can still walk away.'

And Isaac said, 'No, that isn't what I want to do.'

Soon Isaac moved in with Angy and became the stepfather to her three daughters, and for a time, to Boipi and Lulu, two young girls who Angy had taken in and who were later reunited with their families. They all lived in Angy's home, on the site she'd been awarded at Bardale, next to the sandy field. On weekend evenings shebeens in the neighbourhood blasted house music, and on Sundays shacks in the nearby informal settlement shook and rattled with the noise of ardent worship. On Mondays those with jobs walked down to the Mfuleni taxi rank. There Toyota Quantums jostled for spots next to women rotating glistening meat on coals. When the minibuses were full, they headed at speed towards Table Mountain.

Throughout 2010 Isaac boarded a run-down Golden Arrow bus in the early hours of the morning and trundled to the Bellville Mall to start his shift at Mr Price. The commuters from Mfuleni used the bus ride to gossip, to compare the fortunes of their soccer teams, and to complain about that albino boy, the one who'd taken their handbags or broken into their shack. And that was how Isaac first heard about Rowan du Preez.

Chapter Three

All the public traces that Rowan du Preez left in the world were bureaucratic, official, and disturbing. Ten arrests and three successful prosecutions in his 22 years, including a spell at a youth reformatory. Documents in which he was sometimes known as Simphiwe Ndevu, sometimes simply as Roy, though he was most commonly called Rowan. There was one picture of him in print, taken at an odd angle at a distance and out of focus. He was carrying a backpack and wore a zip-up jacket and a white bucket hat. He was either scowling or straining to hear what a companion was saying.

According to Rowan's aunt, Veronica,[3] when he was born, on 28 January 1989, his mother was dismayed to find that her baby was albino. She wanted to leave him behind at the hospital, but her sister wouldn't let her. In Cape Town's townships albinos were sometimes called, colloquially and without affection, *ingawu* – monkeys. Some people believed their condition was the manifestation of a curse. During her pregnancy with Rowan, Yolanda had lived in Site C in Khayelitsha, next door to an albino woman whom she was always teasing. Much later the family would say: that's the reason you had one.

Veronica never knew who Rowan's father was, and no matter how often she asked, Yolanda would always deflect the question. Throughout his childhood Rowan too tried to get his mother to tell him. She never did. Du Preez was the name of the husband she had left before her pregnancy with Rowan. At times, frustrated with

Rowan's questions, Yolanda would point at her own father, John Ndevu, and say to the boy, 'That man cares for you, he looks after you, feeds you. He's your father.'

When Rowan was a child, the family would be told by neighbours, again and again, that he did 'silly' things on the street. The family dismissed this as the normal behaviour of an energetic boy. The first time they knew he stole was after his mother's boyfriend left her. He had been the family breadwinner and had provided for her children's needs. Deprived of this income, Rowan took an armful of his mother's clothes, sold them, and bought himself a new outfit.

Veronica tells a story about when John Ndevu ran into a neighbour, the father of another albino boy, at the local spaza shop. The neighbour took John aside and said, 'How is your boy doing? Because mine, he's *stout* [naughty], he's up to all kinds of mischief.'

'Mine too,' Rowan's grandfather replied. 'He's up to nonsense.' The man's comment reassured John Ndevu that Rowan's behaviour was just a characteristic of albino boys.

Right from when Rowan was a child, John Ndevu couldn't tolerate anyone beating the boy. Rowan's skin was pale, almost translucent, and his grandfather imagined it was stretched thin, too delicate to protect the child within.[4]

❖ ❖ ❖

John Ndevu moved to Cape Town in the 1950s. Born in the Eastern Cape in the mid-1930s and educated up to Grade 7, he was a young man, perhaps even a teenager, when he left his rural Xhosa village to find work in the city or on its peri-urban farms. He returned to his rural home a handful of times and in 1960 married a woman, probably called Adelaide[5], with whom he had three children, including Veronica. He left again when they were still young children. Veronica next saw him when she was 18, at the time of her own marriage. At some point in that absence, Ndevu had taken a second wife, a coloured woman whose name may have been Sylvia. He formed a new family in Cape Town, with two daughters, Desiree and Yolanda, and a son, Alistair.

When John Ndevu moved to Cape Town, black workers were treated as a necessary evil by the Union government[6]. Their labour and movement needed to be tightly controlled, and they were not allowed to feel rooted in any city. Later, under apartheid, black men had to carry a *dompas*, their passport to urban areas, where their presence was tied to formal employment. Their families were forbidden to join them. As such, this was not only a labour policy and an anti-urbanisation policy but also a policy of forced family breakdown.

What would this have meant for John Ndevu? For one thing, it meant that for most of his adulthood many of the fundamental aspects of his life were illegal and that all the places where he lived were dysfunctional. For a black man to move to Cape Town without an offer of employment, and so official sanction, was illegal, as was any job he did without a pass. Loving a woman of a different race was a transgression against the country's colour bar laws. Finally, to make matters worse, they lived together. In the 1950s and 1960s, the Group Areas Act had gradually divided the city into racial zones and made it illegal to reside outside of your racially designated area. Mannenberg, where John Ndevu lived with his wife, was scheduled as a coloured-only neighbourhood.

Living in Mannenberg meant having to pass as coloured, which Veronica says meant her father changed his name. Perhaps he took a month – September, January, October – as a surname as these were common among coloureds. These names had been given to their ancestors by white settlers who didn't understand or care what their slaves' and workers' real Malaysian, Indonesian, Madagascan, Khoi, or San names were. Jonny September – with a complexion on the pale side and the Afrikaans he learned at the workplace – he could have passed with that.

Then, at some point in the 1980s, when John Ndevu couldn't cope or wouldn't put up with his wife's drinking problem, he left her and returned to his old name, and a black neighbourhood, Site B, in the middle of Khayelitsha. He took his three children with him, and he raised them alone, trying to provide stability.

Through the 1980s Khayelitsha bore the brunt of apartheid's endgame chaos. People filed in, fleeing violence from state-supported vigilantes who attacked the youth and anti-apartheid activists in the townships of Crossroads and Nyanga[7]. At a moment's notice, four-wheel-drive mine-resistant vehicles would pour out riot police. Strikers and protesters would close off the exit routes if the police didn't do it first.

John and (his first wife) Adelaide's children, now adults, made the same journey he had from the Eastern Cape. Like him they struggled to find stable employment and were shunted from one township to another. He introduced them to his children by Sylvia, and encouraged them to see themselves as one family.

❖ ❖ ❖

And that family included the 'nonsense' boy with the thin skin. In his teenage years, Rowan was twice suspended from high school, and finally expelled. The first suspension was for stealing from other children; the second, for stabbing an ex-girlfriend with a ball-point pen. At the age of 14 he was expelled for slashing the tyres on the school principal's car in retaliation against a teacher who had told his class about the girlfriend-stabbing incident. Rowan's criminal record showed that at 15 he was arrested for theft and sent to reform school.

After his release from reform school, things deteriorated. His mother, recently promoted as the manager at a Zebros fast food out-let in Bellville, died suddenly of food poisoning. At 16 – before or after this, I don't know – he was charged with the rape of a teenage girl, for which he was later given a suspended sentence of five years. Rowan's criminal record noted that he went by two nicknames, though really they were one, given to him by other boys in Mannen-berg: White/Nigger. This was inlaid on his skin, probably through makeshift methods, along with two other tattoos: a $, possibly gang insignia, and the name of his mother, Yolanda.

Veronica was seemingly the only member of the Ndevu family to experience good fortune at that time. In 2010, she was awarded a plot in Bardale, Mfuleni. Independent, no longer married, working as a domestic for a white family in Somerset West, and now com-manding a precious resource, a title deed, she was in a position to invite her father to live with her, along with the two orphaned boys now under his ward, her nephews, Rowan and Nathaniel.

They found that Mfuleni was like the other townships they'd lived in. Few people had jobs, groups of laughing children played on every street, and so that they might do so in safety, residents hacked deep troughs into the roads to slow down any cars. Mfuleni was a place where young men were idle, and everyone knew where the meth houses were.

❖ ❖ ❖

When Angy Peter first saw Rowan du Preez, he was pinned face down on the bare *hlabeni* outside her house, and men from the neigh-bourhood were kicking him. She told them to stop. In turn, they told her to get lost. 'What did he do to you?' she said. 'Let the police handle it.'

Rowan, about 20 years old then, was pressed against the ground that had often been the site of public spectacles. It was a place that might have been reserved by the authorities for some well-intentioned purpose: a playground or a school. But Bardale was only two years old and the government hadn't yet built any houses, let alone community amenities. So the field went untended. Low-hung sedans and minibus taxis began to cut across it. In winter cars got stuck in the soft, wet sand and men gathered to lay down planks and push. Here community meetings were rabble-roused by loudspeaker; here boys kicked a ball in summer and, more and more often, here criminals were beaten.

The men who kicked Rowan were convinced that he had broken into one of their homes. Their possessions were still missing, which meant the beating would continue.

If they didn't stop, Angy warned them, she'd call the police and the authorities might be more interested in the assault than the theft. One of the men turned to her and shouted: *'Impimpi!'* This was one of the worst insults. Formerly reserved for apartheid collaborators, it now denoted a spy, a snitch, a traitor.

Angy left to alert the 'satellite' police station, which consisted of two bored constables in a radio kiosk next to the taxi rank. This was the only way within walking distance to reach the police.

When she returned to the field she found that the police hadn't responded but that the small mob had dispersed. While she had been away Rowan's grandfather had arrived. And John Ndevu, a short man with bright eyes, had offered to pay the men for the goods they had lost. And so, once again, they'd handed him back his grandson.

Chapter Four

At the age of 17, Angy said her family went through a traumatic period, and she became listless and withdrawn. She dropped out of her final year at high school, and inhabited a quiet fury. Her father heard about a naval training programme at the Waterfront in Cape Town and suggested she apply. Angy wouldn't know anyone in Cape Town, but she liked the idea of being a female pioneer in a boys' club. As her mother's choice was that she train to be a nurse or a nun, Angy found the idea of being a sailor far more attractive. When her father located a place for her to stay with friends of his in Sea Point, she was off.

Angy took to the training well, but before she had finished her first year, Tlokotse had a stroke and died. Unable to pay the fees herself, Angy had to quit the course. She managed to hang onto her foothold in the city centre by working at the V&A Waterfront as a bar lady on a ship that was permanently docked near the Robben Island ferry terminal. But without financial support from her father she couldn't maintain her rent and had to look for cheaper accommodation. And that was how she came to Khayelitsha.

Also some 25 kilometres from the city centre, Khayelitsha sprawled on the other side of the N2 from Mfuleni. It was only slightly bigger than Mfuleni but eight times as densely populated. From the highway it spread towards the ocean, thrumming with people on any given day, loud with music and arguments, a place of poor roads and bad driving.

Steve, her first serious boyfriend, lived near the initial shack she rented, and soon they moved in together and became parents to two girls, Thumi and Ntobokeng. The relationship lasted until his unruly drunken behaviour got them thrown out by their Khayelitsha landlord, and then by the next one in Nyanga. In 2007, she left Steve to find somewhere to live with her children. Her family had grown and now included another daughter, Hope, and Boipi and Lulu, who she had adopted.

Khayelitsha was expanding through the piecemeal occupation of unused land: sometimes this took the form of premeditated overnight operations, sometimes it was shack-by-shack. Around the country the government was calling such bids 'invasions' and the poor were hanging on, in the face of fierce eviction units, by sheer numbers and persistence. Friends encouraged her to take part in the occupations, but Angy felt uneasy about the illegality, and waited until she could buy a shack in RR Section, an older, more established neighbourhood. This decision proved to be fateful.

In RR, Angy got involved in community meetings and, given her ability to speak her mind, was elected chairperson of the street committee. One of the other committee members was also involved in the local branch of the Treatment Action Campaign (TAC), a social movement advocating access to medication and health care for HIV-positive people. She convinced Angy to join the TAC. Angy hadn't heard of the NGO before, but when she walked into their meeting she found a group of people openly discussing their HIV status and it thrilled her.

At first she was just a TAC branch member and an unpaid volunteer. Because she left home early in the morning and returned late at night from her bar job, she had to arrange her day off to coincide with branch meetings. Not having free time wasn't something that bothered her. She focused on her kids and her job, and did not have or want friends. Other people felt like a waste of time; they were superficial, pleasure-seeking, and had an annoying propensity to tell her she was stubborn and difficult. That was not something Angy enjoyed being told, and so she kept her distance.

Soon she was asked to work for the TAC on a more permanent basis, and she agreed. Throughout her teenage years and her young adulthood she'd been at odds with her schools, her family, her community, her bosses. Most of her battles involved fierce and sometimes dirty fights against anything she perceived as sexist or destructive to her community. In high school, she had spread rumours that vindictive nuns were pregnant, and as an adult, she scared away the clientele from shebeens that served teenagers. The consequences had ranged from beatings to school expulsion to social isolation. Now, for the first time, Angy felt she'd found a place where she belonged, a place where she had allies in her fights with the system. Her energies were directed at a common aim, and their techniques were more effective.

The TAC at its height was a powerful model for a type of activism based on the membership of poor and working-class people, guided by the country's constitution, and committed to research, evidence, and educating the movement and their communities. At the height of the AIDS epidemic, it had successfully campaigned for and coerced the South African government into rolling out antiretrovirals — the drugs that prevented all of Angy's children from contracting HIV and kept her from developing AIDS. They also took multinational drug corporations to court in an ambitious legal gambit to get drug prices lowered.

In its weekly branch meetings and its grassroots campaigning, the TAC was also a democratic and empowering body. Women bore the greatest burden of the epidemic as they were more susceptible to HIV infection, and were on the front-line of the care of people suffering from AIDS. And in the TAC, women became leaders and decision makers too, and this, especially, endeared the organisation to Angy. She described the person she was before she joined the TAC as 'tense and tough'. She 'took no nonsense' from anyone, anger brimmed inside her and she would vent it at anyone – a stranger, her boss, a colleague. The word she used for how her job at the TAC made her feel was 'relief'. Life felt easier.

❖ ❖ ❖

Working for the TAC was a tall man with a deep voice called Mandla Majola, who quickly saw potential in Angy Peter. He'd grown up in a two-bedroom matchbook house in the old Cape Town township of Gugulethu. His mother worked as a cleaner in a clothing factory and his father was a municipal street cleaner. Mandla had gravitated towards the TAC after a short stint in local politics and became one of its foremost leaders. When he and Angy worked together, he appreciated her dedication, hard work and talent for mobilising. He decided to recruit her for the Social Justice Coalition (SJC) where he was also actively involved.

This organisation came about in reaction to the xenophobic riots that swept the country between May and August 2008. In those four months, in hundreds of wildcat incidents, migrants from African countries were attacked and their stores and homes looted. Sixty people were murdered in the course of the violence, and 50 000 migrants and refugees fled their homes and settled in temporary refuges within the country.[8] Several of the founders of the SJC were TAC veterans, like Mandla Majola. They soon established a membership base in the townships which could give the organisation its direction. To this end, Mandla recruited Angy to help him establish SJC branches.

The SJC, according to another founding member, Gilad Isaacs, began with a broad premise, 'that people's lives were precarious, and how do you address that?' Through discussions with the membership, a number of campaigns gradually took form, one of which had policing at its heart.

To start building evidence for this campaign, the SJC began collecting affidavits from the residents of Khayelitsha about their experiences with the police. The majority of these were sought out and taken down by Angy Peter. To collect them, she traipsed to the far corners of the township, following leads to the informal settlements which abutted railways, ran up sand dunes and spilled into the ocean.

Affidavit from NN

I am an adult woman living in Khayelitsha. In July 2012, I was at my cousin's brother's house, where he sells alcohol. He was so drunk that he was unconscious, so I was selling the alcohol on his behalf. At about 3 o'clock in the afternoon, the police arrived looking for my cousin's brother. Soon they discovered him, still unconscious, in another room in the house. It was the same room in which we keep the proceeds of the sale of the beer, and my cell phone was charging.

After the police had left, I found out that the cash and the cell phone were both missing. Suspecting that it was the police who stole the items, we took down the registration number of the police car. But I do not have the registration number of the police car anymore. The same day when I went to report the matter to the police, I was told that I could not lay a complaint. The policeman on duty said that because we had not ourselves witnessed the theft, they could not help us.

❖ ❖ ❖

When Angy and Isaac met he was working for Mr Price, doing stock inventories at one of their retail outlets. The job was boring, providing activity only in bursts, interspersed with long hours when nothing had been delivered or needed recording. In between deliveries Isaac amused himself by walking the floor in his uniform, responding to shoppers who asked him for advice with a quick, 'I don't work here'. Angy introduced him to the world of activism, and he began to spend his days off at SJC protests and pickets.

In 2011, he quit his retail job to care for his mother, who was dying of diabetes. After her funeral, he looked for work again, and Mandla Majola tried to recruit him to the SJC. At first Isaac brushed him off. The position Mandla was offering was a volunteer role, with the possibility of a paid job if funding allowed. Angy had been the sole breadwinner while he cared for his mother, and Isaac was eager to earn a salary again. 'I don't mind spending time here, doing whatever it is that needs to be done, you know,' he told Mandla, 'but as soon as something out there comes up, I'm going to take it, you know. I'm not going to be here with the SJC forever.'

Isaac found an opening at the airport and began training to work as a security guard. But his conversation with Mandla nagged at him and he gave up the security position to try things out at the SJC, where he soon became salaried. The income was a little less than he'd earned at the airport, but for a change it was a job he enjoyed. The fulfilment he derived from the work was important to Isaac because his new role at the SJC was hardly the picture of glamour – he worked on the sanitation campaign.

After the xenophobic riots, the SJC's research and consultation had led them to put an unexpected issue at the top of their agenda in 2009: toilets. Though the majority of the informal settlements in the township were older than a decade, porta-loos and other chemical toilets, which had been installed as 'temporary' measures, were still in use. In some places a hundred homes shared one toilet. Because flush toilets received no maintenance, and porta-loos only sporadic cleaning, throughout Khayelitsha communal toilets were in such deep disrepair that they were often unusable. As a result people walked into the bushes at night to relieve themselves and were often mugged, murdered or raped. More permanent structures were similarly neglected and poorly lit, making them prime locations for brutal crimes.

Isaac worked on the independent monitoring of a janitorial service for all the city's informal settlements. It was a job that involved repeated trips to toilets around the township trying to get residents to report on the quality of maintenance, and the cleaners to share details of their employment. He would leave his house in the morning and not know how long his work day would be. Frequently it ran into the late hours of the evening, and he could still be called back to work out-of-hours at a moment's notice. But he found meaning in the work and no longer watched the clock.

❖ ❖ ❖

Affidavit from SM

I am a 19-year-old woman living in Site C, Khayelitsha. I work as a volunteer at the Social Justice Coalition.

Having grown up in Khayelitsha I have witnessed so many crimes, I have lost count. In August 2012, I was a witness to extreme police brutality. Hearing shouting out on the road outside my house, I went outside to see the police beating one of my neighbours, who they believed to be a member of a gang. There were six policemen who arrived in three vans. They dragged him out of his house, punching and kicking him. Then they dragged his pregnant girlfriend out of the house. She was entirely naked and they were punching and kicking her, too. Eventually they took both of them away.

❖ ❖ ❖

The SJC's other major campaign had slowly coalesced around the quality of policing in Khayelitsha, as well as the dysfunction in the broader criminal justice system. This was not just a straightforward interpretation of what it meant to address 'safety' in a township. To a large degree, it drew on the personal experiences of activists in the organisations who had lost colleagues through horrific crimes during their time in the TAC. The first was Lorna Mfolana, a 21-year-old single mother. In December 2003, after the TAC end-of-year party, she'd gone to a tavern in Khayelitsha, where a group of five men had gang-raped her in a nearby toilet. The SJC believed she was killed because after the rape she had told her attackers that she was HIV positive. In a rage they had kicked her to death. When her body was taken to hospital, medical staff did not do a sexual assault test because her injuries were so severe they assumed she had been run over by a truck.

Eventually, two men were convicted of Lorna's murder, despite huge problems with the evidence collection on the scene, and numerous court postponements. Mandla Majola, who was closely involved with the trial of Lorna Mfolana's killers, and had supported Lorna's family during this time, said about the experience: 'The failure of the SAPS or the prosecution to inform the victim's family [about events in the case] caused great consternation and contributed to a loss of faith in the criminal justice system and, particularly, the police. Personally, I was shattered and came to believe from the experience of Lorna Mfolana's case that the system is broken. Every postponement led to disappointment for [Lorna's] family, friends, and comrades ... and added to the tension of the family and friends of the accused. Delays, loss of evidence, failure to conduct proper forensic investigations including timeously photographing of the crime scene, all led to frustration and anger.'[9]

Then there was Nandipha Makeke's murder, which came only a week after Mfolana's killers were convicted. Nandipha Makeke had joined the TAC at the age of 12, and was made a branch leader in 2005, at the age of only 18. That December she too was raped and murdered, her body dumped in a toilet.

In Nandipha Makeke's case, after two years on the court roll and more than 17 postponements, two men were sentenced to 20 years in prison, but the other two were acquitted due to lack of evidence, among other problems.[10] Throughout these trials the TAC were a constant presence in court, listening to proceedings or picketing and singing on the court steps. They led march after march through Khayelitsha to demand justice and attention, not only for the murders of Lorna and Nandipha, but for the rape and abuse of other women and children. Mandla communicated with the families of the victims; the police, largely, did not. It was the TAC who badgered the police for updates on the investigations or to find out why and when suspects might be released on bail.

Angy had been present when the TAC protested on the court steps and in her JSC role was put in charge of mobilising people for court attendance. Increasingly, she was assigned to work on criminal justice issues. She attended community policing forum meetings, justice cluster meetings at the Khayelitsha court, and submitted complaints for discussion at police cluster meetings. When residents came to the SJC with cases the police refused to open, it was Angy who accompanied them to the station and refused to leave until they had a docket number. When women complained that they had seen the man arrested for their rape back on the streets, Angy found out if he had been released on bail and if he was in violation of the terms.

In SJC meetings the activists strategised about how to make these disparate activities translate into a change in the justice system. After years of marches and complaints to various authorities they had seen murderers convicted, thanks in part to their sustained pressure on the police and courts, but they had made no systemic changes. Each time they had to go through the whole process all over again. Zackie Achmat, who was one of the founders of the TAC and the SJC, recalled that in each incident the only anti-crime protest messages they encountered were the death-penalty voice[11] ('and it was loud') or the shoot-to-kill voice[12]. 'That was essentially the only message on safety,' said Achmat, 'so clearly we had to change strategy.'[13]

Out of these discussions came a decision to petition the premier of the province to hold a commission of inquiry, which would force open access to information, and leverage change at a national level. They drew together evidence – including Lorna Mfolana's and Nandipha Makeke's cases – into a complaint which was submitted along with those of five other organisations[14] to the premier of the Western Cape in November 2011.

As they waited for a response, they continued to collect evidence that could be used in the prospective commission. Angy was made the head of a Criminal Justice Task Team, the focal point for the commission, and together with another colleague, stepped up the SJC's work collecting affidavits from Khayelitsha residents.

❖ ❖ ❖

Affidavit from SZ[15]

I am an adult male resident of Green Point, Khayelitsha. My mother was a domestic worker and the breadwinner in our family. In 2002 my mother left Cape Town to return to the Eastern Cape, her traditional home where she married a man who is not my father. I have five siblings and I am the second oldest.

I never met my father. I grew up in Khayelitsha, playing soccer in the bushes. In the summer we would go to the beach on Baden Powell Drive. I was aware of small crimes. The first time I saw serious crime was during 2005–2007 when people in the community burnt criminals because of theft. On one occasion a man was burnt to death when people poured burnt plastic over him. If I can remember correctly the police just watched.

As children we weren't safe because we had to share toilets in the informal settlement and people had to go to the bushes to relieve themselves. Our house only had two rooms, and at night the women used buckets to relieve themselves in the room. The men had to go outside.

Someone who is not a black person cannot understand how painful this is.

No one walked to school alone because there would be a 100% chance that the gangs would take you down. If they came to rob us and we were in a group, we could run in different directions and the gangsters would not be able to catch all of us.

I never saw either the Metro police or SAPS patrolling.

We never felt completely safe. My personal experience of the police and the courts as a resident of Khayelitsha shows that one cannot get justice from them.

❖ ❖ ❖

Liat Davis, a lawyer and researcher from Sea Point, worked with Angy in the early days of the SJC, and got to witness her mobilising abilities at first hand, both through her interactions with colleagues on campaigns, and at public events. 'People don't want to fuck up when Angy's around,' said Liat. 'Her passion for the campaign feeds into people.' Liat had seen an aimless, bored crowd, impatient for a free meal, suddenly whip to attention when Angy began to talk. Her attitude was 'very honest. It's very raw. It's like: "This is who I am and fuck anyone who cares. I'm willing to campaign until I die on this issue."' Liat admitted that she was 'enamoured, enthralled really'. But others worked more uneasily with Angy, who developed a reputation for having a temper.

Gavin Silber, who was the Research Coordinator and Deputy General Secretary at the SJC from 2010 until 2013, recalled how Angy did not like to be managed. Gavin was adamant that Angy was 'an incredible asset', who was 'in many ways responsible for building the SJC', but also 'passionate to the point of being incredibly head-strong'. Her way of working brought to the fore all the tensions the organisation felt between reacting to crises in the lives of its members and engaging in long-term campaign work.

29

'Because you are a membership organisation you'll have someone come into your office and say my daughter was raped or someone was murdered in a toilet,' recounted Gavin. One of Angy's strengths was her ability to react immediately in such cases. 'She would take them to the clinic if they were raped, or she would go to the police station and get a docket opened. If there was xenophobic violence or a vigilante incident, she would set up a meeting within a matter of hours and talk people down.' Angy sometimes stayed with victims in hospitals or waited out a stand-off with a stonewalling police officer until the early hours of the morning.

While Gavin said it was difficult, if not impossible, not reacting to these incidents, their campaign work required continuity and focused attention. Often Angy's colleagues at the SJC would only hear about her interventions later, and many considered that a liability. 'An organisation like the SJC prides itself on making consensus,' said Gavin. 'With even the smallest decisions, we wanted to always follow protocol.' And helping individuals navigate the criminal justice system was time-intensive, sapping resources from the campaign work. As her colleagues watched her flout protocol and take on cases without consultation, her behaviour became divisive. When her managers defended her, other activists felt she benefited from special treatment. And the work fed her anger, and her anger drove her work. In conflict she could scream and shout, and there were complaints from other team members about her temper. By 2012 she had been given several warnings by her superiors.

For Gavin Silber, Angy's difficulties stemmed from the relentless traumas she encountered. 'I have the luxury of driving home and going to my apartment in the city. I can disconnect from what is happening in Khayelitsha.' Gavin, like the other white, middle-class activists in the organisation, lived in suburbs where crime rates were low and social dysfunction hidden. 'But the majority of activists can't escape. You become the go-to person in the neighbourhood.' Back in

Bardale, Angy was never off-duty, and rape victims and relatives of the murdered came right to her front door. 'I think it was genuinely something she struggled with,' said Gavin. 'I don't live in a suburb where I see a 6-year-old child raped and left for dead. I don't know, if I did, if I would be able to say, "Okay, we have to slow down and follow a set of long-term processes about this."'

Angy's anger was not dissimilar to the anger that drove the violence the organisation had been set up to tackle.

Gavin admitted, 'I struggle to see how other people in that situation don't let that anger overcome them. You're exposed every day to an unimaginable level of very traumatic incidents among your family, your friends, and your colleagues.' No one in these neighbourhoods can entirely avoid this trauma, but for activists it was amplified. 'Your job is to gravitate towards crises,' said Gavin, 'not to walk away from them.'

Chapter Five

Rowan's grandfather was retired and probably received a state pension of, at most, R1 200 per month in 2012, and a child support grant of R270 for Nathaniel's upbringing. Desiree, who often helped John Ndevu with cooking and cleaning, had a part-time job and still lived, as far as I could ascertain, in Mannenberg. A family primarily living off one or two welfare grants was not unusual in Mfuleni, though it would not have been easy for them to get by on some R1 400 a month.

No one ever mentioned Rowan, educated only up to Grade 8, having a job. In Mfuleni he had soon developed close friendships with a group of boys, many of them also known to be drop-outs and drug users. These boys explained to me that they would do 'piece jobs' for their neighbours, small tasks involving manual labour, and they would *skarrel*, which meant doing any odd thing to survive – collecting scrap, selling things by the road, asking people for cash or occasionally mugging them to get it. They were not quite a gang, but a group of skollies, in which Rowan stood out. Among them was Rara, his best friend, and Roger. Both were slight and feline. Keeping the group company at local shebeens were girls who at different times were their girlfriends. One was a tall and long-necked teenager called Asavela.

With the move to Bardale, Ndevu's protectiveness continued. If Rowan stole, his grandfather let it be known that the injured party should come to him first and he would find a way to resolve matters.

The problem, Veronica came to understand at around this time, was that once you got a reputation for being *stout*, it didn't matter what you actually did or didn't do, people always came for you. Whenever anything went missing, it was always Rowan who was dragged out of his grandfather's yard to account for it.

In turn John Ndevu would always try to stand between Rowan and punishment. 'His grandfather loved him too much,' said Nomawethu Mbewu, one of their neighbours. 'He couldn't be hard with that boy. He would pay any money to save him.' Nomawethu believed Rowan was victimised for being an albino, and that, to make matters worse, he was motherless. He couldn't draw on a woman's tirade to shift the blame and quell the crowd, when they came for him. '*Mamela* [listen],' Nomawethu said to some of Rowan's old friends in my hearing, 'who of you has a mother? And I won't beat you if your mother is standing behind you, né? But an old man? What can he do?' The boys looked at the ground. 'I want to be clear every time these boys did wrong,' said Nomawethu, 'it was always Roy [Rowan] who was being beaten up by the community.'

❖ ❖ ❖

Angy's and Isaac's activist work didn't stop when they left the SJC offices in Khayelitsha; it continued in their own home. Each week two different meetings would take place in their three-room shack. In reaction to seeing how many teenage girls in Bardale dropped out of school, fell pregnant, or had alcohol-abuse problems, Angy started a 'girl's reading club' called 'The Seven Bs' (Books Before Boys, Because Boys Bring Babies). They would discuss national political issues that had been on the TV news and the adult women would teach the younger ones about how 'female persons can be independent, hygienic, respectful towards their parents, and deal with peer pressure'. With Isaac's support, she had also set up a SJC branch in Mfuleni, and this too met in their lounge.

Angy and Isaac didn't own expensive furniture or flashy goods, except for a flat-screen television. At these meetings, their guests crammed onto and around their worn sofas. If the household smacked of success it was because it had the rare structured calm of a home with two parents, both of them in full-time employment. They were also owners of the land the shack sat on, and landlords to the woman next door – in short, a couple who was able to send their three little girls to schools outside the township. And if those meetings were exceptional, it was because their visitors were told that social movements of people just like them – poor, badly educated, without obvious prospect – had changed the world.

Angy had found her recruits in the neighbourhood. Asavela, the tall girl in Rowan's circle of friends with the large, bright, lemur-like eyes, was one of Angy's first conscripts to The Seven Bs, and in turn she recruited the delinquent girls she drank with. For the SJC, Angy had recruited some of the idling young men she ran into on the streets.

When the SJC started in 2009 it had fewer than 15 members, including its founders. By early 2011 it had around 1 500, with most of the 15 branches in Khayelitsha. Theirs was the only one in Mfuleni, and it numbered about 15 people. A favourite topic of discussion in Angy's and Isaac's living room was how to grow the branch in size and influence. Once the TAC had just been a bunch of hopefuls, now it was a force that demanded attention. With the locus of its power in Khayelitsha, no other civic organisation in the Cape townships could mobilise people the way it could – and people, no less, armed with knowledge about what made a good public health system and the conviction that they were entitled to it. The motley collection of teenagers and adults in Angy's lounge wanted to do the same thing for public safety across the whole of Mfuleni.

In 2011 Rowan had entered the fold. He'd shown up at Angy's

house several months after the incident on the field, and told her he'd been wondering what his friends did at her meetings. A few of them had already joined the SJC at Angy's bidding, and Rowan probably had more of an idea than he let on.

They talked about his life, and Angy told me this later seemed to her like a fateful conversation.

He told her about Yolanda's death, his childhood, the times he'd spent in jail. 'I turned out the way I did,' Angy said he told her, 'because the community would never accept me.'

'That's an excuse,' she replied, adding that there were many albinos who were accepted by their communities, but that his actions conditioned people's responses to him.

She said she was nonetheless moved by his predicament. Angy also detected an intelligence behind Rowan's tough-guy act and because he'd spent so much time in court rooms and in prison cells, he knew the law backwards. And he was a natural leader: if he changed, might not the other tsotsis change too?

If he wanted to join, she told him, he'd have to live clean. She got annoyed when he said he didn't have a choice. 'Crime is not like tik [the street name for crystal methamphetamine],' she said, 'you can change.'

Angy would later explain in court, 'He then told me that he wanted to change,' and in response she told him that she believed he could change because he was still young. Rowan was accepted into the Bardale branch of the SJC.

As part of his rehabilitation, Angy took him to workshops on gender-based violence because he was, in her words, a 'violent person' who admitted he saw women 'not as human beings'. The workshops covered basic concepts such as what rape is and why it is wrong, and what effect it has on the victim. Angy met with him one-on-one every week, to monitor his path to honest living.

Not everyone was happy about Rowan joining the branch.

Some of the younger members told Angy they thought the SJC was supposed to be about supporting the fight against crime, not supporting criminals themselves. She told them to reserve their judgement.

Desiree Jack, when asked in court what she thought of the SJC, said she didn't know much about what Rowan's role was in all that 'anti-crime business', but she thought if it helped young people figure out their lives it must be a good thing. Even though she didn't live in Bardale she knew Angy through community activism. 'Sometimes, when I was off work and I went there to help my father with the housework, then there were people with loudspeakers, holding their meetings. But I wouldn't stay still to listen to what the meetings were about. I didn't take notice of her and that SJC thing of hers.' John Ndevu understood the SJC to be, approvingly, a programme that taught children 'how to carry themselves'.

Rara didn't join the SJC but he observed his best friend's excitement when Rowan told him he'd been elected chairperson – a position he shared with Isaac. Rowan was elated that he'd been chosen, in other words, to be the responsible one.

❖ ❖ ❖

Nomawethu Mbewu, a sometime member of the Bardale Street Committee, believed that Rowan loved being part of the SJC, and it had meant the world to his friends who were likewise involved.

She emphasised that she was not in Angy's corner, per se. '*Mamela*, you see me and Angy: we are not friends. We were never friends. She pushed her mission and I pushed mine. We respect each other, that's the thing.' But in her view Angy and Rowan suffered from the same problem: they were both 'outshining'. In Angy's case because she was 'a very outspoken person, a very straightforward person'. In a meeting she would say anything. She wasn't afraid of how you'd take it, she followed her guts. She didn't mind if someone came from a poor family. She would escort people to court. She was one of those people who stood up for everyone. In Rowan's case, because he was albino, but also friendly, even sweet, in some indefinable way.

In 2012 Bardale had two community resources: a primary school, and a multipurpose community hall, where the ward councillor had his office, an enterprising bodybuilder rented out use of his gym equipment, and elderly women did exercise classes. Angy and Nomawethu both told me a story about this hall, that when it was being built in 2010, the community caught wind of a theft: the construction company's generator had gone missing, and word went out that one Masonwabe was responsible. So people from Bardale found him, and they began to beat him on the field. 'And when the people here *moer* [beat] you,' Nomawethu said, 'they really *moer* you.'

Nomawethu said they might have beaten him to death except Angy called the police, who threw Masonwabe in their van and took him away. 'And the community was angry with her for that,' she said. This wasn't the first time Angy had done something like that, Nomawethu said, recalling Angy's intervention when Rowan was beaten.

There was an instance where a Bardale teacher, Ta Topz, approached either Angy or Nomawethu for help. Both women told me the story independently and both women claimed that the teacher came alone and secretly to her. Ta Topz was the recipient of the generator Masonwabe had stolen and he was terrified that people would find out and turn on him too.

Either Angy or Nomawethu or, more likely, some coalition of neighbourhood problem-solvers, helped Ta Topz. They returned the generator to the construction site and told the company that they'd had an anonymous tip-off.

❖ ❖ ❖

Rowan's role in the SJC did not appear to put him on the straight and narrow. By the end of Veronica Ndevu's second year in Bardale, Rowan had been caught being *stout* far too many times, she said. Her neighbours told her they wouldn't chase her away, because they knew her, she'd been in Bardale since the beginning. But Rowan, he had to go.

John Ndevu sent Rowan to stay with someone in nearby Delft, but within three weeks he was back in Veronica's house.

'Hayibo, Rowan,' she said. 'Why are you here?'

'Because I called him to come back,' said John Ndevu, laughing.

Veronica received no peace from the neighbours. The moment she was on the street, someone brought up the topic of Rowan. Her father was adamant, 'Rowan is here to stay'. Did he approve of what Rowan was doing, she wondered?

Veronica heard that Rowan had been arrested for the robbery of a Somalian store. When the police had questioned the store owner he'd picked up a piece of fruit from his counter and said, 'Like this. One of the robbers looked like this'. That evidence alone was enough to convince the police that Rowan was the culprit. In despair Veronica said to Rowan, 'Why do you rob when you're so identifiable? No other thieves here are the colour of a peach.'

She panicked, called her brother and told him she was thinking of selling her house. She made her arrangements: the house was sold, and she left for the Eastern Cape.

❖ ❖ ❖

Because of her activism, Angy had a dozen senior policemen's personal cell-phone numbers, and only used them to complain.

She told me that in about February 2012 Rowan called her from a police cell. He'd been arrested with two others for the robbery and murder of a Somalian spaza-shop owner in Thembalethu township in George, a town on the Garden Route. The Somalian man was Llyaasi Mohamed. Rowan had most likely been the junior partner in an outfit that included Simphiwe 'Caras' Mdedi and Abongile 'Cheese' Khabiqueya. Ostensibly on a criminal rampage, with the help of two others, they had earlier hijacked a Ford Bantam in Atlantis (near Cape Town) and then driven to George, not only robbing and killing Mohamed but also shooting his friend in the thigh before grabbing airtime vouchers and the shop's takings. They then moved on to shoot another Somalian shop owner in the arm in a second robbery that evening. Two days later they were tracked down to a house in the area by SAPS Thembalethu and the George Dog Unit.

Rowan needed Angy's help. He asked her to get him a police detective, but not just any detective – a special kind, that one-in-a-hundred, good kind.

Angy claimed that when she was recruiting Rowan to the SJC, he'd mentioned something to her that later took on greater significance. No one other than Angy was present for that conversation, or the call from the cell, and he was, essentially, the only person who could corroborate it. It had come out in the course of a meandering conversation about Rowan giving up crime. Angy had insisted, as was her wont, that if he wished to, he could quit. 'It's not that simple,' he'd told her. 'There is this powerful man who uses us to commit crimes for him. He gives us the weapons and the information.'

'So?' Angy had said. 'You still have a choice. You always have a choice.'

To which Rowan said, 'You don't understand.'

Rowan explained nothing on the phone, only that he needed to speak to a detective, and one that could actually be trusted. Angy came to reference this call when explaining her actions on the morning her TV went missing. However, just then, she didn't pay it much attention. She was in the midst of collecting testimonies for the commission,

39

and her hands were full. Essentially, she forgot about Rowan's request. When, after a few weeks, she tried to contact him, the number he'd used was disconnected.

❖ ❖ ❖

Throughout 2012, Angy's troubles with the youth of Bardale intensified. First Asavela was expelled from The Seven Bs reading group. The group had drawn up rules, and punishments for disobeying them. There were rules against getting drunk, leaving school, swearing at your parents or staying out until the late hours of the night.

'And most of them focused on their books,' Angy said later. 'Asavela is the only person that took her own direction.'

Asavela had been caught getting drunk. Her friends in The Seven Bs snitched on her. Angy imposed zero tolerance. 'I personally went to the shebeen and spilled her alcohol. And I asked the owner of the shebeen why she allowed minors to drink in that shebeen.' The punishment meted out to the girls was to sweep the streets of Bardale. But Asavela disobeyed that punishment. While The Seven Bs discussed her refusal to comply with their discipline, she disappeared. As far as Angy was concerned, Asavela dropped out of school, which automatically disqualified her from Seven Bs membership.

As for Rowan, he was back in Bardale. His grandfather had paid R1 000 to the bondsman to get him released on bail for the armed-robbery charge, an enormous sum for a poor man. However, Rowan had been expelled from the SJC branch. 'The members of the SJC were quite upset because Rowan did not stop but continued with his acts,' Angy explained in court. Rowan wanted to rejoin the SJC, and Angy instructed him to write a letter to the branch asking for forgiveness and another chance. 'He then wrote this letter of apology,' she recounted, 'but we told him he should not tell us anything about his case because the case was still pending and that we were not the police or the prosecutors, to judge him.' Rowan was accepted back provisionally, but not welcomed. He did not attend branch meetings again.

❖   ❖   ❖

It was raining in the early morning of Saturday 11 August 2012 when Angy and Isaac's TV was stolen. A hard winter rain. Perhaps this was why they didn't hear the break-in. Some people think that robbers use muti, magic concoctions, to induce a deep sleep in their victims. Khayelitsha residents had also told Angy they believed muti helped criminals survive being beaten, which was why they had to be burnt, and why the practice of necklacing – murdering an undesirable by placing a tyre doused in petrol around their neck and setting it alight – was returning to the Cape townships. But Angy had no time for superstition. Rowan had once given her a more pragmatic explanation for the number of times victims would sleep through a robbery. Thieves knew to push smouldering CD disks into cracks in the wall before they robbed a house, he'd said, and the resulting smoke was a supposed sedative.

On the shelves of the TV stand in Angy and Isaac's shack were pictures of their daughters, 6-year-old Hope's face pressed up to her mother, with sisters Thumi and Ntobokeng in matching pink outfits on the lawns of the Company Gardens, the city centre's public park. There was also a framed picture of Isaac as a teenager with two of his high-school hip-hop crew. The family portraits now surrounded a gaping absence, less than a square metre of negative space where their flat-screen plasma had been.

It was 2 am on the Saturday morning and Angy and Isaac were sure of one thing: if Rowan hadn't done it, he would know who had. So Isaac put on something warm and went out into the cold and went to look for Rowan.

PART TWO: ARGUMENT

Chapter Six

This account of the events that followed the theft of the TV was compiled from the testimony in court of Angy Peter and Isaac Mbadu, as well as from that of the state's eyewitnesses – John Ndevu, Asavela Zici, Ntsikelo 'Rara' Dablantu and Desiree Jack. Apart from Angy and Isaac's account of their alibi and of their arrest, the account of events on the weekend of Rowan's murder are compiled only from the State's eyewitnesses' testimony.

Saturday, 11 August 2012
Bardale

Angy and Isaac discovered the theft at about 2 am, probably not long after it had happened. While Isaac went to investigate, Angy stayed behind with the children: she suffered from severe asthma, which was worse now that she was pregnant with her and Isaac's first child. She'd spent a night at the clinic during the week because of an acute attack.

Isaac walked around the streets, hoping to come across someone suspicious. He knocked on the door of another man in the neighbourhood – not a friend this time, but someone known to be 'naughty'.

Isaac half suspected he might have been involved. But when the man opened the door, it was clear to Isaac that he had just woken up. The man was also looking after a small child, his girlfriend's, so Isaac could hardly demand that he help him search for the thief.

Isaac then walked across the dark field to Rowan's house. He knocked. He got no answer.

On his way back to his own house, he saw a parked police patrol van, and finding two police officers inside, tried to report the theft.

'We're busy with something,' one of them said.

'What are you busy with?' Isaac asked. 'You're just parked here doing nothing.'

They told him to return to his house, and he left them his address and telephone number.

He next enlisted a man in his street who owned a motorbike to drive him around Mfuleni but they found no one.

When he got back home, Isaac received a visit from the police. He showed them the evidence of the break-in, and the place where his television set had been. They suggested he open a case, and when he agreed, asked him for the TV serial number.

'What does the serial number have to do with the theft?' Isaac asked. They insisted it was necessary, and refused to open the case without it.

Isaac decided it was useless to have told them about it at all.

Bardale, Rowan's shack

Angy and Isaac said that at daybreak they mounted another search, this time asking their neighbours to help them look for clues. As they went from house to house – asking if people had seen anything, or if their delinquent children might've been involved – the group accumulated and grew.

The group of 'community members' involved in these events was never clearly defined in court, and it fluctuated over the course of the Saturday morning and afternoon. At most times it involved Isaac, John Ndevu, Asavela and someone called Mzinyathi. Ta Topz and

Cindy were also present for some of the time. With Angy and Rowan present, there were usually at least six people in any crowd or group, and perhaps sometimes more than eight.

Between 9 and 10 am, Angy broke away from the search party and went to Rowan's shack, where she found him in bed with his girlfriend.

Rowan reacted as if the theft of the television was news to him. He promised to ask the local skollies if they knew anything about it. Angy, preparing to leave, asked him, 'Are you sure you don't know anything about the whereabouts of my TV?'

Rowan said, 'Sis, Angy, no. I don't know.'

'Are you sure?'

'I'm sure.'

But there was something in his manner which didn't convince her. 'If you don't know anything, can you give me your phone?' Rowan handed it over.

As Angy left Rowan's shack, she came across Cindy, the girlfriend of Ta Topz (the teacher who'd asked Masonwabe to steal the generator), and stopped to talk. Cindy had heard that Angy's TV was missing and she thought Angy should know that last night she and Ta Topz had received a phone call from Rowan wanting to offer Ta Topz a TV.

Angy took out Rowan's phone and opened the call log. At just past 2 am he'd called two numbers, Ta Topz, and a number saved as 'Nonell'.

Angy's temper was up when she phoned Ta Topz. 'Where is my TV, Topz?' she demanded.

The accusation was unwelcome, and Ta Topz flew into a fury. After he'd hung up, he rushed to the fracas that was building in Angy and Isaac's yard.

Angy and Isaac both say that Rowan made his way to their yard himself, without any coercion.

John Ndevu said that on the Saturday morning of 11 August, Angy came by herself to Rowan's shack to ask about the TV. She returned with Isaac 'quite some time' later, but the same morning. (It was unclear from his testimony if this was in fact after the events that would occur in the yard.) He said she had many 'community members' with her, so many that they spilled out of Rowan's door and into the street. John Ndevu said he stood outside Rowan's shack next to the toilet and heard only fragments of the conversation. Rowan was saying, 'that he doesn't know anything about the TV and he again answered and mentioned a police officer in West Bank [a suburb near Mfuleni]'.

Ndevu denied that Rowan went to Angy's yard willingly. Instead he heard someone unidentified say Rowan should be taken to Angy's yard 'so that he can tell the truth'.

Angy and Isaac's yard

It was a short walk between John Ndevu's plot and Angy and Isaac's house, a distance of perhaps 200 metres. Rowan only had to leave his grandfather's property, which was close to the end of a cul de sac, stroll over the pavement, cross a narrow road and then cut diagonally across the field to reach their house.

Their yard was a sandy patch of about two square metres behind a vibracrete wall and a sturdy metal fence. The entrances of both Angy's shack and that of their tenant, Nolubabalo Zongolo, faced onto it.

Angy said that after talking to Cindy, she had questioned another neighbourhood skollie and only then returned to her house. When she got there she found quite a crowd: there was Ta Topz, John Ndevu, Rowan, Isaac, Asavela and some other neighbours. She claimed she didn't stay long. She had had a very heated conversation on the phone beforehand with Ta Topz, one that left her so angry she couldn't look at him without the argument flaring up again. He, too, was furious. She left to avoid a scene and continued tracking down the rest of Rowan's friends. Angy was adamant that she was not present in the yard when events escalated.

Ta Topz, everyone agreed, was a good friend of the Ndevus. Also, according to Isaac, John Ndevu did not intervene in what happened next but instead appeared to support it.

Isaac said Ta Topz sent Asavela to buy a packet of Omo from the Somali spaza store. With the soap powder in hand, Ta Topz grabbed a zinc basin that was lying in the yard, filled it with water, frothed it up, and then repeatedly dunked Rowan's head in the water. On each occasion when he let Rowan up for air, he yelled questions at him about the TV, before dunking him again. Rowan screamed for help and began to cry. According to Isaac, Rowan begged Ta Topz, 'Let me breathe so I can think, so I can tell you where the TV is.'

Isaac said he then confronted Ta Topz. 'The way you are sorting out things, it is not the same way I would have solved it. I don't like it. If this thing is going to go further, into a very serious assault, I want you rather to take Rowan out of my premises. I don't want anything to do with police cases.'

Ta Topz stopped and the group moved back to Rowan's shack, and Angy said she joined them on the way.

Asavela and John Ndevu both admitted that they were also in the yard when Rowan was repeatedly dunked by Ta Topz. They confirmed that the teacher performed the mock-drowning without assistance from anyone else. But they disagreed with Angy and Isaac's account in a few respects. John Ndevu denied egging on the assault and Asavela denied going to buy the soap powder. They both said that, contrary to her evidence, Angy was indeed present.

Asavela also remembered Isaac and Angy participating by beating and slapping Rowan. John Ndevu did not remember this.

49

Rowan's shack: the unexplained assault

Back at Rowan's shack, after the mock-drowning, Asavela, John Ndevu and Angy all recalled separate assaults on Rowan. Asavela and John Ndevu said that Angy was not involved in the (different) assaults that they witnessed.

According to Asavela, Rowan was beaten by 'members of the community' at the gate to his own plot.

Angy's and John Ndevu's accounts were stranger. They both said that at a certain point an unknown man drove up in a Toyota Venture, got out and demanded to see Rowan. According to John Ndevu, this man asked the group, 'Where is the person you said had stolen?' [It was unclear if this character's eerily archaic constructions were reported verbatim by John Ndevu, or if they were a quirk of the translator.]

'Inside,' someone told him.

The man entered the property and grabbed Rowan with one hand. He turned to the group and shouted, 'You called me for a person who is still alive?' and began to hit him repeatedly with a stick.

Angy recounted something similar but said Rowan was beaten with a belt, not a stick.

No one knew who this man was, or how he had found out about the accusations against Rowan, nor did they explain how this scene ended.

Rowan's shack: the phone call

What Angy and Isaac, John Ndevu and Asavela did agree about was that after the mock-drowning, Rowan told the group that he knew where the TV was: he had sold it to a man in West Bank. This man was 'using' him to commit crimes.

Angy said she asked Rowan, 'Which man?'

'Ta Ager,' Rowan replied.

No one present knew who that was.

Next, all witnesses (Isaac, Asavela, Ndevu and Angy) agreed that Rowan was told to call the man in West Bank. They disagreed about when he mentioned Ta Ager, but didn't dispute it happened. The phone was on loudspeaker, and everyone heard the conversation.

Angy said the conversation went something like this: 'Ta Ager,' Rowan said, 'I have something for you that is even better than the TV. Can you please come?'

The man on the other end of the line said yes, but that he was busy. This wasn't good enough for the 'community members' in the shack. There were several more calls to Ta Ager. Rowan ran out of airtime and switched to Angy's phone. Eventually, Ta Ager agreed to meet him, and told Rowan to wait for him at the side of a road which runs between Mfuleni and the New Beginnings flats.

The group in the shack agreed that he would be accompanied on foot by two people. Another group would follow in Ta Topz's car. As there were still people in the group who wanted to be involved, a second car was sent to wait further up the road.

Shortly before 2 pm they set off. John Ndevu told the court he wanted to know more about 'this person who was using his grandson'. He went in the car that followed Isaac and Rowan, who were walking. Asavela waited in the car up the road.

The meeting point near New Beginnings

When they arrived at the meeting point, the witnesses all agreed, Ta Ager was already there, leaning against his car.

Angy said he jumped at the sight of the people following behind Rowan. Quickly he shut his boot, which, in Angy's opinion, had been open as if waiting to receive stolen goods. According to her, he then opened the passenger-side door, pushed Rowan inside, and sped off.

From his seat in the stationary car, John Ndevu also observed this interaction. He concurred with Angy that Ta Ager had the boot open, and that he closed it and opened the passenger-side door when he saw there were people with Rowan. However, John Ndevu said Rowan got into the car willingly.

Ta Topz's followed Ta Ager's car in hot pursuit. Someone in Ta Topz's car called the second car to tell them they appeared to be heading to Blue Downs Police Station and they should meet there. Soon Ta Ager's car swerved into the parking lot at the back of the Blue Downs Police Station. This was reserved for police vehicles and Ta Topz was unable to follow. They did see Ta Ager take Rowan into the building through the police entrance, so they headed for the charge office.

Blue Downs (aka Mfuleni) Police Station

All the witnesses agreed that inside the police station, Angy and Isaac approached the Community Service Centre desk, and the Bardale group (including at least John Ndevu, Asavela, Ta Topz, and Mzin-yathi) hung back a short distance from the granite counter.

Angy said she gave the officer on duty, Tchangani, the short version: that the man who had just walked into the police station was buying stolen goods from a neighbourhood kid, Rowan, and specifically, he'd recently bought their stolen television set.

According to Angy, Tchangani appeared confused. 'I know that person,' he told them. 'He's Andile, and he's a cop.' Tchangani thought that Angy and Isaac had things mixed up. Of Ta Ager, he said, 'He must've just been doing his job.'

'Is his job to use minors to steal TV sets?' Angy asked.

'He was doing his job,' Tchangani replied.

'I'm aware,' Angy said, 'that you're useless. So call the station commander for me instead.'

'I am the station commander,' Tchangani insisted.

'No, you're not,' said Angy. She told him the station commander was Colonel Damoyi.

This didn't improve his mood. 'You know a lot.'

Angy snapped back, 'Because I come to the police station a lot.' Being a resident of Bardale, she told him, she found herself regularly at the police station to deal with issues just like the one that had brought them there that day.

Then Angy had another idea. She called over Fezile Mzinyathi from the Bardale group. 'Call Ta Ager and pretend to be one of Rowan's friends,' she instructed him, in front of Tchangani. She wanted to prove to the policeman that they weren't lying, and that Ta Ager was a criminal.

Mzinyathi made the call with the phone on speaker. By Angy's account the conversation went like this:

'Ta Ager,' he said, 'where is Rowan?'

'He's at the police station,' answered Ta Ager. 'Can you believe that idiot mentioned my name?'

'What about the TV?'

'I still need to check whether it works. If it does, then I'll get the money to Rowan.' Angy thought this precaution was because the rain the previous night might have damaged the set.

Tchangani was unmoved by this exchange. He told her if the TV was the problem, then she should open a case against Rowan.

But Angy didn't want to. She told him the only person she wanted to open a case against was Ta Ager.

'Then you won't get your TV back,' Tchangani told her and strode away from the desk.

Angy then claimed that Tchangani went into the back passages of the station. When he returned he told them that Rowan had confessed to taking the TV and that it was in West Bank. Isaac agreed to open a case against Rowan.

Angy returned to wait with the Bardale group while Isaac filled out a statement. When he had finished, Angy asked him for the case number.

'They told me they'll give it to me later.'

'It doesn't work like that!' she told him in exasperation.

However, even after Angy complained to the policemen on duty they still would not give her the case number. In response, the Bardale group refused to leave until they did so. Tchangani wouldn't budge so they had to wait until the shift changed, and a different police officer came on duty.

John Ndevu and Asavela were too far away from the Communi-ty Service Centre desk to hear the conversation but confirmed the broad outlines of what Angy and Isaac claimed had happened. John Ndevu stated that Tchangani pretended to be the station command-er, that Angy didn't want to open a case and that Isaac did, and that they struggled to get the case number. John Ndevu did not acknowl-edge that Tchangani told Angy and Isaac that Rowan had confessed. When that was said he might have been out of earshot.

John Ndevu said that while Isaac remained at the desk filling out a statement for the case, Angy returned to the group. When John Ndevu asked why she didn't want to open a case, she said, 'This matter with Rowan is a small matter. I will sort it out on my own. And I will sue that police officer.'

Asavela confirmed those words: 'This is a small matter. I will sort it out myself.'

Angy did not say how she would sort it out. And Ndevu didn't know if Angy wanted to sue the police officer working at the Com-munity Service Centre or the police officer who had used Rowan. She didn't explain the comment further.

The shift change at the police station only happened at 5 pm. Then the docket was finally registered on the system. In police terminology this was known as CAS'd, where CAS stood for Crime

Administration System. It contained a summary of the charge and the case known as the 'A1'. It read:

11.08.2012, 14:30: Complainant: Isaac Mbadu.
Suspect: Roy
Crime of scene: The address of complainant being Isaac Mbadu.
Suspect confirms that he was there. Was the one who broke into the house and he can point out where he sells the TV.

Ndevu said he saw Rowan once more before he left the station. 'Dad,' Rowan told him, 'I'm going to be locked up for Angy's case.' They all assumed that Rowan would be held at the police station until he was transferred to the awaiting-trail section at Pollsmoor Prison.

Sunday, 12 August
The field

Because several of their neighbours had been involved in the events at the police station on the Saturday, news of Rowan's theft was included in a Bardale community meeting the next day.

Angy said the meeting was held, by tradition, on the open field between her house and the Ndevus', on the Sunday. Angy was present and contributed her views, but the meeting had been called by an informal committee and was led by others. The people present thrashed out the issues they had with the police. Angy told the story of the theft of her TV and what happened at the police station, but soon the meeting went in a direction she didn't like at all. Soon people began to talk of violent protests and vigilante attacks.

'No one,' she told them, 'no person is going to break the law. Things are going to be done accordingly. No one is going to prevent the police from coming into our community. And you aren't going to go toyi-toying with my name and my story on your lips.'

She had an alternative. 'Damoyi is the station commander and we never got to see him. He doesn't even know these things have happened. We have to make him aware of what's going on first. We'll tell him about police officers who don't work properly and police officers who don't want to open cases.' This was a clear reference to Ta Ager and Tchangani.

That didn't have a universally positive reception either. So the committee leaders put it to a vote. Everyone was told to raise their hands in favour of option A or option B. Option A was going to see Damoyi, to raise these issues directly with him. Option B was burning police patrol vans.

Option A won. They agreed they'd take their petition to Damoyi, and, after struggling to get a meeting date agreed, Damoyi finally accepted their petition on 20 August.

Asavela also gave crucial testimony for the state about this community meeting. In places she agreed with Angy's version: Angy spoke during the meeting; the topics covered by the residents that day were criminals and the police, and the many complaints residents had about both; the meeting was held on the open field between Angy's house and the Ndevus'; this meeting produced a petition – signed by those present – to be delivered to the Blue Downs station.

However, in Asavela's version the meeting was not held on 12 August, but on 8 September, almost a full month later.

According to her version, Angy featured as the star speaker. Angy told the people gathered that her house had been broken into and her TV stolen, and the culprit was Roy. She had called the police but they hadn't arrived, in fact, they'd been very late.

Others chimed in: 'Ja, the police are always late!'

'Or they don't come at all!'

Asavela said Angy had provided a solution: 'If we catch a thief, we should burn them straight away.'

A safe house

Angy said that on the same day as the community meeting some of Rowan's friends called her. They warned her to leave Mfuleni or Ta Ager would kill her. Angy and her family took this threat seriously. The SJC arranged a safe house for them in Athlone.

But Angy didn't give up on her complaint. She wanted Ta Ager arrested, and Tchangani disciplined for refusing to help them. First she called the office of Provincial Commissioner Arno Lamoer, and when she didn't make headway there, she called the Independent Police Investigative Directorate (IPID). This was the police body mandated to investigate complaints against its members. IPID staff were expected to conduct their own investigations into complaints received from the public. A woman who worked for IPID came to the SJC offices to speak to Angy, but she did not take notes when Angy told her the story. In Angy's presence she called the station commander at Blue Downs, Colonel Damoyi, and told him to deal with the complaint. In turn, Damoyi appointed his head of detectives, Lieutenant-Colonel Redelinghuys, to sort out the matter.

The Wednesday after the TV was stolen, 15 August, Angy and Redelinghuys had the first of several meetings, and Redelinghuys began his investigation.

Early August to early October
Bardale

It was either that Sunday or the following Tuesday when John Ndevu returned home to find Rowan in the house.

'How did you get out?' Ndevu asked him.

Rowan replied that the policeman had said he could go.

Rowan was already out on bail for another charge, the armed-robbery case in George. That day Rowan didn't report to the station as per his bail conditions, or the next, or the one after, and so on, right up to Monday 20 August.

So Ndevu said, 'Go and report at the police station.'

He then went with his grandson, and waited outside on Eerste River Way while Rowan filled in the bail book. He waited a long time. Rowan didn't come out because he had been officially arrested for the theft of the TV.

Now Rowan was sent to Pollsmoor Prison, where he remained for six weeks until he was granted bail on Monday 8 October, which his grandfather again paid.

Delft Clinic/Tygerberg Hospital

In early October, Angy was five months pregnant and weighed nearly 100 kilograms. Her asthma flared up again on the night of Monday 8 October, and Isaac called an ambulance. The ambulance took her to a clinic in the township of Delft and she was hooked up to oxygen. The next day she was told to remain there to be seen by a doctor when the new shift started. But she was tired and hungry and wanted to go home, which she did. That night she had another attack. Again an ambulance was called and she was taken back to the clinic at Delft, and in the morning referred to Tygerberg Hospital where she remained for the rest of the day. It was after her return, and four days before Rowan's murder, that Angy heard about Rowan's release on bail. By this time, they had replaced their stolen TV. The week or two after the theft, Isaac had gone to a Cash Converters and replaced it with a similar model. Angy remained determined to get answers about Ta Ager's involvement.

Wednesday 10 October

When Angy found out about Rowan's release she called Blue Downs Police Station. There had been a series of meetings with Lieutenant-Colonel Redelinghuys about the Ta Ager matter and Tchangani's behaviour in the police station. In the process Angy had found out that Ta Ager's real name was Andile Tshicila and that he was an officer in the Crime Intelligence Division. He claimed Rowan du Preez was his informant. He'd gone to Bardale that day expecting to get information and instead found himself rescuing Rowan from a community beating.

But Angy was not satisfied with this explanation, and now Redelinghuys was no longer answering her calls. She went straight to his superior, Station Commander Colonel Damoyi, to get more information. She asked him if Tshicila had been arrested yet. The answer was no, and that the investigation was continuing. Angy wasn't buying this. 'You're giving me empty promises,' she said.

Lieutenant-Colonel Redelinghuys also gave testimony about this, but said that Angy didn't call Damoyi, she called him. During that telephone conversation she complained to Redelinghuys about Rowan's release, and that he was not in jail for stealing her TV.

Thursday 11 October
Rowan's shack

Angy went to Rowan's house after spending the day at the SJC offices. She claimed she made this visit to tell Rowan three things: that she wanted them to continue having their meetings; to apologise to him for the repeated dunking, with the assurance that if she had been in the yard she would have stopped Ta Topz; and to tell him that she hadn't wanted to open a case against him herself.

She was surprised to find Ta Topz and two of Rowan's friends in the small shack. She had to stand just inside the door as there was no space to sit inside. She saw no sign of Rowan's family members, and denied that Desiree Jack could have overheard this interaction.

She asked to speak with Rowan privately.

In response, he said, 'Didn't you open a case against me? You backstabbed me.'

'I'm not after you, Rowan,' Angy replied. 'I'm after Andile [Tshicila] because he used you.'

She heard footsteps behind her, and turned to see John Ndevu approaching.

Rowan got angry. 'You went to the police, so go back, go back to the police!'

'The person I followed to that station was Andile. Not you.' She was raising her voice now. 'I can't speak with you if your behaviour is like this. When you feel less angry, come and see me at my house.'

And with that, Angy left. It was the last time, she claimed, that she saw him alive.

John Ndevu also gave testimony about this incident. He claimed Angy arrived at his house the day after Rowan was released and began shouting, 'Rowan! Where is my TV!'

He replied on Rowan's behalf. 'Madam, did you not open a case? Why now come and shout? Why don't you just wait for the law?'

'Did you see my name on the docket?' said Angy, perhaps in reference to the fact that Isaac had opened the case and not her.

'I don't look at dockets,' said Ndevu.

After that Angy left.

In Desiree's account, she heard the conversation between Rowan and Angy while she hovered at the door. Her version was largely the same as John Ndevu's, but she claimed Angy shouted, 'I'm going to show you a thing or two. I'm not some Somalian that you're used to murdering'.

The weekend of Rowan's murder

Angy and Isaac claimed they were at home with their children on the night Rowan was attacked, and had no knowledge of the incident until they were arrested. This alibi never changed, and neither did their account of what happened after the TV was stolen and Rowan named Ta Ager as his fence.

The following details were compiled from the various testimonies given by John Ndevu, Desiree, Rara and Asavela in court. It was not straightforward putting their testimonies into a unified narrative, but allowing for some contradiction and inconsistency, not impossible either. This was more or less what was accepted as the state's version of events. It differed substantially from the statements that were made in the immediate aftermath of Rowan's murder, and also from another set of statements made before the trial. There was one person who featured frequently, Roger, who was never called to testify, and his actions were narrated by the other witnesses.

Saturday 13 October

Asavela woke up on the morning of Saturday 13 October with a hangover. She was at her aunt's house in Khayelitsha, and started her day by joining a boy she knew at a local tavern for a beer. She wanted to spend the day relaxing, but her friend Aphiwe would not stop calling her, telling her to come back to Mfuleni.

At around 9pm, Asavela gave in and returned to her home in Bardale. There she found out why Aphiwe was so insistent: their local crew were all gathered at the Pink House, an unlicensed shebeen on Khaya Walk in the centre of Bardale, and there was a good party going on. Asavela's mother also told her that Rowan had been looking for her earlier that afternoon, which meant he must have been released from jail. Asavela was excited to see him, but a neighbour, Nosibenzele, acting the disciplinarian, argued that Asavela should stay in that night. So Asavela snuck out of her mother's house in order to join her friends.

When she got to the Pink House everyone was there already. The boys – Roger, Rara, Rowan, Thandolethu and Thobile – and their girlfriends – Aphiwe and Thobela.

The boys were taking turns to play pool while while the girls chatted on the side, drinking quarts of Storm Cider.

According to John Ndevu and Rara's testimony, Roger, Rara and Rowan had spent the afternoon and evening at a traditional ceremony that John Ndevu held at home for 20 of his family and friends. They had gathered in the afternoon and the young men had been given food, some bottles of Castle lager, and two litres of home-brewed *umqombothi*. By 7.30 pm the booze was finished and they had sat around smoking until about 10 pm, when Rowan had asked to go out.

Desiree also recounted this scene, saying that Rowan asked 'Tima,' – their nickname for Ndevu – 'can I go play pool? I'd really like shoot some pool.'

'Rowan, you do like to play at night too much, don't you?' Desiree had cut in. 'Go to sleep, man.'

'Ag, leave him be,' said John Ndevu. 'He's a youngster. Let him go shoot some pool.'

Rara said they had joined the girls at the Pink House, but that Roger's girlfriend was at a different tavern, Maxaba's Place, on the other side of Mfuleni. At some point between about 10 and 11 pm, Roger wanted to see his girlfriend and left with Rara in the direction of the other tavern. Just around the corner from the Pink House, Rara said they passed two taxi drivers, who asked for Rowan. The boys lied to the men, telling them that they hadn't seen him that night, and continued on their way to Maxaba's. In court, these taxi drivers were not mentioned again.

Rara said that when they got to the tavern Roger's girlfriend wasn't there, so they stood around while Roger phoned her. They couldn't have been there long before Thobile burst in to tell them Rowan was being beaten up.

Asavela claimed that she witnessed the fight between Rowan and his attackers break out. After Rowan finished his game of pool, he asked her to come outside with him. In the sandy yard in front of the shebeen, Rowan and Asavela leaned against the concrete wall of the toilet. 'Man,' Asavela asked Rowan, 'where is the TV? Sisi Angy is looking for that TV.' Rowan said nothing. One of them moved the conversation on, and Thobela joined them. Asavela asked about jail. He'd enjoyed his time there, Rowan told her; he didn't even want to leave.

According to Asavela, they then talked about Bardale itself, township life and general matters. Asavela said it was in the midst of this conversation that Azola Dayimani approached and grabbed Rowan by the neck of his shirt, yanking him aside and into the street. 'Where's the TV, boy?' he shouted in Rowan's face.

Things escalated quickly, Asavela said. Chris Dina, who didn't know Azola but lived across the road from the Pink House, saw the confrontation. He too approached, saying, 'What's going on here?'

Rowan broke away and ran up the road, but Chris and Azola caught up with him on the corner of Sipho Street and Khaya Walk. They began to slap him, yanking and grabbing at him. Asavela ran back to the Pink House, where she found Thobile outside. 'Find Roger and Rara,' she told him, 'and tell them what is happening.'

Asavela said she then went back onto the street and looked towards the corner where she saw Angy and Isaac taking a night-time stroll on Sipho Street. Seeing that Chris and Azola were roughing up Rowan, Angy and Isaac also rushed to the scene. Angy began to slap Rowan, who was crying, demanding her TV. Isaac helped, slapping and kicking him too. Trying to get away, Rowan moved towards a nearby crèche, but got pinned against the gate where they continued to slap him. He called out for someone to fetch his grandfather.

Asavela returned to the Pink House and continued drinking. A little later, she went back to the street corner and saw that Isaac, Angy, Chris and Azola were still assaulting Rowan outside the crèche. Back at the Pink House, she asked Roger and Rara to fetch John Ndevu.

According to Rara, after hearing from Asavela about the attack on Rowan, he and Roger went to the crèche. Rara snuck up close to a door on the side of the shack, and peeped in as the door was slightly ajar.

Inside he saw two men he didn't know and 'Boet Isaac'. They were standing still. He couldn't see Rowan. Someone was asking about a television.

John Ndevu said he was woken sometime between 11 pm and midnight by loud knocking on his door. Outside, he found Rara and Roger. They told him Rowan was being beaten by Angy and her husband, Azola and a taxi driver. John Ndevu sent them away.

Rara also said that he and Roger had gone to Ndevu's house and told him Rowan was being beaten, but didn't say by whom. Ndevu had sent them back to get more information. Rara returned to the Pink House where he told Asavela that John Ndevu had refused to leave his house.

'Who took Rowan?' Rara asked her.

'Angy, Isaac, Azola and Chris,' Asavela replied. In his account, Rara stated that this was the first time he knew the names of the attackers.

Rara asked Asavela to return with them to tell Ndevu what she'd seen. Asavela refused. She wanted to continue drinking.

Roger and Rara left again for Ndevu's house. This time they took shortcuts, weaving between plots, and again knocked loudly, using their shoes to beat the walls of the shack.

According to John Ndevu, it was only a few minutes after he'd sent Roger and Rara away that he was woken for the second time to loud knocking on the walls of his shack.

'What?' he screamed out.

'Old man! Open the door! Open the door!' said the voices outside.

Desiree said that, realising the voices sounded familiar, she asked her father, 'What is it, Dad?' He didn't reply. She lay in her bed in the kitchen, stiff and awake. He spoke with the people outside, but she couldn't make out what they were saying. Leaving the callers at the door, John Ndevu went back to his bed, and she called out to him, 'Tima! What's going on? What's going on? Tell me what? What is it?'

John Ndevu said that the boys once again begged him to save Rowan, and this time he agreed. He woke Desiree, and left the shack.

Desiree said her father told her, 'Des, you have to get up, because Angy and her husband and their friends, they're beating Rowan.' Desiree pulled on shoes and followed her father, Roger and Rara.

Outside his shack John Ndevu told Roger and Rara to wait at the corner of the park on Sipho Street for Desiree. He set off down Minister Street to find a friend whose cell phone he could use to call the police. At the corner of Sipho Street he stopped. From there he saw Rowan, about 40 metres away, being beaten outside the crèche by Azola, wielding a golf club. He saw Angy punch Rowan continuously on the shoulder, and Isaac and Chris delivering blows too. Rowan was not fighting or screaming, but cried and struggled to get out of the clutches of his assailants. John Ndevu hurried on to find a phone. When he phoned the police they were blunt: there was more crime that night than there were policemen, and he'd just have to wait for a van.

Asavela said that at some point in the evening she left the Pink House for the fourth time and walked to the corner of Khaya Walk and Sipho Street. There she watched the quartet push Rowan down the road, away from the crèche. After a while she returned to the shebeen.

In Rara's account Asavela was already back at the Pink House dancing, when he and Roger returned from John Ndevu's house. They asked her in which direction Rowan had been taken. In Asavela's account, they met in the road as she walked back to the Pink House.

Asavela said she pointed out to the two young men and John Ndevu, the direction the vigilantes had taken Rowan. They asked her to accompany them but she refused, saying, 'I'm thirsty, and I want another drink.' At about 1 am, a time that couldn't be placed in relation to the assault, Asavela said someone had been stabbed in the Pink House and it had put the owner, Vuyisile, in a foul mood. He'd kicked people out and shut the door, so Asavela had to knock on the door and ask to be let back in.

Desiree said she made her way up Minister Street, and hearing a loud hubbub on her left, turned into Sipho Street to investigate. She stopped next to a pink house near the park. There was a crowd milling around. She continued down Sipho Street towards the voices.

She stopped at the rear of the crowd next to the crèche gate. From there she could see three males and a female in a pink gown inside the yard. She recognised one of the men as Angy's husband. He was holding Rowan down. She said the rest of them were hitting Rowan. Chris had a golf club. As she watched, Rowan broke free and the men chased after him. Isaac caught him again and during their struggle Rowan's sweater was ripped off. Desiree looked to see what Angy would do, but she was too tired to chase him, her pregnant belly obviously weighing her down. Desiree's thoughts at that moment were, 'Oh, jinne! They're going to kill him.'

It was not clear how Rara's and Roger's conversation with Asavela dovetailed into this, but Desiree said after she witnessed the scene at the crèche, she ran towards Minister Street, where she found the two young men. She asked Roger, with whom she could communicate in Afrikaans, 'Where is my father?'

'He's gone to call the police,' Roger said.

'Roger, you stay mos near these people. Won't you please talk with them, ask them only to leave Rowan alone? Please.'

Roger said he would see what he could do.

According to Desiree, the three of them then jogged back to the crèche, but Rowan and the crowd were gone.

Desiree said that she, Roger and Rara then walked in the direction of Zakhele Street. As they turned the corner into Counsellor Street, she saw Rowan running towards them along Zakhele Street, topless, wearing only a pair of black Nike tracksuit pants. He was running for his life, first into Counsellor Street and then towards Thobela

Street. Thobela ran parallel to Sipho, and they both intersected with Minister Street.

Rara thought Rowan must be running towards his home, which was on the cul de sac off Minister. He turned and raced up Sipho Street towards Minister Street, thinking he would join up with Rowan.

Rara said he had watched Rowan turn into Counsellor Street and had run towards him, only to watch him struggle with two men – Chris and Azola – who jumped out of a white Quantum outside Darasabo Cash Store (also referred to as 'the Somalian store'). (Toyota Quantums were ubiquitous in Cape townships at this time as minibus taxis. In court, the words 'taxi', 'minibus', 'Quantum' and 'white Quantum' were used interchangeably.)

Rara did not place Angy and Isaac at this scene. He said he had watched helplessly as the taxi sped off. Only then had Rara noticed Desiree in Minister Street, weeping. He said John Ndevu joined them from another street, asking, 'What's happened? Where's Rowan?'

Desiree claimed she saw a half-naked man run out of Zakhele Street. She thought this was Rowan, as he was bare chested when she last saw him, and so she ran towards him. Rowan turned into Thobela Street and she ran behind him and as she began to catch up, she shouted 'Rowan, run into one of these houses!'

She said Rowan refused, telling her, 'Aunty Des, it won't work, they'll just haul me out full force!'

They ran faster, until a white Toyota Quantum sped past her.

Desiree said two men jumped out of the minibus at the corner of Thobela and Sandile streets. She watched Isaac and Chris grab Rowan, and again Rowan struggled out of their hands and sprinted away, with Isaac and Chris in pursuit. Again Desiree ran behind them towards Minister Street.

Azola was shouting, 'Catch him!' Soon Isaac managed to grab Rowan around the torso and Chris his legs. Rowan struggled, but he was surrounded. Bleeding, exhausted, beaten, he began to flag in front of her, as the white Quantum pulled up outside the Darsabo Cash Store. Isaac and Chris dragged Rowan to the minibus and forced him inside.

Before the Quantum pulled off towards Rotterdam Road, Desiree claimed she saw Angy sitting in the second row of the minibus's benches.

After Rowan was kidnapped, Rara said he and Roger hurried to the satellite police station at the Mfuleni taxi rank, about ten minutes' walk from Bardale. They asked for a police van. The duty officers told them one had already been called by Ndevu. They waited but no van arrived.

Again, they asked the police officers to call a van. Be patient, they were told.

In desperation, Roger and Rara set off on foot for Blue Downs Police Station, a cold 45-minute walk from Bardale. Here they again asked the police to send a van to Mfuleni, and were again told one was on its way. It never arrived.

Desiree said that after the kidnapping, she stood in the road, thinking, 'Did that really just happen?' Afterwards, back at her father's house, she stood in the night air at the basin and washed the tears from her face. She and her father were talking outside when a white Quantum drove past, music blasting from its speakers. Taking out her phone she recorded the registration number: CA860006. The taxi turned at the Darsabo Cash Store and disappeared from sight. Leaving her father, Desiree ran through her neighbour's yard, and stopped at the edge of the field. From there she saw the taxi draw up outside Angy's house, and watched Angy and her husband climb out. (The implication here was that they had just returned from murdering Rowan.) John Ndevu did not mention this in his testimony.

Walking from the police station to John Ndevu's house, Rara said they saw the white Quantum parked outside Angy and Isaac's gate, blaring music. At Ndevu's house they told him what they'd seen.

Asavela said she saw Azola and Chris again at about 1.30 am. She was at the Pink House when they parked on the sidewalk at the tavern, loud music pumping from their white Quantum. Asavela said Azola was in the driver's seat and Chris in the passenger seat, both of them drinking.

Azola said to her, 'You should come with us.'

She didn't reply.

'Don't you want to drink? We could go and enjoy ourselves somewhere.'

'No,' Asavela said, 'I don't want to drink with you.'

After leaving John Ndevu's house, Rara said he and Roger walked passed Zakhele Street and saw the white Quantum parked outside Azola's house, surrounded by empty cider bottles.

Sunday 14 October

That morning, according to Desiree and John Ndevu, they went to the police station to ask about Rowan. No one there knew anything about him. They were taken to a crime scene where John Ndevu struck up a conversation with another policeman. This man told him what had happened to Rowan.

Angy said she was in Khayelitsha collecting testimonies for the commission of inquiry into the police that Sunday, accompanied by Isaac, who was still concerned about her health after her recent asthma attacks. Late in the morning, she received a phone call from a policeman at Blue Downs station saying he needed to see her. She said the call did not alarm her, as she was following several cases and complaints, and was often in contact with policemen from various stations around Khayelitsha and Mfuleni. They agreed on a meeting spot and Angy was there waiting when the police van arrived. Some members of Rowan's family were in the van. Angy and Isaac were arrested. At the station they were told the charge was attempted murder. Later, the charge changed to murder.

John Ndevu and Desiree said that after Angy's arrest, they made statements, and then tried to find out where Rowan was being treated. They went to the Mfuleni taxi rank intending to take a minibus to Tygerberg Hospital. At the rank was an ambulance. Desiree asked the driver if he had heard anything about Rowan's case. She used a local slang word for an albino – a Pink Pop. Based on that information, the driver established that Rowan was in the ICU ward at Groote Schuur Hospital. He was comatose.

John Ndevu and Desiree Jack made their way to the hospital. There they were told Rowan would not survive his injuries. Separately they said their goodbyes.

That evening the hospital informed them that Rowan had passed away.

❖ ❖ ❖

Rowan du Preez was found alive, lying on his back by the side of the road in the desolate undeveloped scrubland outside Mfuleni, where he had been necklaced.

Ten days later Western Cape provincial spokesman Lieutenant-Colonel André Traut signed off a press release – only issued in the case of exceptional crimes – headed: MEMBERS OF THE SOCIAL JUSTICE COALITION.

It is believed that members from the Social Justice Coalition, 32 years old Angy Peter, 26 year old Isaac Mbadu, 25 year old Christopher Dina and 24 year old Azola Dayimani was arrested on 14 October 2012 shortly after a murder case had been lodged at Mfuleni [Blue Downs]...

A postmortem found evidence of an assault involving 'sharp and blunt trauma'. The burn wounds would have obscured most bruising and scratches, but there was a 33-millimetre stab wound in Rowan's right chest wall. There were also two blunt-force marks on his head – each a v-shaped mark – and another stab wound in his back which had not penetrated beyond soft tissue. X-rays revealed no broken bones and no haemorrhaging in the muscles beneath. These wounds were deemed 'non-fatal'.

What had killed Rowan was the burning. The pathologist declared that the entire surface of Rowan's body had been burnt, and there was charring of his genitalia, lower legs, feet and soles of his feet, and his lips and nose. It appeared two tyres had been used, one placed near the ankles, which had been charred badly enough to expose bone, and one around his midriff. However, at the scene only one tyre was found, smouldering, some distance away from his body. There was no explanation for the position of the tyre, except a painful deduction: at some point somebody, probably Rowan, had removed it from his body. It appeared the other tyre had burnt down completely. A subsequent test by an expert witness deduced that these tyres would have been alight for between 12 and 25 minutes, during which Rowan would have had to breathe, and would probably have inhaled fire and hot gas. The temperature of the flame would have been upward of 500 degrees centigrade.

Chapter Seven

It was clear that there was both much agreement and drastic diver-
gence in the stories told by Angy and Isaac, and those told by the
eyewitnesses in the trial and at intervals until Rowan's death about
what happened in the twelve hours after the TV was stolen. Going
over the versions of John Ndevu, Asavela, and Desiree Jack, I was
surprised by how much they corroborated Angy and Isaac's story,
and by how one line of dialogue, or even just its interpretation, could
re-colour a scene.

It was far from straightforward putting these accounts – delivered in court in fragments and bursts – into a coherent narrative.
The witnesses' stories threw up the most inconsistencies when two
of the witnesses crossed paths, and contained timings, movements
and lines of sight that were improbable. Rara said he met Desiree
before she went to the crèche, whereas Desiree's account was different. Timing was also at variance in Desiree's and Asavela's accounts. Asavela claimed to have seen the four vigilantes pushing
Rowan down Sipho Street and away from the scene, before or
roughly at the same time that Desiree said she watched the four
beat him in the yard of the crèche, and then watched him break
away, only to be re-caught. In Rara's account, Asavela was already
back dancing at the Pink House when he and Roger asked her
which direction Rowan had been taken. In her account they met
in the road as she walked back to the shebeen. Rara didn't mention

going to the crèche with Desiree, but did say he sent her in that direction, which Desiree said didn't happen. She didn't first meet the boys at the park, where Ndevu had told them to wait for her, but rather ran to them after first witnessing the assault at the crèche.

Angy's defence advocate also made much of Desiree's claim that she ran with Rowan as he was pursued. The major point here was plausibility, but also that her account was inconsistent with Rara's testimony. In his heads of argument the advocate called it her 'Zola Budd' impression – 'running and keeping up with Rowan who was half her age and running apparently for his life. If she is to be believed she ran 100 metres in the same time it took Rowan to run less than 50 metres. Rara [young, fit and uninjured and unimpeded by a crowd] ran up Sipho Street and according to his account arrived at the corner of Sipho and Minister streets at the same time Rowan arrived at the corner of Minister and Thobela.'

But once I had massaged the eyewitness testimony into chronological order all the incongruence I'd struggled with was easy to forget, and, on the surface of things, the problems with the witnesses' accounts weren't entirely unusual. The human mind tends to focus on the centre of danger – like a weapon – to the point of filtering out all other details. We are bad at estimating the duration of events, and bad at estimating distance. Actions tend to be well-remembered, but other details, like the position of other witnesses, clothing, setting, can fall by the wayside. Even the most accurate accounts can throw up contradictory information, and leave gaps that are unexplained. These are, of course, also the problems with accepting eyewitness evidence. There is a joke that does the rounds among memoir writers, apparently a Russian proverb: *nobody lies like an eyewitness*. Numerous psychological studies have shown how easy it is to change someone's memories (even get them to fabricate memories) by asking them misleading or suggestive questions when they are debriefed.

❖ ❖ ❖

In imagining how each of the stories played out, it was the behaviour of other people that I found most unusual. In the townships – and in much of the media – vigilante attacks were referred to primarily as 'mob justice'. And indeed a large proportion were committed by groups of people, with many individuals delivering the blows that added up to severe injury or death. The psychology of crowds played a large role in whipping up anger, in diminishing responsibility, in providing a spectacle that played a rhetorical role in enforcing community norms. While it was also true that some vigilante attacks were premeditated, took place over extended periods and were organised, these tended to be conducted discreetly. This was because everyone taking part in a vigilante attack was aware that, even if they had the tacit support of their neighbours, they were still breaking the law.

The version of Rowan's attack put forward by the eyewitnesses suited neither strategy well. The attack was done publicly, in a place where Rowan was known and resented as a criminal, but no one other than the four accused took part. And even though Angy and Isaac, at least, were well versed in the possible legal consequences of mob action, they seemingly made no attempt to hide their activities. And the part of the assault which involved real brutality, the kind of brutality associated with mobs, took place on an empty and isolated road, far from the community.

Desiree described the four of them as a volatile mini-mob, when she stood within touching distance of their attack on Rowan in the yard of the crèche. She said they were so angry they would've turned on anyone related to the victim.

'What I always do,' the defence advocate said to Desiree, 'I look at what an ordinary person would've done under those circumstances. And you aren't an ordinary person, you're the [mother-figure]. I put it to you, you would've screamed, and said, "Stop! Don't beat him! Angry, what are you doing?" Or words to that effect. Did you?'

'You, sir, you have a point there,' Desiree replied, 'but you don't mess with a mob. Because if Rowan had seen that I was standing there, then my life would've been in danger too.'

Yet, they were not egged on by baying crowds, or helped by their neighbours. The crowds in these testimonies were strangely passive. When the defence advocate cross-examined Desiree about how she had kept up with Rowan, her explanation was that he was impeded but not stopped by crowds 'thick' on the street that stood in his path. John Ndevu, too, said a crowd formed around the assault and lined each side of the street, entirely quiet but nonetheless intimidating.

And with all these people in the streets, and all the people at the Pink House, people who were neither involved, nor clearly in favour of the assault, strangest of all, there was not a single independent witness to the crime.

What difference would 'independence' make? Surely people as grief stricken, as tortured by Rowan's death would remember all the better, would want the truth to come out all the more?

Desiree Jack vibrated with a bitter anger whenever I saw her in court, and her pain came through in the transcripts.

'Are you angry that Rowan is now deceased? Is that right?' the defence advocate asked her in the midst of his cross-examination.

'Should I laugh, sir?' she replied. 'That isn't a question that the gentleman can ask me,' she'd said to the judge. 'If he had a heart, then he wouldn't ask that question.'

'Don't be angry,' the judge said. 'You aren't happy about the fact that Rowan was killed?'

'I am not happy, sir.'

John Ndevu and Desiree only ever referred to Rowan's behaviour as 'naughty'. They denied knowledge of the true extent of his crimes.

Whether they were lying primarily to themselves or to the court wasn't clear. Even Veronica, who doesn't deny his criminal history, was adamant that Rowan was a sweet, loving son. He cooked for them, made jokes, had charm. He chastised his younger brother if he was disrespectful to Ndevu. He was easy to be around, dutiful like a child, and even when he grew up you could still send him on errands and he would go without complaint, return, and help with the chores. 'One child inside the house, and another outside the house,' the judge offered, as a compromise between the family's evasions and the version already on record.

For Rara too, I did not doubt Rowan's death was a tragedy. When I first met him in Mfuleni, after his testimony, taciturn as he was, he told me that they were best friends. 'He was like a brother to me,' Rara said. He hadn't slept the night Rowan was kidnapped, only drifting off at dawn. A few hours later the police woke him when they came to collect him to make a statement. Taking a slight detour to the police station they drove him to Blueberry Hill and told him that was where Rowan had been set on fire, pointing out the exact patch of earth.

Asavela, at first take, presented as the most removed of the four. She was one of Rowan's friends, but she was also not sufficiently disturbed by his assault to stop dancing and drinking. But of all of them, she was the most connected to the defendants.

In her evidence-in-chief she presented their relationship as slight: yes, she'd been a member of the SJC, but she'd only attended a few marches. Under fire from the defence advocate, a more complex picture emerged. Before joining the SJC, she had been part of The Seven Bs book club. But Angy had found her drinking at the shebeen.

'And Angy caught you there,' said the advocate, 'and took away the liquor, and chased you out, and had words with the shebeen owner.'

'Yes, that is correct. She chased me away.'

Their interactions were not limited to community activism,

either. Asavela confirmed that in 2011 she lived with Angy and Isaac in their home. After a particularly bad fight with her mother, who had objected to her daughter's affairs and her heavy drinking, Asavela had decamped and moved in with Angy. At Angy's house, in turn, she was kicked out when she abandoned babysitting Angy's children to go drinking. Angy had been furious and excluded Asavela from her friendship, and her links to the world outside Bardale, perhaps the only links for drop-outs and teenage mothers. These – by Asavela's admission – were the terms on which their friendship became strained.

Asavela's teenage life appears to have been one of consistent chaos. Throughout her teenage years she repeatedly fell out with her mother and other care givers. She had lived at her aunt's house in Philippi for a time, then been forced to leave when she 'accused her [aunt's] husband of sleeping with her'. Nosibenzele, the neighbour who thought Asavela should not go out the night Rowan was murdered, had also taken Asavela in, after another fight between Asavela and her mother.

The defence of Chris and Azola also rested heavily on the idea that Asavela had implicated them out of spite. Chris had once been in love with Asavela but had broken up with her after a few months of dating because of her heavy drinking and mood swings. Azola claimed Asavela had tried to get his phone number in order to initiate an affair but he had refused to let her have it. A previous driver for the SJC had lost his job for having an affair with a school child in The Seven Bs and he didn't want the same fate to befall him. He believed she was bitter, a woman scorned.

Angy argued, privately, that the eyewitnesses had taken money, and Isaac moderated that slightly by saying that a potent mix of grief and poverty had laid the ground for an approach by the police. The defence advocate never mentioned money, but rather implied that vulnerable people had been given a suggestion which brought them closure, and with it, revenge. Those vulnerable people were a pensioner and a part-time care worker who had lost a beloved child; and two unemployed youth with substance-abuse problems, who had been Rowan's friends. No one on the stand lived a secure and resilient life.

The state advocate probably felt confident that his four eyewitnesses would be accepted. Their accounts of intimidation and assault corroborated each other fairly well, so well that the defence was left with little option but to argue that all four were, more or less, liars. So did they come off as trustworthy? 'Speaks to credibility' was one of the defence advocate's catch phrases and he questioned that credibility through fair means and foul. He tried to place Desiree's history of depression, post-divorce, on the record, and to dwell on Asavela's 10 am beer drinking and history of affairs, at a later point calling her 'a drunken slut'. All this appeared to have annoyed the judge and drove his sympathies towards the Ndevu family.

In the box, John Ndevu came across as humble and bereaved, an elder in slacks and a sleeveless jumper, grey haired and harmless; Desiree was confident and upright, her hair in a bob, plump, a soft face, a gentle, high voice, a knee injury preventing her from sitting, so she faced off squarely with her cross-examiner. But Rara and Asavela were so soft-spoken the translators appeared to be considering a strike. 'I'm begging her,' one of them said during Asavela's cross-examination, 'to speak up.' The judge made jokes about giving her nutritional supplements 'to wake her up', and told her that, if it would help, she could turn her back to the gallery, who he told off at least once for laughing, in a jeering way, during her testimony. (In those first weeks of the trial the audience was largely comprised of Mfuleni people.)

Repeatedly combing over the transcripts of their testimonies, I found it difficult myself to really work out when key events had happened. That there were contradictions was clear, that they were fatal was not. On the face of things their accounts on the stand, together, sketched a plausible series of events.

❖ ❖ ❖

I would have liked to write more about Angy and Rowan's first meeting on the field, but Angy was not good with details, and there was no one else to ask. Rowan's immediate family – John Ndevu, Desiree, Nathaniel – would not grant me an interview, though I asked many times, and through various channels. They did not say why, but the people who delivered their refusals speculated: they did not trust journalists, and they believed that, like everyone else, I was on Angy's side. And, in investigating this story, many things I asked and heard had to cross boundaries of race, class and language which increased the chance of misunderstanding, lessened the chances for trust.

I should also mention that some of the things that Angy told me did not add up. Angy told me that at 18 she came to Cape Town in a state of deep alienation, having dropped out of school after the murder of her twin brother. Mpho had been shot in the street in a drive-by, she said, in an act of retaliation. Her uncle was a criminal and had double-crossed his fellow thieves after a heist, and absconded with the money. Their uncle lived with her father – his elder brother – and had no children of his own, so Tlokotse's children paid the price. First Angy was kidnapped and released when the uncle paid a portion of his debt, but then Mpho was murdered when he didn't put up the rest.

Angy also told me that at 15, she and other students had burnt down the principal's office at her high school in protest against the treatment of a classmate, who had been humiliated by a public beating with a belt.

Two stunningly dramatic stories, but I could find no one in Khutsong to confirm them. None of the teachers at Badirile High who had been there throughout the 1980s could remember the headmaster's office being burnt down. Neither could the teachers who had been at Badirile at the time but had since moved on to other high schools. In fact, they were fairly convinced it had never happened and I was fairly convinced that if it had they would've remembered.[16] I could find no classmate or teacher who could remember Mpho's death either. Angy's face looked familiar to some of them but so many students had moved through the school by that time, and Khutsong was a tumultuous place where politics and crime and gangs had claimed the lives of a lot of young men over the decades, that one murder might not stand out.

Khutsong was a black township which adjoined a formerly white mining town called Carletonville, now in terminal decline as South Africa's gold industry shrivelled. In a small office above a parking lot, I looked through three years of the *Carletonville Herald* covering the year Mpho was murdered as well as those before and after. I found no answers, though a pattern did emerge. The front page would feature a large photo of a white person, or a white couple, who had died in some accident, usually a car crash, or through an untimely disease. Then there would be fillers about cross-country races, white boys and girls who won maths Olympiads, littering in the town centre, and adverts for agricultural machinery. The back pages would feature one or two stories about Khutsong, and if any deaths there were mentioned they were murders, and the victims were only counted, rarely named. There were no other publicly accessible records about the life and times of Khutsong, no searchable death notices or even birth records. Badirile had no register of the students who had attended the school.

At the Khutsong Police Station, Nanette, a friendly human-resources officer, searched the police database for details of Angy's mother's employment. This database contained information about everyone who worked or had worked for the police force, and there was no record of a Matseleng Peter, even under alternative spellings. 'Maybe she worked here,' Nanette offered, 'but not as a policewoman.' As a cleaner, she implied.

When I told Angy she was incensed. Her mother had been in uniform. 'And I'm sick of this!' she said. 'This isn't the first time this book of yours has made me upset.' Our phone conversation ended unpleasantly. Later, she said she would take me to Khutsong to verify her story, but it proved hard to find time for that.

None of this background information was material to the accusations against Angy. The stories she told me were consistent, and she told the same ones to her husband, friends, and later to government officials. She gave me the names of her family and told me where to ask about them. She never hindered me from looking. But it should have been possible to verify these stories, and I couldn't.

The stories I heard from people who lived in any of these townships – Mfuleni, Khayelitsha, Khutsong – seemed to be only coherent at a distance. They were unrecorded, so poorly integrated into any system that looking at them up close seemed to make any story fragment, and the pieces drift away from each other. By the time I got to Khutsong it was a puzzle that was already familiar. What did the absence of an answer mean? That one must make do with ambiguity? Or that there was a lie afoot? This was a game of trust, and that question was important.

;

PART THREE: EXPERT OPINION

Chapter Eight

For all the years I researched these events around the murder of Rowan du Preez and their aftermath, there was a general consensus, among those disposed to have opinions on the matter, that the causes of the high crime rates in Cape Town's townships were: unemployment; alcohol abuse and unlicensed taverns; ineffective or non-existent visible patrolling by the police; poor detective work by the police; non-response to emergency calls by the police; lack of indoor sanitation for many who were then vulnerable to attack when relieving themselves in the open or in portable toilets without adequate lighting; poverty; inequality; the existence of informal settlements whose small alleyways did not permit the entrance of emergency vehicles; and the explosive growth of the crystal-meth market.

The causes were always in an explicit hierarchy, one that changed from person to person. And if, in those years, I knew which causes someone would place greatest emphasis on, then I'd also know who they voted for. Or, at least, who they didn't want anyone else to vote for.

Around the time that the SJC was formed, the city's politics were reconstituting. Cape Town had always been a fussy city, and since the democratic transition one that was ruled by coalitions, floor crossing, and surprises at the ballot box. But in 2006, on the basis of a volatile coalition, the Democratic Alliance (DA), a centre-right party then cobbled out of various minority interests and otherwise spent political forces, wrested control of the city from the ruling African National

Congress (ANC), the centre-left party of erstwhile liberation. The DA then slowly strengthened its control of the city council by juggling desirable and undesirable partners, floor crossings and mergers. In 2009, the DA won the entire province of the Western Cape.[17] While the DA's share of the national vote was still a paltry 16.7% next to the ANC's 66% it began to more aggressively project itself as the 'official opposition', as if in a two-party state. The party leader, Helen Zille, a white woman who had been a political journalist before entering politics, became provincial premier and soon perhaps the most recognisable opposition politician in the country.

The powers of provinces in relation to national government were not particularly impressive, but for the DA this victory expanded its influence over Cape Town, giving it control, though limited, over public housing, education, and health. Any success in the country's second-biggest city could be more fully owned as a DA coup, something that had increasing significance as criticism of then President Zuma and his administration became more and more vocal.

Certain ANC politicians did not take this defeat gracefully. Many years later, it emerged that President Zuma had met with Cape gang leaders to ask them to mobilise votes for the ANC to re-take the city. He also authorised the creation of a National Intelligence Agency project called the Principal Agents Network (PAN) to re-take the province for the ANC, though it was hard to know how sincere this aim was, as the primary activities of PAN staff were looting state coffers under the pretext of 'covert activities'[18]. On the ground, mercurial characters like Andile Lili and Loyiso Nkohla, then members of the ANC Youth League, dressed in camo fatigues and characterised the DA administration as inherently racist and colonial, declaring at public rallies that they would make the city 'ungovernable'. The DA soon went into siege mentality, and began to force the extension of the political reach of provincial and city powers.

The Western Cape – and especially its capital, Cape Town – also became the chief display in the DA's shop window, the centrepiece of a campaign to entice voters in other parts of the country who were looking for a new provincial or local vehicle for their vote. A mantra arose: The Western Cape is the best-run province, Cape Town is the best-run city – look what DA rule can do for you.

But one of the greatest weaknesses in this pro-DA narrative was crime. It should be pointed out that between 1994 and 2012 the murder rate[19] in South Africa plummeted, something which often went unsaid when talking about crime. National murder rates were at 67 per 100 000 in 1994, but had dropped to 30 per 100 000 by 2012[20]. This was mirrored by the decline in many other serious crimes. While always above the national average, high crime rates in the Western Cape saw the same steady decline as the rest of the country up until 2009.[21] Cape Town's violent crime situation was also successfully obscured by an effective campaign to reduce inner-city crime (which had fallen by some 90% since 2000), where business and residential property values were sky-rocketing, and the fact that crime was concentrated in poor, peripheral neighbourhoods such as Khayelitsha, Mfuleni and Mannenberg. This allowed Cape Town to successfully project an image of being *the* safe city in South Africa, where you could drive with your windows down and tourists could saunter through the inner city at dusk inhaling the smell of frangipani and the ocean breeze. But in 2009, the murder rate in Cape Town rose again, so fast and steadily that by 2012 Cape Town had the highest murder rate in the country. It was such an outlier, in fact, that it accounted for almost half the national murder rate increase between 2009/10 and 2014/15.[22] Cape Town began to feature regularly on 'most violent city in the world' lists, and the bad press made the DA leadership spitting mad.

National government, however, alone held the mandate for policing, and provincial and city governments had no operational control over policing powers. Using a limited provision for provincial oversight over the police, Premier Zille began to vigorously stretch the limits of what her administration could control, and publicly stated her ambitions for more provincial control of policing.[23] The Cape Town Metropolitan Police Department was put on steroids. Once primarily known as traffic police – there to arrest illegal drag racers, breathalyse suspected drunks and monitor the streets for parking violations – they expanded into aggressive anti-gang operations and a force for land evictions. National police management responded with threats of legal action, and a war of words. In parliament, the DA shadow minister for police repeatedly implied that national decision makers were deliberately understaffing the Western Cape police force, which held 60% of the entire country's vacant posts. Their critics responded that crime rates were high because the DA administration favoured white ratepayers and neglected basic service delivery – street lights, roads, sanitation and housing – in the townships. Crime and policing in the Western Cape became a political battleground.

So when the SJC, along with several other organisations, submitted a complaint to Premier Zille in late 2011, painting a picture of gross police dysfunction in Khayelitsha, they framed the responsible parties carefully. Calling for a commission of inquiry, they catalogued a long list of systemic problems that Khayelitsha residents faced in getting justice in the wake of a crime, and underscored these with the cases they had documented through their affidavits. This was not a well-worn path. The premier would have to use untested powers across enemy lines. The activists were calling for her to exercise the power of the provincial premiership to call for a commission of inquiry headed by a retired judge, and they asked that it have the power to subpoena, which gave it a coercive edge.

Anyone reading the complaint with an eye to the city's politics would have noted the way the document drew attention to its inclusion of the Metro police, particularly their most controversial and biggest unit, the Anti Land Invasion Unit. This unit ostensibly existed to stop people from illegally occupying city- and province-owned land that had been identified for public housing. 'This is in fairness to the majority of law-abiding people on the list,' the city's website explained. Activists claimed the main role of the unit was to – unlawfully – lay waste to the shacks and possessions of people living in those informal settlements which happened to feature on the unit's hit list, which they did at the rate of about 300 shacks a month.

In the scheme proposed by the SJC, the commission would be holistic and impartial: it would include the police, the lawyers, the courts, the prisons,[24] the neighbourhood watches and community policing forums. It would span national and provincial responsibilities, ANC and DA, state police and city police.

Premier Zille tried for eight months to get top police officials to respond to the complaint. In July 2012, she went ahead anyway and set in motion formal procedures to approve a commission, officially announcing that it would go ahead a month later. As the activists requested, the commission she proposed would be headed by a retired judge, Kate O'Regan, formerly of the Constitutional Court, and by an eminent advocate, Vusi Pikoli. The hearings would be public and would take place in Khayelitsha, so that residents could attend. But the premier also narrowed its focus. Only the responsibilities of the national police force would be examined, while other government departments and the Metro cops were excluded. In short, no entity under DA direction would face scrutiny.

Nathi Mthethwa, the minister of police, immediately went to the Cape High Court to seek an urgent interdict against the commission. When the High Court set the police's case aside, he took it to the Constitutional Court, the country's highest authority. Here, too, he was unsuccessful.

❖ ❖ ❖

Affidavit from TB

I am a 40-year-old male resident of BM Section, Khayelitsha. The submissions in this affidavit are made on the basis of my personal experience with vigilantism, both as a resident of Khayelitsha and as the brother of a victim of a vigilante execution. In September 2012, my younger brother was beaten and burned to death on Lansdowne Road after he and two friends were caught trying to steal from a man's house.

They broke into his house to steal his belonging while he was out. The man came home and he caught them in the act. He managed to call upon the community members for help. The two men my brother was with had lived in Khayelitsha for a long time and knew how to escape from the area, but my brother was new to the area, so did not know how to get away. He ran in the wrong direction and had to turn around. Many members of the community were waiting for him when he came back. They grabbed him and dragged him back to the house he had been trying to rob, where he was brutally beaten.

While he was being beaten, my brother begged for his life. The crowd didn't listen. They dragged him to Lansdowne Road, poured petrol on him, and burned him to death.

The next day I didn't hear anything from him. In September, I was in [the centre of town] when I received a call from one of the residents of BM Section, who told me that he had witnessed my brother's killing.

When I returned [to Khayelitsha], I went to Site B Police Station. I told them that I had heard my brother had been killed and asked if they knew anything about it. The police told me that they had received a body, and had sent it to the mortuary in Tygerberg.

At Tygerberg, I was taken to identify my brother's body. I came with two other people, and when they saw his body they ran away.

His face was beaten so badly that I couldn't even recognize him. His body was burned from neck to torso. I only knew it was him because I noticed a scar on his hand from childhood, and because I had given him the tracksuit pants he was wearing.

I didn't cry when my father died or when my mother died, but to see how horribly my brother died did make me cry.

When I came back from Tygerberg I went back to Site B Police Station. The police said they had opened a case and asked for contact numbers from my brother-in-law and me. They told me they had arrested some people in connection with the murder, and would call to let me know more details and update me. That was on Tuesday, 4 September 2012. The police never came to interview my neighbour or me.

I am still waiting for that call. I still don't know who killed my brother. The police never let me know anything about who they arrested. Because of the prevalence of vigilantism, his murderers could be anyone, even one of my neighbours.

❖ ❖ ❖

Two experts, the psychologist Pumla Gobodo-Madikizela, and an anthropologist, Kelly Gillespie, compiled reports for the commission, based on interviews in Khayelitsha. Drawing on their respective expertise on issues of justice and trauma, that sought to explain what drove the violence. Both would deny a straightforward link between policing and vigilante murder, though they gave powerful explanations about how policing, and the lack of it, helped to shape the phenomenon.

For the commission, Professor Pumla Gobodo-Madikizela, a senior research professor in trauma, memory and forgiveness at the University of the Free State, wrote a report on the causes of vigilante violence in Khayelitsha. Gobodo-Madikizela, a small, elegant woman with short hair and glasses, was perhaps most famous for her book *A Human Being Died That Night* [25]. This recounted her conversation with apartheid-era state-death squad commander Eugene de Kock, and with the perpetrators of politically motivated vigilante necklacings in the 1980s in the Eastern Cape. As such it was a chronicle of the insidious ways the conscience could be silenced.

Gobodo-Madikizela drew on theories of 'social anomie' to describe how poor policing contributed to a feeling of abandonment. The urban conditions of Khayelitsha were the basis for this anomie, such as the size and density of informal settlements, where people felt anonymous in the constant flux of their neighbours, and dehumanised by the government's neglect of their basic needs, where there were no reliable safety nets. But the crux of the anomie was the sense that rules were never enforced. 'This lack of enforcement of rules is at the heart of many testimonies presented to the Khayelitsha Commission: police are never there, and even when they are within visible distance of a crime, they rarely take immediate action, and when they do take action, the criminals are released or the case struck off the roll.' In such conditions, people feel they have no stake in society, and so are not bound by its codes.

During her testimony she read out a quote from one of the interviews she conducted in Khayelitsha in May 2013:

'We heard a woman screaming, "I-bag yam! I-bag yam! Nal'isela!" ("My bag! My bag! Here is a thief!") In no time, I mean, in no time, everybody was coming out, slamming doors behind them. And they were all dressed in their clothes, not pyjamas. It was as if they were waiting, ready all night for exactly this kind of thing to happen. Then they descended upon this man – they came with all sorts of weapons to assault him. Rocks on the street were thrown at him. In no time, the man was gone, they had finished him. Think about it, in a matter of a few minutes, perhaps seconds, a man is dead, killed by a group of people in my community for snatching a woman's handbag on her way to work. Glancing at his body lying on the side of the street, I saw that a large concrete slab – you know those slabs used to divide freeway roads – had been thrown on the back of his head to finish him off.'[26]

Like the necklace murders she had studied in the 1980s, the vigilante attacks in Khayelitsha,[27] Gobodo-Madikizela said, had most of the typical hallmarks of crowd violence: 'The fact that there is a trigger event that mobilises the crowd, the crowd acts spontaneously,

not in a planned fashion, the violence seems irrational and dispro-
portionate, there is no evidence of a leader, the harm is inflicted by
a group of individuals, not by one or two, and very rarely does it
happen that anyone tries to stop the escalating crowd action.'

But what was remarkable about the Khayelitsha incidents was
that they lacked any build-up at all.

By contrast, in the crowd violence that Gobodo-Madikizela had
studied in the Eastern Cape in the 1980s, 'spontaneous' violence was
often preceded by a period when a crowd 'hung around', deciding
what to do, or a period of escalating punishment and dehuman-
ising treatment, such as the degrading and insulting songs which
denounced *impimpis* in political necklace murders. Such escalation
was found in many other international examples of 'spontaneous
violence'. This build-up seemed to be central in predisposing a
crowd to cross the final boundary from beating to killing. In contrast,
in the incidents reported in Khayelitsha, 'from the very onset ... the
intention is to inflict maximum harm'.

For her, this sat at the crux of the problem that vigilante murders
presented in Khayelitsha. 'How can we understand the brutality of
the pattern of this vigilante violence? How is it that a group of community members, who do not usually do things together, can come
together without any prior planning and act in such a unified way,
albeit in a violent manner?'

Gillespie spoke about the feeling of compounded disappointment, hopelessness, and anger that pervaded the Cape townships
as a result of systematic failures in democratic South Africa to provide safety and dignity for its citizens. 'It is this systemic failure, and
the deep anger that ensues from it, that erupts in moments of mob
violence,' she wrote. '[Mob violence] says as much about the conditions of township life more generally ... as it does about the failure
of the criminal justice system to protect residents.'

Gillespie also drew attention to another remarkable feature of the mob attacks: there was no consensus on the use of 'mob justice' in Khayelitsha. 'Some residents are completely convinced that it is the best way to stop crime in the township, while others are horrified by it. Some think it is far preferable to the formal criminal justice process, which to them is opaque and inefficient, others see it as a "barbaric form of justice",' Gillespie explained. A representative survey of Khayelitsha residents had found that 73% of residents did not approve of vigilantism.[28] Yet there were many incidents and many participants: people who thought it was a good thing; people who had taken part but felt remorse afterwards; and people who hadn't wanted to be involved in the first place but had been unable to safely extricate themselves. 'What everyone shares,' said Gillespie, 'is a sense that "mob justice" is totally understandable given the conditions of life in the township.'

While the misery of those conditions was not only about crime, crime had become 'a sign, an instance, of a systemic set of problems in the township. A criminal act becomes a moment that crystallises a host of social ills into an obvious and addressable dilemma. Its punishment, then, becomes a means of funnelling anger about a range of different matters into a single instance, onto the body of an individual culprit.'

Gobodo-Madikizela saw psychological resonance between Khayelitsha mob violence and the necklace murders she had studied in the Eastern Cape. In the 1980s communities had felt a need to remove 'traitors' from their midst, with the act performing the role of an exorcism, as much as a judgment.

A year later a paper would be published independently by Dr Celeste Herbst, giving a vivid quantitative illustration of these acts.

As her time conducting autopsies at the Tygerberg Forensic Pathology Service came to a close, she decided to devote her remaining tenure to a study.[29] Tygerberg was one of two major pathology labs in Cape Town, and its catchment area included the police precincts in the north, taking in crime-ridden townships such as Khayelitsha, Mfuleni, Delft, and Nyanga. Herbst went through ten years' worth of pathology reports, and drew up findings on a matter that had been a marked feature of her time there: the rising number of deaths by 'community assault', or, as the police often called them, kangaroo or bundu courts.[30]

'Multiple injuries' was the key feature of the cases she looked at: contusions, lacerations, abrasions, fractures, stab wounds and internal organ injuries. These injuries were caused by fists, stones, sticks, sjamboks and bricks. Out of 8 634 murder postmortems between 2004 and 2014, she found 424 deaths were caused by community assault – almost five per cent.

Among the trends Herbst picked out were the geographical concentration of these murders. More than half of the 'community assault' murders had happened in the Khayelitsha precincts (Khayelitsha, Lingelethu West and Harare). But when she sorted the data by population size it was highest in the Blue Downs precinct (which included Mfuleni) which had the third highest number by precinct, and the highest per-capita rate of mob assault in the Tygerberg catchment at 73 community assault murders per 100 000 population.

Herbst's pathology data also revealed a pattern of injury which dovetailed with Gobodo-Madikizela's reading of 1980s necklace murders as an act of purging evil elements from society. It suggested that, more recently, township residents didn't want to murder criminals so much as erase them, to kill them so thoroughly that it was as if they never existed in the first place.

❖ ❖ ❖

Premier Zille often invoked the recent rise in vigilante murders as a reason for the commission. When the fight over the commission erupted in the press, vigilante 'justice' was already widely in use in comment pieces as a symbol, something that brought together in one swoop both lack of faith in the police and the threat of anarchy this evoked. No one would have said vigilante violence was hard to explain, and no one seemed to doubt its popular appeal. The understanding of vigilante murders that seemed to emerge from their media treatment was of a problem caused by the police's absence. And that given an absence and the press of a crowd, people in the townships spontaneously filled it with violence. The solution then was more policing, and policing with a stronger hand, all the better to feel the presence of the state.

The police vehemently rejected the idea that vigilante murders were directly linked to their performance. In court, their lawyers argued first that the phenomenon had been 'sensationalised' and wasn't nearly as prevalent as the premier implied, and that a naive public confused gang retaliation for vigilante attacks.[31] In the commission, when both of these claims were disproved, they argued that it arose because people didn't understand bail, because they wanted quick justice, because they wanted their things back. At their best, these police denials had at their heart dismay – dismay that the police should be held accountable for a great and ubiquitous social dysfunction, one which they felt they had no control over.

The treatment of vigilante violence in the complaint that sparked the commission was more nuanced in this respect: to the complainant organisations it wasn't just a symptom, but a concern in its own right.

Nonetheless, vigilante 'justice' and the commission became intertwined concepts in the press and the legal proceedings that followed. Its complexity was reduced to one simple equation (bad police equals many vigilantes), and the phenomenon was inextricably bound up with the SJC activists, their request for the commission, and the allegation that the police were failing.

PART FOUR: JUDGMENT

Chapter Nine

The Western Cape High Court's facade was austere and neo-classical, and more than a little bit ugly if you stepped far enough back from the building to gain an overall impression. Inside, once past half-hearted security guards scanning briefcases and boxes of legal briefs, you got to the core of the old building. Beneath you were corridors used by clerical staff, and the entranceways to the galleries of the old, colonial-era courts. Most of the court rooms, however, were to be found down a drab, linoleum-lined corridor that served as a bridge to a newer, brutalist building.

It was in one of these newer courts, Court 17, that the majority of the trial of Angy Peter and Isaac Mbadu would take place. The defining feature of that unremarkable room was plenty of oak: the walls were covered in asymmetrical, pale planks of irregular depth which hid sound baffles. The decor was modern but basic, neither particularly cheap nor particularly expensive.

Dwell further on Court 17, sitting there day after day, and you might decide it was bunker-like, in as inoffensive a way as possible. Perhaps it would be kinder to say it was laid out like a windowless, cast-concrete church. There were double volumes above the judge's seat, cloister-like side areas blanked off by pillars, with pew-like benches for the audience. This, together with the various visual cues instructing you to sit still and remain silent, gave Court 17 excellent acoustics: no echo, no shuffling, no ambient noise – all the better to hear justice take place.

The main actors in the trial included the judge and the advocates and lawyers representing, variously, Angy and Isaac, Azola and Chris, and the National Prosecuting Authority (NPA). The judge, Robert Henney, sat in red robes on a wooden throne, beneath a state crest carved out of Rhodesian teak, a middle-aged man with a square face, who had begun to thicken around the middle.

Henney was a born-and-bred Capetonian, and had grown up on the Cape Flats in Athlone where his widowed mother had struggled to make ends meet. He'd registered for a law degree at the University of the Western Cape without knowing how he would pay his fees. Benefactors stepped in for his first and second year. In his third year, he told me in an interview after the trial, he'd taken a government scholarship that committed him to becoming a state prosecutor upon graduation. 'It was always my intention to assist people. But friends and students I studied with were being arrested [for political activism]. So it was one of the most difficult jobs. Not in the sense of not enjoying it. But you worked with policemen, the people you hated, the people who were oppressing you, and you had to work with them! Many lawyers from impoverished communities had to do that.'

Henney, who gave interviews to the press at the time of his appointment to the High Court in 2011, told the *Cape Argus* that in his early career he 'envisioned a judge as someone who had integrity and who was humble, honest and "fiercely independent"'. He said he had entered law out of a desire to bring justice to the poor. But in criminal matters in the lower courts the business of law was primarily sorting out the rights of poor victims of crime and the rights of the alleged perpetrators of crime, who were also poor and also largely victims – of violent, broken families, and dysfunctional schools, and a justice system that never rehabilitated criminals. And many of the cases that came to court had already been compromised by shoddy police work. In those courts judges worked closely with policemen and prosecutors, and saw how they struggled to build strong cases while being overburdened and under-resourced. There was huge public pressure on judges to lean towards a view of justice that was biased towards victims, sympathetic to the state's case, and delivered a harsh sentence. In his time at the High Court, Henney was known as a man who did not shy away from strong convictions.

Arrayed on one long bench facing Henney were the lawyers and advocates, with their clients behind them. The defence of the accused was split into two teams: Angy and Isaac's legal team were drawn from private firms. This was only possible because their fees were paid in part by Amnesty International, who had been brought on board by the SJC, and also by funds raised by the SJC itself. Azola and Chris were represented by a legal aid lawyer – the second who had been assigned to them.

Angy and Isaac's team was by far the more intimidating. Their attorney was Joshua Greeff, an Afrikaner in his forties who worked for the city's largest criminal law firm, Mathewson Gess Inc. Greeff was tall with light blue eyes, wore suits which were sharply pressed but not showy, a crew cut, and a clean shave. He greeted people frankly but was scrupulous in his hellos and goodbyes and when asked how he was invariably responded, *'Ek kannie kla nie'* – 'I can't complain'.

Though considerably older, Advocate William King gave off a more maverick air. King was tall and slim with a full head of white hair, and arrived in court each day with a large leather hold-all worn down and brimming with papers. This entrance communicated some disorganisation, yet when cross-examining he was thorough and exact. He brought to the case four decades of legal experience, including a spell as a local magistrate, and was highly seasoned in arguing both civil and criminal matters in the High Court.

Advocate Israel Ndlovu, assigned to represent Azola and Chris by the NPA through a legal aid scheme, was in his early thirties, rotund and bald with an inconspicuous goatee. He had grown up in a Durban township and was the first person in his family to get a university degree. When court was not in session it was rare to find him not chuckling and giggling with his clients, witnesses, or the other lawyers.

Despite their friendly lawyer, Azola Dayimani and Chris Dina were themselves enigmas to me. Azola declined to be interviewed, while Chris only granted me 15 minutes while I drove him back to Mfuleni one day. Their own explanations of how they had become mixed up in the trial were never entirely convincing. I saw them much as the court saw them: two men as likely as any others to be there.

Ndlovu's affable manner was also not much at odds with his performance in leading evidence or cross-examinations. While his questions were delivered in a booming voice that rose and fell poetically in isiZulu, few of them were ever put to witnesses, and he seldom objected.

The state was represented by Advocate Phistus Palesa, a short man with a petulant face. Palesa was the kind of lawyer whose enjoyment of the court-room game, by his own admission, lay in technical wrangling over finer points of law. The NPA never granted me permission to interview Palesa, and he wouldn't discuss a thing without it, so I can't tell you much more than that. He led his witnesses without much fuss, though he could be raised to a flustered, hurried voice in cross-examination.

Lastly, there were the translators. The trial was thoroughly multilingual, with witness testimony in both Afrikaans and Xhosa, in addition to English, and lawyers delivering questions in all of those languages, as well as Ndlovu delivering his in isiZulu.[32] This required the services of two translators who took shifts in the seat beside the witnesses translating English and Afrikaans into Xhosa, and vice versa. One was a dour man in a leather jacket and tie, whose deep monotone flattened out the most emotional testimony, and the other a pint-sized young woman, whose falsetto took the edge off the sharpest accusations.

❖ ❖ ❖

By the time the trial came to court 18 months had passed since Rowan's death – a long time to remember events with crisp detail. An eyewitness would usually have their memory jogged by the statements they made at the time of the crime, except in this case, where they all denied some or all of the content of those statements in court.

The first statements made by John Ndevu, Desiree Jack and Rara are dated to the morning of Sunday 14 October – the morning after the assault, when Rowan lay in a coma in Groote Schuur Hospital. Asavela gave her first statement ten days later on 24 October. These first statements were, in some cases, almost entirely repudiated by the witnesses.

Statement-taking was and is still a notorious weakness of the police force. The problems the witnesses had with how their stories were recorded might not have looked so odd if they hadn't also denied core components of a second round of statements that were taken at the behest of the prosecutor only three weeks before the trial. These were intended to correct the errors of the first statements.

How could these second statements, which the statement-taker knew would be used in a high-stakes criminal trial, still be repudiated by the people who had made them less than a month before? There was no honest incentive on either side for the statements to be taken down so poorly.

'Your grandson had been abducted and burned,' King put to John Ndevu in his cross-examination. 'You were a witness. You had walked all the way to the police station. Can I accept that this was important to you? That you wanted the police to help you?'

'Yes.'

'You wanted to tell the police what you knew of the case?'

'Yes.'

'The police wanted to know it as well. [Investigating officer] Muthien wanted to know what you had seen?'

'Yes.'

'And you told him?'

'Yes, I told him.'

Ndevu's first statement had not mentioned that he witnessed the assault at first hand. It said that he received news of the assault and abduction from Desiree. It did not mention the names of any of the people who Ndevu claimed he knew. Yet Ndevu was adamant that when he made the statement to the investigating officer, he hadn't left anything out. Curiously, the statement also contained Azola's address. John Ndevu repeatedly said in his testimony that he had only been shown Azola's and Chris's houses several hours after he had given this statement. Yet there it was on a page that contained a signature he said was not his.

In John Ndevu's second statement there was again no mention that he had directly observed the assault. There were also several details in it that Ndevu had not included in his evidence-in-chief. Under cross-examination from King he either said he'd forgotten to mention them or, much worse for the state, completely denied ever telling them to the policeman who took the statement.

The problems with John Ndevu's statements were not a special case. Every eyewitness version of events changed radically between statements, and then again when they testified in court. Some of them said that the involvement of Angy or the other suspects was left out of their first or second statements – others said their names were added in. The locations of separate assaults moved and so did the site of the kidnapping. The potential murder weapon – the golf club – was only mentioned for the first time in court. The substance of the changes was almost always incriminating for the accused. One of these unexplained 'additions' to John Ndevu's statement was that in the aftermath of the TV theft he overheard Rowan telling

Ta Ager to rescue him: 'Rowan asked, said he asked for help, because the group of Angy is killing him.' [33]

John Ndevu was 76 years old at the time of the assault – in other words, six years past the year at which it was assumed, in forensic terms, that human sight and hearing degraded dramatically. Indeed, his eyesight was poor and it had never been treated. It was so poor that in court John Ndevu was unable to make out the contents of the police photograph album of various locations. In fact, he could neither confirm nor deny that a particular photograph was of his own house. Likewise his eyesight prevented him from being able to draw a rough sketch of the roads around his home. Yet according to his testimony he was able to identify people he did not know well, or at all, at a distance of 30 to 40 metres at night.

Night-time was an issue that affected all the accounts, no matter how young and sharp the eyes. Bardale was an electrified part of Mfuleni but it had no street lights, and the shacks generally only had internal lights. On that Saturday there was a waning moon, a crescent, and it only rose at 3.16 am. Without illumination it would have been too dark to see your hand in front of your face.

John Ndevu was adamant he could see the scene clearly because of the light provided by an Apollo light, installed in Bardale not long before the incident, as a temporary measure before streetlights were installed. Apollo lights had been a feature of South African townships since the 1980s. At thirty metres high – nine storeys – they were out of all proportion to the sea of shacks around them. Their bulbs were an unsparing ring of incandescence that illuminated whole blocks – yet King was able to prove in court that Bardale's had been broken when Rowan's assault occurred.

All subsequent witnesses referred to other lights – ordinary light bulbs – outside the crèche or the Somalian store that illuminated the scene.

Desiree also claimed that the time stamp on her statement was wrong, and therefore her father's too. Their statements were recorded as having been commissioned between 9 and 10 am, yet both were adamant they had only made their statements after the arrest of Angy and Isaac, which happened at about noon.

Further problems emerged with Asavela's first statement. This was made on 24 October 2012, ten day after the murder, when Desiree took her to the station. Desiree had translated Asavela's statements from Xhosa into Afrikaans for the investigating officer, an example of such dire police practice that Judge Henney, in his decades of practice in the lower courts, had never come across it before.

Asavela said no one read the statement to her, but she signed it anyway. She said she thought parts of it later 'might be wrong', and that was why she gave a second statement in January.

'So I am correct in saying this first statement was discussed with the prosecutor and with the police and then it was decided to make a second statement?' King asked her.

'Yes.'

'So you corrected the mistakes made in the first statement or the problems?'

'Correct.'

'Why did you have to make a second statement? What was wrong with the first one? What was recorded wrongly?'

From the record, when King asked her this, it appeared that Asavela studied the original statement, one Palesa had been asked to hand her, quite slowly. A small snafu ensued because she was looking at a copy of her statement in which the 'wrong' parts had been highlighted. Asavela was then handed a clean copy but she seemed to have trouble picking out the differences. When King slowly drew them out, Asavela admitted most of these details had been added by Desiree.

The second statement accorded more closely with Asavela's testimony in court, though it retained an erroneous reference to a 'taxi guy'. This figure did not at first appear to be Azola or Chris.

Secondly, her statement mentioned only one person by name – Angy – and another indirectly – 'Angy's husband'. In this regard it was no different to the other four statements that were made that day.

'Out of all five of you,' King noted, 'not one of you mentioned Azola, Christopher, in any way, in any identification, nor a third or fourth person, that Sunday afternoon. What do you say to that?' None of the five people, including Nathaniel and Roger, who gave statements on the Sunday, mentioned the names of Azola and Chris. At least three of them – John Ndevu, Asavela and Rara – admitted they knew their names.

King fought this battle alone. Why Azola and Chris hadn't been named in those first statements was only of tangential relevance to his own clients, and direct relevance to those of Ndlovu, who added little to this line of enquiry.

The events recounted in the statement also suggested other key eyewitnesses from whom the police never took statements. These included Malwangi, the occupant of the shack adjacent to the crèche; Vuyisile, the owner of the Pink House tavern; and Thobile, who had called Roger and Rara from Maxaba's Place to tell them about the assault. The docket also contained statements from eyewitnesses who were not called as witnesses: Nathaniel, Rowan's younger brother; and Roger, who had, according to Rara's testimony, witnessed the entire night's events with him.

King put these on the record himself, by reading out Roger's statement to the court: 'On Saturday 13 October 2012, that evening at an unknown time, I was with Rowan du Preez and also Rara. Rara and I walked to a girl. We left Rowan at the Pink House. Then my friend came, known as Thobile, and told me that they were chasing down Rowan. Rara and I then left. I then heard outside that they were busy beating Rowan in a house. I therefore went to Rowan's house and informed his father and sister. I therefore took his sister where they were beating Rowan. I couldn't see anything. Rowan's sister went closer.'

King also read out Nathaniel's statement: 'On Saturday, 13 October 2012, around 20.00 I went to the Pink House, Bardale Squatter Camp and met up with two known males, Rara and Roger. Roger and Rara, upon seeing me, informed me that my brother Rowan du Preez was kidnapped by unknown people and was being assaulted somewhere. As I entered the Pink House, a friend of mine known as Manyoliso, informed me that Rowan, my brother, was being assaulted at Anele's house. I suspect that Anele was involved in the kidnapping and assault on my brother Rowan du Preez.'

Was kidnapped by unknown people.

I couldn't see anything.

Anele's house. I suspect Anele was involved.

These assertions would have made for interesting cross-examination, along with the fact that none of these statements mention Angy or Isaac.

❖ ❖ ❖

Desiree testified last out of the eyewitnesses and was by far the state's star witness. By the time she took the stand, the stakes were much higher. For the defence, the evidence-in-chief contained a degree of corroboration. For the state, the evidence-in-chief displayed a growing number of suggested evasions, implausible scenarios, and inconsistencies. Desiree's testimony tied up a lot of loose ends. These might have been incompatible with the memories of other witnesses, but her recollections dispelled doubts about identification because she claimed to have been within arm's length of the assault, and close to Rowan when he was kidnapped. Other details which seemed erroneous in John Ndevu's testimony were confirmed in hers.[34]

In fact Desiree's testimony was so full of detail it sharpened the whole evening of the murder for the first time, and unified the different accounts.

Yet, for all the detail she remembered in court, her original statement was threadbare on the day after the attack – a statement which she said was read back to her, giving her an opportunity to point out mistakes. Desiree had also accompanied a policeman, a Captain Kenneth Speed, around Bardale to compile a record of the locations of the assaults and the abduction that she had mentioned in this first statement. John Ndevu has also accompanied them, to help with the exercise.

Captain Kock and Muthien, the investigating officer, were also present. King summed up the problems with the photographs with unusual simplicity. They were simply 'all over the place', he said.

Speed was a well-known detective although he was not based at Blue Downs Police Station. Both Henney and King agreed that he was a 'top cop' and absolutely 'paraat'. 'Paraat' means 'ready', but figuratively it connotes someone upstanding who operates by the book. An advocate told me that it was considered bad luck to defend someone in a case where Speed had collected evidence, as he was so meticulous that none of the usual loopholes around poor police procedure could be worked.

When it came to recording the location of Rowan's kidnapping, Speed hadn't just photographed the location, he'd taken a GPS reading of the abduction point contained in the first round of statements: the corner of Sandile Street.

Yet in court Rara said, for the first time, that he'd seen Rowan bundled into the taxi outside the Darsabo Cash Store on the corner of Thombela. The store's lights had illuminated the scene.

Then Desiree, who testified next, differed from her previous statements. Instead, she said she'd seen Rowan caught by the men on the first corner (Sandile Street), but he'd escaped briefly and was only forced into the taxi on the next corner (Thobela). She said she'd told Speed this, and couldn't account for why Speed had photographed an otherwise random street corner and labelled it 'abduction point'. The wrong pink house had also been pointed out by John Ndevu in these photographs. (Wrong in the sense that while it was a pinkish house, it was not the shebeen.)

What could you make of so many mysterious mistakes?

'Accused 1 and 2 say they were at home that night with their children in bed when you say you saw them,' King said to Desiree at the end of her cross-examination, 'the night of the assault and the abduction and the burning.'

'It's a lie and they know it. It's a lie.'

'If you say they were there, then you are trying to mislead the court purposefully, with intent.'

'Sir, I stand under oath. I have no reason to lie.'

'Or you are mistaken. You've made a mistake in your identification.'

'I know what I saw and I know what I saw. So I haven't made mistakes, sir.'

'And I put to you, you are motivated by a need for revenge in what you wrongly believe they did to Rowan.'

'Mister, point number one, I don't know these people. I never wanted to know them. I have no vendetta against them.'

Ndlovu repeated this exercise for his clients, walking her through their alibis. Again and again Desiree said, 'they lie'. They lie and they lie and they lie. When Ndlovu said that Chris Dina didn't know Angy before or at the time of the assault, she shot back: 'God will judge him. That's all I have to say. He should – before he thinks, before he lies – he should look upwards.'

As suspicious as the major changes in these statements were, as implausible as I found some aspects of their accounts, their stories were so full of detail, some of it as random and unaccountable as life, that it was hard to believe that they could be entirely false. So, too, was it hard to accept that four people would get up and lie repeatedly when surely most of them wanted the truth. Without a doubt, John Ndevu, Desiree and Rara wanted the people who killed Rowan to pay.

Re-reading their testimony I would often be struck by a feeling that was unsettling and unresolvable. Were they telling the true versions of what they saw but filling in gaps in areas they didn't remember that well? Or was this wholly invented, or based on other people's accounts, a now lurid hallucination of Rowan's last moments, which they repeatedly tortured themselves into imagining? Or was it a mixture of the fabricated and the lived? They saw the abduction, shadowy figures beating Rowan in the dark, but invented the faces? Had that mixture now been repeated so many times they could not separate the two parts?

Chapter Ten

Most of the eyewitness testimony took place while a different legal proceeding occurred at the outer edge of the city. Officially it was called the Commission of Inquiry into Allegations of Police Inefficiency and a Breakdown in Relations between the South African Police Service and the Community in Khayelitsha, but colloquially, people called it the Khayelitsha Commission. In part this was because the name 'Khayelitsha' was so closely associated with images of violence and dysfunction that people would just fill in the gaps themselves.

The commission began in February 2014, the hottest month of a hot summer, three months before a national election. There was a febrile air in the city, as if the intensity of the political campaigning were ramping up the air pressure. From the viewing platform on the sand dunes behind Lookout Hill Tourism Centre, where the proceedings took place, you strained your eyes and wondered if you saw haze above Khayelitsha, which was sprawled out beneath you. The commission had actually been due to begin in November 2012, but after a series of court bids to halt the process, two years, three adverse judgments, and R10 million later, the police had rolled over and made all their people available to the commissioners.

The police's opening statement denied a 'systemic failure of policing in Khayelitsha'. They claimed they could not operate in the poorest parts of Khayelitsha, and the solution lay in housing and street lighting and jobs. Their argument was that you couldn't be inefficient in an impossible situation. Later, in questioning a witness, one of the police lawyers would say 'the biggest criminals in Khayelitsha are poverty and under-development'.

While they had opened bullishly, even cross-examining the geographer on his competency to draw a map, they soon took a softer, more conciliatory approach to the proceedings. This happened when a procession of Khayelitsha residents testified to their experience of trying to seek formal justice. Many of the horrific crimes they spoke about were highly personal in nature, committed by people they knew, many of them spurned husbands or jealous ex-boyfriends. The police often complained that the public expected them to prevent such crimes, yet they could not patrol bedrooms or tell parents how to raise their boys. Yet in these complaints there was little sense these people in Khayelitsha had expected the police to prevent the crime.[35] The nub of their complaint was about the response of the police after a crime was committed. The crime was not investigated or investigated so poorly it was laughable. Even when an investigation did take place, the victims talked about never being informed about the case or about court dates. Nor were they told about bail granted to people who might have cause to hurt them. A surprising number of complainants talked about feelings of heartbreak when they were dismissed by police officers to whom they had tried to bring evidence. 'It feels like nobody cares,' one of the complaints stated. These were the words of a woman whose brother had been killed in a deliberate arson attack, 'as if it is just dogs that died in that fire'. Almost everyone mentioned emotional closure as the reason they wanted to pursue cases many years after the tragedies had occurred. At least one person revealed that they had to talk their relatives out of seeking revenge.

At the beginning, police management was nowhere to be seen and no rank-and-file police officers joined the proceedings, unless they were waiting to testify. As the weeks went by this began to change, and the odd policeman dropped in to watch the proceedings. In the months before the commission sat, the police hierarchy had cooperated fully, handing over all their minutes and evaluations, and all the case dockets the commissioners had requested. Most academics who studied the police believed it would be easy for them to brush off the allegations no matter what happened. In the exhibition hall at Lookout Hill, rows and rows of plastic chairs were set out behind the lawyers' desks, and were routinely filled by Khayelitsha residents. Brown paper-bag lunches were doled out to everyone at the midday recess, and the NGOs set up impromptu pickets and toyi-toyied at its gates. When I looked around the hall I tried to see it through the eyes of the police: a bunch of lefties in shorts and sandals, women breastfeeding at the back, some thin, hollow men who'd hang out near the free lunch distribution asking for a job. Hardly what power looked like.

For me the question was: What relationship did this commission have with the Rowan du Preez court case unfolding in the city centre?

Often, back in my room after a day of testimony at the commission or the court, I found myself unusually exhausted, and drawn to mid-afternoon naps that were always fitful, with fragments of testimony playing back to me.

It is like it is just dogs that died in that fire.

I did not understand how anyone could be so cruel.

Often an image would appear to me, not really a dream, and always quickly dissipated: shadows on a carpet and a bar of light, and in it the tip of the tail of a snake, moving. What alarmed me most about this vision was its high kitsch. (The snake! The shadows! The afternoon torpor!) In fact, I feel embarrassed even now. But it came again and again. Eventually I did get it, did realise what some part of my mind wanted me to understand: that this was what conspiracies always looked like – the little bit of snake you got to see. What you didn't or couldn't know was if it was a mole snake or an adder.

Many of the individual complainants at the commission had been helped by Angy Peter, or were recruited by her to bring their stories to the SJC and the commission. Her name was on many of the documents submitted to the commission, in the minutes of various meetings, on affidavits taken from the community, and her cases had been included in the original complaint bundle. Yet Angy was not on the list of witnesses for the first phase of the commission.

Her bail terms prevented her from any public speaking appearance. Nor did the SJC consider her psychologically fit to be put through the stress of giving testimony. Or at least that was what they told me. It was hard to know what to make of this at the time. I had called the SJC spokesperson to say I wanted to interview Angy Peter again, and been told that she did not want to speak about the case. Considering this a courtesy call, rather than a formal request, I was surprised by the response, given the easy interview I'd had with Angy a few weeks previously. When I called Angy personally to confirm that this was her attitude, there was a long pause after I put the question to her. Just when I was sure she was about to tell me never to call again, she said, 'Fuck the SJC. They never asked me.'

Chapter Eleven

I joined the gallery in Court 17 during the first police testimony about Rowan's hearsay statement. It was the end of March 2014 and autumn was approaching.

Much to my surprise the court was never full during the main proceedings of the trial. A bench for the press, against the wall to the right of the lawyers' pew, was almost always empty. Towards the middle of the trial, GroundUp, a small, online-only news site that was funded by donations, sent a journalist on a regular basis. On some days a handful of girls would fill up the audience pews, providing support for Angy. Their taxi fare was paid by the SJC. Occasionally curious lawyers sat for a short stretch between other cases. Sometimes Joel Bregman from the SJC would drop in to confer with Angy and Isaac's legal team, sometimes accompanied by a representative from Amnesty International.

The most consistent presence on the audience benches was a weary, whippet-thin policeman wearing the name tag 'Adonis'. He had landed the easy but tedious task of guarding the court. This man was pigeon-chested, with sallow skin, a deeply lined face, and a uniform which appeared to be several sizes too large for him. He had a policeman's typical neat upper-lip moustache. I had occasion to study him closely because on many days we were the only people observing the trial. Officer Adonis tried very hard to stay awake.

❖ ❖ ❖

The first item of evidence collected in the case against Angy Peter and Isaac Mbadu – A1 in the dockets' numbering system – was a statement from a policeman of a conversation he'd had with the victim shortly before the ambulance arrived. Later, months later, two more statements were added from other police officers, describing what they had heard. These were damning, but Rowan was dead, which made the statements 'hearsay', reported speech. As such they could not be tested on the stand, and so were ordinarily inadmissible.

There were circumstances in South African law which allowed for a hearsay statement, one which passed certain standards, to be admitted. The most compelling circumstance was when the statement was deemed a 'dying declaration', an exception based on the rather dubious premise that dying men and women have no reason to lie. But Rowan's statement was not submitted as a 'dying declaration' because it gave no indication that he believed he was in the last moments of his life.

The statements submitted by the police officers were put to the regular test provided by the Law of Evidence, a set of infernally vague guidelines that the court should 'take regard to'. In summary it read: here be dragons, use your own discretion and be kind to the interests of the accused.[36]

King called for a 'trial within a trial' to sort this out. It was a sophisticated battle manoeuvre that allowed the defence to call in experts but complicated the narrative line of the trial immensely. For instance, some witnesses gave testimony that fell partly within the main trial, and partly within the supposedly distinct 'trial within a trial', or 'hearsay trial' as I came to refer to it. It also dwarfed the main trial: eleven witnesses, to determine the validity of a few minutes of alleged speech, versus ten witnesses, covering everything else from the TV theft, to the assault, to the arrests.

The hearsay trial kicked off with the testimony of Captain

Lorraine Kock. She'd been in the police for 23 years at the time of testimony, and a captain in the Visible Policing (VisPol, for short) division at Blue Downs for seven years. Kock was short and wide, and her eyes moved little as she spoke, as if she were vacantly reciting a report to a senior officer. She gave the impression of a tank, a follower of orders, schooled to implement them with blunt force.

The story she told started at 1.15 am on the morning of Sunday 14 October. She and a student constable, Barnardo, were on duty patrolling in a marked police car, which she was driving. While travelling on the main road of Mfuleni she noticed an oncoming red Tazz flash its lights. She pulled over next to the car.

The driver told her that as he drove past Blueberry Hill, he heard screaming from the bushes. They followed him to the scene. The road was straight and bleak, thick with bush scrub on one side, and flat, empty wastes on the other. The man stopped at an unremarkable point and she and Barnardo, after ramping the curb to park in the bushes, climbed out of the vehicle.

'There we found a naked man covered in burn scar. My colleague, Constable Barnardo, communicated with the male. I stood next to Barnardo.' They both stood over him.

'Constable Barnardo asked the male what his name is.' Kock could hear the man say that his name was Rowan du Preez and he lived at 24541 Minister Street, Bardale.

Next, Barnardo asked, 'What happened to you?'

The questions and answers were both delivered in Afrikaans, and Kock said he spoke '*duidelik*' (clearly) and she could clearly hear.

Rowan was lying at her feet. She stared right into his face. His burns were serious, and skin was peeling off his arms, chest and lower torso. From his waist down to his upper thighs his skin was burnt black. The night was dark. They were several metres deep into the bushes. There were no streetlights. Kock had left the vehicle lights on to illuminate the scene, and they also had their torches.

'The person then answered that he was kidnapped from his house by Angy and her husband, who live nearby him. He also, further, said that they put him in a white Quantum minibus, and that they took him to the area where we'd found him. And he also said that they beat him, and took a tyre, and put it on his body, and set fire to it.'

In cross-examination she described how he spoke 'in one go', 'without pauses', 'in full sentences', '*nie rus-rus nie*', without mumbling, and she heard it perfectly clearly. She asked him no further questions and radioed for an ambulance. Kock didn't take a statement from Rowan. With burnt hands, she explained, he was in no state to sign it. However, she made notes of what he said.

Kock went to radio 'Ops' – the operational control room for her station – from her vehicle. At the same time, she looked for the man in the Tazz who had alerted them to the victim, but he had left the scene without a trace.

The area where they found Rowan did not fall in their precinct, so she radioed the appropriate Kleinvlei Police Station. They arrived in a patrol vehicle a few minutes later to take over the case. Kock and Barnardo then left the scene and drove to a nearby Sasol petrol station to fill up.

While they were there, she called the duty officer for that evening, and told him what had transpired. He instructed her to call Captain Coetzee, who was on stand-by. Captain Coetzee didn't accept their handing over the crime scene to Kleinvlei. While the victim had been found in Kleinvlei's precinct, he told her, the crime had been committed in the Mfuleni jurisdiction and they would have to return and take over the docket.

They did as ordered and waited for the ambulance. It arrived about ten minutes later and took Rowan away.

The next police officer to testify, Constable Raul Vince Barnardo, made a striking impression in the witness box. Like Kock, he was in uniform. Barnardo's face was young, round and soft, like a teenager.

He struggled to grow the obligatory police moustache and his youth-fulness was only offset by a slightly receding hairline. What really set him apart was something in his manner: a mixture of posture, speech, and confidence, that showed he was acutely alert to his role on the stand. He stood as stiffly as a soldier on parade, his shoulders pulled back so that his body resembled, almost comically, a bow pulled taut.

Barnardo described the same scene as Kock, but added more de-tails to his account of Rowan's statement. Narrating Rowan's words in the first person, he told the judge, '"And they put a tyre and tube around my body. They then set it alight" – M'Lord – "and then they left me," M'Lord.'

The man was clearly in pain, he shuffled on his back, attempting to roll over. He shouted out *'Help my! Help my!'* (Help me! Help me!)

Hoping it would calm him down, Barnardo told the man they had radioed for an ambulance.

He then explained how they handed the scene over to the Kleinvlei police.

The second day Barnardo testified was a miserable autumn day. It had drizzled since morning, then pelted down over lunch time. Coming back into the High Court for the afternoon I was shuffling through security when a woman ran up breathless behind me and I turned at the disturbance. Although I glimpsed her face briefly, the image stuck with me for the rest of the afternoon. The woman had a grey shawl thrown over her as protection against the weather. It cov-ered half her face as well as a tiny bundle, a shockingly small baby. The woman's face, panicked, was striking. Though it was composed of harsh features – a sharp nose, deep-set eyes – her face had, perhaps due to a sprinkling of freckles, something inexplicably delicate about it. She pushed past me and rushed down a corridor, leaving behind a smell of rain. I wondered what case she had to get to. Was it a hus-band or brother in trouble? Was she there to give moral support to a victim? Was she the victim of some crime?

The next day I recognised Constable Chandré Nadia Wilhelm as this woman the moment she stepped up to the witness box. She was the third police witness and she came from the Kleinvlei Police Station. Wilhelm was on maternity leave but her husband had a court order excusing him from his duties – he was also a police officer – so that he could look after the baby while she testified. I saw him jigging the tiny baby on his prominent belly outside the court room, looking almost as nervous as his wife. Wilhelm had arranged with the judge to take regular breaks to breastfeed.

Of the police officers who were on the scene with Rowan that night, she spent the shortest time on the stand. Throughout she looked unhappy to be there. She sat rather than stood, and often bowed her head, using a normal and unremarkable number of *Edelagbares* – M'Lords.

Her evidence-in-chief was brief. At 1.20 am Kleinvlei got the call: there was a man, burnt, lying beside Blueberry Way. Constable Chandré Wilhelm and Officer Sers Fortuin responded. Arriving on the scene, Wilhelm saw another patrol vehicle with both its emergency and headlights on. A tyre lay burning in the brush. Immediately Wilhelm focused on a human form illuminated by the other van's lights. She approached the man, who lay on his back not far from the tyre, and asked him in Afrikaans, 'Who burnt you?'

'Angy and her husband,' he said, also in Afrikaans.

'Where do they live?'

'They live in the same street as me.'

'Which street is that?'

'I live in Minister Street, in Bardale Squatter Camp, Mfuleni.'

The man continued, 'Angy and her husband and two other men forced me into a white taxi.' Then pain overcame him and he screamed, 'Help me! I can't any more, help me!'

'What's your name?' she asked.

'Rowan du Preez.'

She asked him no more questions.

In the meantime her partner was on the phone with someone at Mfuleni station. He was told that they would take back the crime scene. Wilhelm radioed Kock to tell her. Rowan continued screaming until the ambulance came. '*Help my! Help my! Ek kannie meer nie!*' (I can't any more.)

❖ ❖ ❖

When I arrived at the court for the first time, I hadn't known what the state's case would be. Angy had told me a few months before that she did not know either, only that at the bail hearing the prosecutor 'had talked about something that Rowan had told the police'.

On the face of it, I'd been sympathetic to Angy's story, but it was jarring seeing the police give evidence. Never before had I been so acutely aware that witnesses on the stand made an oath: you staked your testimony on your reputation, stood up in front of the judge in your skin, and if you did not tell the truth, then afterwards you would be known as a liar. And you would have committed a crime, for which you might serve jail time, and for which you would probably lose your job. Why would these people take that risk?

When people pronounced it obvious that Angy had been framed, they weren't drawing on a large pool of similar incidents. In the democratic period there had, at this time[37], been no known and celebrated cases of police stitch-ups, except perhaps the prosecution of Fred van der Vyfer for the murder of his girlfriend, Inge Lotz.[38] In Van der Vyfer's case, the police, perhaps desperate for a conviction in a sensational murder case, planted evidence and manipulated expert forensic opinion to bolster their case against a hapless actuary.

Go back further in our history and you find rich accounts of false confessions, manipulated evidence, and the testimony of askaris, former liberation fighters turned collaborators with the apartheid police torturers and used to betray their comrades.[39] These statements were routinely used to convict political activists of violent acts that they may or may not have committed.

But the full details of the Van der Vyfer case and the sham cases of the apartheid era were unknown or forgotten. When they pronounced Angy innocent, the people I came across drew on a contemporary conviction: that the democratic project to reform the police had failed, and activists who lived and worked in poor neighbourhoods were once again at risk.

This was not a conviction that Judge Henney shared. In fact, the idea that the police were generally corrupt, an idea so widely accepted on the streets outside the courthouse that it was effectively banal, was one that Henney vehemently rejected.

It was clear to me on my first day in court that Henney did not have a huge amount of patience with the defence that King was arguing. It involved long and tedious cross-examination on several events, some of which were not directly connected to the murder. It implied corrupt practice among both constables and generals. And King had only a patchy explanation of how this conspiracy would actually have worked. Henney wanted evidence that the police had been corrupt, individually and demonstrably. He did not want shadowy theories that rested on the police force at large having diffuse motives to persecute or silence a sole activist.

Much of this related to the fact that any conspiracy against Angy was genuinely hard to understand. How much was it about the policeman Tshicila and the corruption inquiry against him? How much was it about the Khayelitsha Commission? The former had powerful individual and personal interests at stake; the latter was either about petty but vicious political competition or the backlash of a powerful institution. But who cared enough, individually, to make something like this happen? And when you added up the harassment that Angy was alleging she experienced, it was hard to know what resources it would have required or how many people would have had to have known about it. For Angy to be entirely innocent, four of her neighbours and three of her local police officers had to be convinced by someone to lie under oath. And many others – at several levels in the hierarchy – had to at least look the other way. When you started toting it up like that it seemed so complex as to be absurd.

Near the end of Kock's cross-examination, Henney flew into a rage with King, when he tried to probe the issue of Blue Downs taking the case back from Kleinvlei. It was a platz, a red-faced, neck-veined platz, the platz from which all subsequent altercations flowed daily. It started and ended in what would come to be a typical iteration: 'On what do you base that question?' And, 'No, no, *no.*'

King's response was to recount the premise of Angy's plea. 'M'Lord, I base it on a number of reasons. Firstly, the background to this matter as regards who the accused are, and what they were doing at the time, what the political scene was at the time.'

Which caused Henney to break in, 'You have been saying this all along, but I'm not seeing how it's tied together. It's all speculation, it's all based on suppositions, nothing concrete, except that the accused was critical towards the police and has voiced concerns against that.'

King recounted again several reasons why he was asking the question, but this angered Henney even more.

'I still don't get it! I still don't see how you tie up this allegation on the one hand and how it's linked. It's all pure speculation. It's all baseless.'

If King didn't 'tie things up' his clients would be torn apart by the prosecutor when they testified, Henney warned, and in the meantime he was tormenting the witnesses. 'I've been waiting for you to tie it together. It's not being done. It's assumptions. It's speculative.

It's not based on anything and you cannot cross-examine a witness on that. If there's a possibility, then it should be tied up with evidence, and there's no evidence.'

Angy herself affected a fatalistic air. 'I am so tired. I am so tired of this now,' she told me during the recess after Henney's 'baseless' comments. 'What difference does it make? Prosecute or not, either I'm in jail for life or I'm dead. The judge is God. If the judge has it in for the defence or the prosecution the case is lost. I wish they would just go ahead and convict me.'

❖ ❖ ❖

The defence were fairly confident that evidence from Kock and the other police would be easy to discredit. For a start, though they all claimed to have made notes, all of these notes were now lost. This gave the defence room to explore several possibilities. Had Rowan, suffering from brutal injury, said anything at all? If he had spoken, had he been at all coherent? If he had spoken and been coherent, or somewhat coherent, did he perhaps say something different to what Barnardo's statement recorded? Could he, perhaps, have said something garbled which incorporated bits of what they recorded ('Angy', 'TV', 'taken from Bardale') which had since been massaged into a clearer narrative?

They could also explore if there was anything about the conduct or memories of the police witnesses that would throw the rest of their testimony into doubt.

In his cross-examination of Kock, King first established what she and Barnardo did after they left the scene. They drove back to the station, Kock said. Barnardo's statement was time stamped at 2 am so he would have sat down to record it straight away. Kock, the commander of the shift that night, did the duty parade with the VisPol team and went home at about 3 am. Later, she took a police photographer to the crime scene.

' "Protect and Serve" is the police motto, isn't it?' King asked.

'Yes, M'Lord.'

'Now, did you go and tell the family that their son was lying in Tygerberg Hospital?'

'No, I didn't do that, sir.'

In fact, the police hadn't pursued any of their leads that night – despite having the address of the victim, his full name, and the name of his attacker 'who stays near me'. Even Henney joined in on grilling her about this. 'It's all very good and well that you followed procedure … but you're on the scene and Bardale is on the way. You have to go past it in order to return to the police station.'

Kock's answer to this was simply that it was at the end of her shift. The detectives had the information, which was contained in Barnardo's statement, the A1, made at 2 am that night, and it was their job to do something about it. It was lazy, she admitted to the judge, and, looking at her inert face, I thought, quite believable. But King argued there was more to it than that: 'The statement that I make to you is that it wasn't a dereliction of duty.' He argued that she didn't have any leads to follow up after she left the scene and neither did the detectives because 'Rowan said nothing about those things'. With the same lack of emotion to which she'd agreed she'd been lazy to Henney, Kock denied this.

Kock's third day of cross-examination was tedious and frustrating, and it went on for hours. Ndlovu cross-examined her on the flagging down of Kock's van by the unknown man, but got neither his nor King's clients anywhere. King got Kock to run through Rowan's declaration again, in the first person, combing over any change in word order or vocabulary. She stumbled and King jumped on every change: 'Wait, wait, wait, "they brought me here, beat me" – was the beating before or after he was brought there? No, no, no. Don't say "he also said at a later stage". I want the precise words. You mustn't leave anything out. Stop, stop, stop. You are running ahead now. I only want to know the first sentence. Now you speak of "put in a taxi", and now you speak of "loaded in". Which one is right?'

'"White Quantum taxi"?' he said to her. 'Because earlier you said "Quantum white taxi".'

Was she sure he didn't say, '*they* brought me here'?

As she continually rebutted his criticisms and allegations, her testimony and her physical presence seemed aligned in a formidable solidity. The defence got little support from the judge in trying to pin down the statement. '*Belaglik*,' said Henney at one point, about King's performance that day – laughable. And so King seemed the pedant, grasping for inconsistencies.

King's lack of traction did not seem to defeat him, and eventually he found a more fruitful angle. On Kock's second day on the stand, a short one, King had spent most of the time getting her to describe their actions on the scene after speaking to the victim, which she did, slowly and confidently. She had stood next to Rowan while she radioed the Ops room for an ambulance. They said they would send one. Then she walked to the vehicle and radioed Ops again to get Kleinvlei to the scene. Then she and Barnardo spent five to seven minutes walking around, found the half-burnt tyre, and Kleinvlei arrived. She watched a male and female police officer approach the victim. Then she went back to the car to check where the ambulance was, and at about this time she saw it arriving. Barnardo spoke with the ambulance staff, asking them which hospital they would use, and then she watched them attend to Rowan. In total this took 25 to 30 minutes.

She was made to go over it again: she was certain Kleinvlei came first, and then the ambulance. The Kleinvlei cops were with Rowan for about eight to 10 minutes. Then she saw the ambulance park, the staff get out the ambulance, and they joined the Kleinvlei cops with the victim.

'And then he was loaded into the ambulance.'

King said, 'You saw that?'

'Correct, Your Honour.'

'Now, how long after you arrived on the scene did the ambulance take to arrive?' he asked her.

She wasn't sure. 'Round about a half hour, Your Honour.' She again confirmed the sequence of events she had already described. King checked with her how long it would take to get to the Sasol petrol station: about three to five minutes. And how long did they spend there? Long enough to fill a whole tank. While there she received the radio call from her superior to take back the case and they returned to the Blueberry Hill scene and waited for the ambulance, which hadn't arrived yet?

'That's correct, Your Honour.'

King then handed up the Emergency Medical Services report, which detailed the time the request was logged and the time the ambulance got there. 'Incident: 01.21.' Then: 'Arrive scene: 01.32.' It took the ambulance eleven minutes to get to Rowan and the Blue Downs police officers. The ambulance's records also clearly stated that they were only on the scene for 13 minutes. Kock's story changed: actually they went to the Sasol petrol station after the ambulance had arrived. 'Your Honour, I could be wrong, they could first have come and then we went to put in petrol.'

She then said they filled up and returned to the scene before the ambulance left. This version did not account for all her previous memories of the ambulance staff attending to Rowan, and it was still improbable. They would first have handed the scene over to Kleinvlei, and then it was a six- to ten-minute return-trip to the petrol station, where they filled up a whole tank – a lot to happen in 13 minutes.

Suddenly her recollection became shakier. She had already admitted it might be Captain Jonker she spoke to, rather than Captain Coetzee, when presented with evidence that it was Jonker on stand-by that night. Next she flipped on whether Barnardo asked his questions in English or Afrikaans. 'Your Honour, I could be confused. It was a long time ago. I could be wrong.'

And though this was the point King ended on – her improbable version, her suddenly fallible memory – it did not seem like a fatal blow. She was simply that solid a presence. 'And again, just to emphasise the point, the reason why you're so uncertain,' said King, 'is that it happened a long time ago, a year and half, and you did not immediately make an affidavit or write it down?'

Kock, glumly, patiently, seemingly unperturbed, confirmed King's analysis: 'Yes, Your Honour.'

❖ ❖ ❖

Something about Barnardo, on the other hand, communicated a quick intelligence, and in his attitude towards the court's authority, ambition. Unlike most witnesses, he faced the judge directly, spoke to him alone, and bookended each sentence with a 'M'Lord'.

Barnardo had been at Mfuleni only six months at the time of the incident and it was his first stint in the field out of police college. He was still in training, a one-stripe student constable. He walked onto the scene with little experience and was very much the junior to Captain Kock. Yet on the stand he came off as the brighter of the two, and talked with an air of purpose and control that contrasted with Kock's dull, seemingly thoughtless 'I don't knows'. And, though he looked only at the judge, when it came to cross-examination it was clear that there was a true duel between him and King.

King began by worrying at a familiar point: if Rowan could so easily relate his story, as it appeared in their statements, why hadn't they been able to get more out of him, such as the names of the accomplices? Barnardo's responses demonstrated one of two things:

either that he was a bit thick, which might have washed except he couldn't quite hide that he wasn't, or that he had a talent for almost answering the question.

'M'Lord, there are questions that I did ask him, M'Lord, but he didn't respond to all my questions, M'Lord, due to being in pain, M'Lord.'

'Did you ask him, for example, who was with them, this husband-and-wife team?'

'No, M'Lord. I didn't ask him that.'

'Well, tell us what you asked.'

'M'Lord, I asked him what has happened to him.'

'What else?'

'That's what I asked him, M'Lord.'

'Okay, constable. You said you asked other questions – or did I mishear you?'

'No, you heard me correctly, M'Lord.'

'Then what other questions did you ask?'

'M'Lord, I can't remember what other questions I asked him, M'Lord.'

As King questioned him on the actual statement, various discrepancies emerged between what Barnardo said each time he repeated Rowan's words in court. So King tried to nail down his exact words. For example, Barnardo's statements and version in court repeatedly mentioned that Rowan said 'Bardale Squatter Camp'. But when King pressed him on this point, in a way that suggested there was something strange about Rowan describing Bardale in this way, he explained that he had added the words 'squatter camp'. Later, when I visited Bardale I saw exactly why this was important. The people in Rowan and Angy's Bardale were not squatters: they had been legally settled on their sites, which came with piped water and electricity connections. Around the corner was a truly informal settlement, with higgledy-piggledy roads and no piped sanitation, and the difference was clear and important to everyone there. In Barnardo's testimony 'squatter camp' emerged as being how the police distinguished between two different 'Bardale' zones in the Mfuleni jurisdiction. They saw one as a formal suburb of single-storey houses with neat front lawns, while the other Bardale consisted of shacks and concrete sinks. Barnardo ended up taking 'squatter camp' out of his version of what Rowan had said.

The differences between his account and Kock's were less easy to smooth out. Kock said Barnardo had asked his questions in Afrikaans. This was unremarkable, as all of them, including Rowan, were fluent in both languages. But Barnardo maintained he asked the questions in English, while Rowan replied in Afrikaans. Most importantly for King was the issue of fluency. While Kock maintained Rowan spoke with no pauses, fluidly, perfectly clearly, Barnardo claimed there were pauses. King tried to get clarity on how much his injuries and general condition had affected his speech.

'Is it fair to say he spoke with difficulty?'

'M'Lord, I said it is fair to say that he spoke in pain, M'Lord.'

'Let me repeat the question. Maybe you didn't understand it. Is it fair to say he spoke with difficulty – not pain, with difficulty?'

'M'Lord, I can say it is fair that he spoke with difficulty due to his pain, M'Lord.'

'What do you mean? Explain to the court.'

'I mean, M'Lord, that the pain that the victim has obtained, M'Lord, was difficult, because he was screaming for help, M'Lord. I don't know for how long he was at the scene, M'Lord, or for how long he had been laying there, M'Lord. So what I am saying is: it was difficult, he was in pain, M'Lord.'

'Difficult for you to hear and understand, or difficult for him to talk?'

'M'Lord, I heard exactly what he was saying, M'Lord.'

'So you are saying it was difficult for him to talk?'

'I am saying I heard what he said, M'Lord.'

Judge Henney intervened at this point, though not unkindly. 'No, no. Not what you heard. Was it difficult for him to talk?'

'M'Lord, I believe it was difficult for him to talk because he was in pain, M'Lord.'

King took over again. 'Constable, I am not interested in what you believe. I am interested in what you observed and heard. Was it difficult for him to talk?'

'Yes, it was difficult for him to talk, M'Lord.'

'How was that difficulty expressed? Explain to the court what you saw and heard that was difficult.'

'What I observed, M'Lord, is that he was screaming but he was talking as well, M'Lord.'

'So what you are saying is he didn't say "I am Rowan du Preez and I reside at 24541 Mfuleni". He was saying "I am Rowan – *scream* – du – *scream* – du – *scream* – Preez – *scream*". Is that what you are saying?'

'M'Lord, what I am saying is he told me his name is Rowan du Preez, M'Lord.'

❖ ❖ ❖

One of the more curious aspects of Barnardo's and Kock's stories was the moment at which Mfuleni station decided to take back the case it had successfully palmed off on another station. If there was a moment when the senior leadership were first alerted to Rowan's attack then it was when Kock radioed the incident into the Ops room. That would have given them several hours to hatch a plan before Angy's arrest. The duty detective and the senior officer on stand-by could have alerted Redelinghuys, the head of detectives.

Police stations all had (and still have) targets to achieve, targets which were important measures of their performance in the eyes of the police hierarchy and its rewards system. These targets ranged from the number of arrests made, to the number of cases solved, to how many knives were confiscated or shebeens raided. Vigilante murder cases typically had abysmal conviction rates – witnesses were often complicit, or felt solidarity with the murderers, and unless a whole crowd was arrested it could be hard to identify a primary perpetrator. And by Kock's account she didn't tell her superior anything about the case when she contacted him. She did not say that Rowan had made a statement, or that he had mentioned Angy's name. It was not obviously the kind of case that was going to help Mfuleni achieve its numbers. The fact that Kock said she gave Coetzee (or Jonker, Kock was unsure who she actually called) no details on the phone made the decision stranger still. How then did he (Coetzee or Jonker) know that the crime was committed in Mfuleni?

King was never explicit but the theory behind his questioning went something like this: that October night the police found Rowan on Blueberry Hill, burnt, still alive and crying out for help but not coherent. Because he was an albino they knew it was Rowan – Roy, as they called him at the station, where he made frequent appearances including to do community service in the grounds. This explained why the ambulance staff only had one personal detail about him in their records – his first name, which they got from the police. Kock, not wanting extra work, handed the case to Kleinvlei but in the meantime radioed in to report the murder, telling her bosses who it was: 'Roy's been necklaced.' After Kock signed off the radio, senior police officers called each other and conferred. Maybe they didn't know what they wanted to do yet, but they told Kock to keep the case in-house, and spoke to Kleinvlei to give them the same order. When the witnesses arrived at the station on Sunday morning no one could tell them anything because the police really didn't know who necklaced Rowan, and hadn't decided yet who it would be. That was why no one was arrested or questioned the night before. When most of the senior officers met at the (unrelated) Gusha Street crime scene at 8 am on the Sunday morning – more on that to come – they talked as a group and reached a decision. Then Barnardo's statement Barnardo's statement – the A1 – was made that afternoon and backdated to the early morning. (Kock only made a statement three months after the murder. Wilhelm made hers five months after the murder.) If you entertained this 'conspiracy', it was interesting to think about what role Barnardo might have had: an ambitious, fledgling constable, who put his name down as the first and primary witness to Rowan's declaration.

This conspiracy theory could be easily dispelled if more of the documentation was available. Wilhelm might have recorded something in her pocket notebook like – 'attended crime scene on Blueberry Hill. Victim gave statement and named suspect "*Angy en haar man*". Mfuleni took the case back because crime began there'.

Above all, usually you'd be able to understand a little more about the lines of decision-making or the thinking behind a move like that by looking at the Occurrence Book. According to the police's own standing orders, the Occurrence Book is 'the most important of all the registers used in the Service. It must contain a complete record of the history of a police station, besides serving as the control record of all other registers'. The opening of all dockets, the start and end of all shifts, the booking out of cell phones, firearms, and hand radios, arrests, all domestic violence incidents, the handing in of prisoners' property, the payments of fines and bail, visits by officers from other precincts, and complaints against police: all of these things were recorded in the Occurrence Book. Each entry was numbered consecutively, and cross-referenced to other relevant entries, with the name of the person who made the record and the time it was made. Have an Occurrence Book in front of you and you had a searchable index of every major and minor event that happened at a police station.

But Mfuleni's Occurrence Book didn't record this decision, and Kleinvlei's for the night of 13 and 14 October was missing. Kock's pocket book also might have been of some help, but this too was lost. And so was Barnardo's, which might not have recorded the decision to hand over, but would have recorded the incident. The defence had asked the stations involved repeatedly to search for the Occurrence Books and the pocket books, which by law should be handed over to the station for safekeeping when they are complete. Barnardo had even made a formal statement in response to one of Greeff's requests, saying his pocket book was untraceable.

But not all lost documents stayed lost. After Kock's second day of cross-examination, almost all of which King spent going over the order of events at the scene and trying to recreate the decision to hand over to the other station, the court went into a two-week recess. Upon its return Prosecutor Palesa gave an exuberant report: the pocket book of Constable Raul Barnardo had unexpectedly resurfaced.

❖ ❖ ❖

Discovered mid-way through Kock's testimony, Barnardo's pocket book was King's number-one problem. Now that it was tendered as evidence, it provided more or less contemporaneous corroboration of Barnardo's story, and a reason why Rowan's words could be reliably recalled. Either the defence needed to argue that the entire book had been reconstructed or that the specific entry relating to Rowan had been inserted in a open space, later, when they knew what it needed to say.

King read from Barnardo's pocket book on the night of the incident: '... Street arrest: suspect arrested for possession of dagga. 2 x stop weight. 0.002 grams. Exhibit was booked in SAP13 [Occurrence Book number such and such] ... 00:10 Roadblock operation at Mandla Road opposite Silversands robots. All equipment was used. Cones, reflectors and stop signs. Vehicles pulled off: White Nissan TDI (searched vehicle). Silver Ford Figo (searched vehicle). Black Tata (searched vehicle). 01:50 received a complaint by un-known black male hearing screams from bushes. Went to investigate. On arrival in Blueberry Hill I heard a scream near the road.'

'Then,' King said, 'the incident with Rowan. Then you go on to say you attended the crime scene.'

He continued reading Barnardo's notes, which matched the constable's statement. So far the pocket book seemed a reasonable list of the events and records taken that night. 'Now, however, it gets strange, seriously strange,' said King. 'On the next page, page 47, it said, "continued late entry. Establishment of the composition of the CPF [Community Policing Forum]. Outcomes: improved stakeholder communication, improved and re-affirmed stakeholder relationships..."'

Immediately after the entry on Rowan there was a long series of notes about a Community Policing Forum meeting that Barnardo had attended as part of his training. These notes were dated on the night of Rowan's attack. The date of the meeting had been eight months previously on 22 February 2012.

'Now, did you fill that in and the following one and a half pages after you had completed the docket?' King asked.

'M'Lord, when I completed the docket, I wrote the pocket book up, M'Lord.'

'You see, your evidence is that you were rushing to complete the docket so that you could go off. Now, it doesn't make sense that you would have had the time to fill in something like this that relates back eight months. Do you understand what I am saying to you? Can you explain it?'

'I understand, M'Lord. M'Lord, the entry I made was important, M'Lord, it was requested.'

'Let me make sure you understand me correctly. In the light of your evidence that you had no time to do anything else, like find the accused or tell the family or do anything else but fill in the docket and go off duty, that entry seems bizarre. That is what I am putting to you.' King's point was clear, but this was where it ended and it did not seem fatally damaging.

Later, King picked up on something else in the pocket book. If it told the truth, he said, then Barnardo was indeed working the next day, from the afternoon onwards (which he had previously denied). What was more, he was on duty guarding the cells. According to the pocket book, he fed the prisoners, who would have included Angy and Isaac. Did he remember?

'M'Lord, I don't remember feeding prisoners, but if it states in my pocket book then I was working in the cells, helping the cell guard feeding the prisoners.'

'Let me try and jog your memory. The accused said she saw you there.'

Barnardo remained silent, his face impassive.

King continued. 'Accused 1, Ms Peter. She says she saw you and she spoke to you that evening because she was trying to get medication for her asthma condition. And when she asked you, you laughed.'

'That is incorrect, M'Lord.'

'You see, the reason I am asking you all these questions is the accused was subsequently hospitalised for the asthma or shortly thereafter. She was taken from Pollsmoor, where she was lodged, and placed in hospital as a result of this asthma condition. And you say you know nothing about anybody asking you for medical help?'

'M'Lord, I know nothing about anybody asking me for medical attention or assistance.'

❖ ❖ ❖

Chandré Wilhelm was an important witness for the state. According to her statement, Rowan told the story of his attack on two occasions, the second being to her alone. She was not a Mfuleni cop and consequently uncontaminated by the Tshicila business. Her statement corroborated both Rowan's ability to talk and what he said. It was important in other respects too. It was such an important piece of evidence that you had to wonder why it hadn't been recorded at the time. Instead, it had taken the investigating officer five months to obtain her statement. Her pocket book, too, was missing, as was the original folio on which she had made her notes. The Kleinvlei Ops room Occurrence Book for the period was also missing.

King picked at the edges of her story, trying to find a weak point, but couldn't. 'As I told you, Your Honour, my focus was on the man. All I could [see] was a horrifying sight for me, someone who is burnt out,' she told King, explaining why she hadn't asked any other questions. 'That's all that attracted my attention.'

She repeatedly said she couldn't remember anything apart from his words, because the sight was grotesque. This was a reasonable explanation, and a wall King could not penetrate.

King returned to what was either a meticulous or a pedantic attempt – depending on your view of his defence – to reconstruct the exact words Rowan uttered, with their exact pauses and exact torturous inhales and exact cries of pain. Wilhelm, like the others, took this exercise badly and it progressed slowly, through one assay after another, with King's patience wearing thin.

'In the answer he gave, was there anything yelled between the answer or was it smoothly, consecutively given to you?'

'He said "Angy and her husband". These were his words.'

'You do not listen to the question.'

Henney stepped in: 'Did he shout when he answered, or did he answer in between screams?'

'No, he just said: Angy and her husband, Your Honour.'

King went at it again, and again got no answer. Henney too took another turn. King started a question, 'Do I understand...?' but was interrupted by the interpreter. Annoyed, swiftly, he turned towards his table and exclaimed to Greeff: 'It's like cross-examining in a wet bag!'

Palesa leapt up. 'I have just a humble concern, M'Lord. Counsel said "cross-examining a wheat bag" behind his back and I could hear it from here. That is uncalled for, M'Lord.'

'No, no,' said King explaining that he said 'in a wet bag' because of the interruptions caused by the translation.

Palesa was not satisfied. 'He passed to his instructing attorney: "like cross-examining a wheat bag".'

'No,' said King, '"in a wet bag". *In.*'

Henney defended King. 'It's frustrating if you want to cross-examine, and then you want to get into momentum and there's an interpretation, then you have to stop.' The judge tried to get the process started again, but King, uncharacteristically, did not follow his lead and resume. He remained in an odd pose, stiff, looking downwards, one hand on the front bench.

'M'Lord, might I take a short adjournment at this stage?'

'Sure, what time is it?'

'It is frustrating and I want to get myself,' he took a breath, 'under control again.'

After a short adjournment, Wilhelm was brought back in.

King was his usual energetic self. 'You heard the prosecutor, who sits three steps behind me, say that I tried to call you a "wheat sack". You heard that now, né?'

'I heard a bit of the "wet sack". I didn't hear anything further, Your Honour.'

'A "wheat sack", that's what he heard. He didn't hear at all that I said "cross-examination is like arguing in a wet sack", because...'

'I only heard a bit of wet sack, Your Honour.' She looked at him nervously, as if scared she'd be in trouble somehow.

King pushed on: 'The problem is, that is precisely the problem that the defence sits with. Because it's *the interpretation of something that wasn't heard right* that's the problem. Now you have an example of what can happen. That's why it's so important that we are sure about precisely what was said. Understand?'

'I understand, yes.'

Yet the answers to his questions remained evasive. It was unclear if she said Rowan only screamed between statements, or in the midst of them. King asked the question so many times and in so many ways it was amazing this remained a mystery. Was he not explaining clearly enough for the witness, was she not able to understand the question even if it was clearly put, or was she simply refusing to answer it? It was incredibly frustrating to listen to. King asked her eight times before Henney stepped in, rephrased the question in terms that were neither more nor less clear, and she defaulted to, 'I don't remember.'

One of the strangest exchanges between Wilhelm and King happened when he asked her to explain how the decision was made to give the scene back to Mfuleni.

She wouldn't answer and eventually King said, 'I invite you to make your own decision over what might have happened.'

But Wilhelm looked aghast at being asked to ad lib. 'I'm not going to… I'm sorry. I can't make my own things, Your Honour.'

'You can not think for yourself. Why?'

'No.'

When King pressed, she followed this with: 'I just followed orders at the time, M'Lord.'

In the end, I was left believing she had deliberately evaded his questions, but had done it in a hesitant, nervous way that masked it even more thoroughly than had Barnardo's performance. By mixing in admissions of poor recall with strenuous appeals to how traumatising the scene was she had managed not to commit herself.

But what did this mean? Perhaps it really happened, but she didn't take notes, and on the stand she couldn't remember the details, and so found herself trapped in a corner by what her statement said and was too scared to improvise. Perhaps investigating officer Muthien really was just too lazy to drive to her station in the five months since the incident to collect her statement. Or perhaps Muthien had really spent that time wearing down a woman who didn't want to lie.

Wilhelm was 30 years old at the time of the murder. She'd been out of police college for two years, spent one of them as a student constable, and been a fully fledged police officer for a year. King tried to leverage her junior rank, her lack of experience, and perhaps her feminine attitude on the stand, to show she was too overwhelmed by the scene to remember it clearly. Inadvertently he stepped into something that would damage him instead.

'Let's accept,' he said, 'it was in the beginning of your career as a police officer.'

'If you want to, accept it as so.'

'Had you had any other incidents where people were burnt?'

'No, Your Honour, it's the first.'

'Tell the court in your own words what you went through when you see this incident. What was, what effect did it have on you?'

'Your Honour, afterwards – Your Honour, at that time I couldn't say exactly what went through my mind. But I know that in the evenings I began to have nightmares. It was after we attended the scene. It…'

'Was it shocking?'

'I will say, the shock, after it all then the shock took me, Your Honour.'

Palesa was worried about this enough to revisit it in re-examination. He tried to spin her lack of experience as an explanation for why she had not kept the notes she had made on the scene. Once he was done there was a palpable sense of immanent relief, that Wilhelm was about to be released from days of long, hard interrogation, and Henney himself stepped in to clarify a point.

'It seems to me this incident touched you deeply?'

She mumbled something out of which only a weak 'Your Honour' escaped.

'And did you get psychological treatment after what you experienced?'

'No, Your Honour.'

'And did you come to the attention of your superiors? I see you are now emotional.'

Wilhelm didn't weep. She just hung her head forward and wiped her eyes. Her voice was strained when she spoke again.

'You, M'Lord, if someone repeatedly has to say what happened then it all plays back once again.'

'So you relive the nightmares, as you put it?'

'Yes, Your Honour.'

Later, after all the medical evidence, after everything else had run its course, I linked two contradictory things to this exchange. One: that for a long time I couldn't stop thinking, day-dreaming, really, about what it meant to be burnt alive – to feel cold liquid on your face, the petrol stinging your eyes, leaking into your mouth, and the awful wait between the sound of a match lighting and contact from an approaching bud of heat.

Two: that for me I was most likely to cry in public at times of anger, helplessness or relief. Wilhelm's tears came right at the end, when she was about to be released from the stand to join her husband and baby in the corridor outside.

Chapter Twelve

On the days when I wasn't at Angy and Isaac's trial, I drove out to Khayelitsha and attended the commission's hearings at Lookout Hill. During lunch breaks, I'd sit on the stairs of the hall's outdoor amphitheatre and try to find answers to the questions Angy's trial brought up in the proceedings I'd heard that day.

Many policemen testified at the commission, from Provincial Commissioner Arno Lamoer, to the men and women who led specialist units and police departments within the province. Former policemen who had served in Khayelitsha and around the country came to give expert opinion and draw comparisons from their tenure. But most revealing of all, and first on the block, were the men then working in Khayelitsha, the commanders, and head detectives from the three Khayelitsha stations, Harare, Khayelitsha (also known as Site B), and Lingelethu West. They were white and coloured and black, Afrikaner and Zulu, fat and thin. The quality of their answers, the sincerity of their defences, the degree to which you believed they were overwhelmed men doing their best or defeated men whiling away the days until retirement, varied from testimony to testimony. Yet as you noticed consistent turns of phrase and habits of thought, let alone the ubiquity of moustaches, they seemed increasingly of a piece. Perhaps in this respect, I thought, the police were the country's greatest non-racial success: police culture was so overriding, so undeniably, even dangerously, unifying.

Under questioning from the evidence leaders, they floundered. Many of these men had submitted their documents late and incomplete, yet they'd known this commission was coming for months. On the stand, they seemed unprepared, sweating as they testified in the close air of summer. It was easy to imagine their internal contortions, trying both to deny personal responsibility and avoid embarrassing their superiors, while also not throwing juniors to the dogs or scrabbling for some kind of answer to questions about their station's dire performance.

Despite any evidence of a conscious strategy, and perhaps through sheer ideological inertia, they all marshalled a similar set of arguments. They deferred to the specifics of the case and claimed they'd have to look at the docket. They said they couldn't possibly generalise. Pushed further to comment on recurring problems, they argued that individual policemen might have made mistakes – they were only human – and there would always be, they stressed, a few bad apples. Most of all, they were doing the best they could, in difficult circumstances.

It was true that despite working in three of the stations fielding the worst crime rates in the city – in the country, even – they did it with startlingly inadequate resources. The numbers of police officers per station were low given the population densities. There were too few detectives. Vehicles were permanently out of action because they weren't repaired. The stations were physically too small to house their offices, while requests to various government departments to release land for expansion went unanswered. Station Commander Dladla, talking about how overburdened his detectives were with murder dockets, said, 'In the movies you see a team of detectives descending on a crime scene. Here you have a team of dockets descending on a detective.' Yet people only noticed their failures. 'Always,' Dladla said, 'we are the whipping boys.'

Off the record, a very senior police official complained bitterly at how the Khayelitsha officers were being portrayed as the detritus of the force. 'When I worked in Khayelitsha, I worked with the best sons and daughters. *The best.*' A former Khayelitsha station commander, an Afrikaner, in response to criticism from the police counsel, replied, his voice wavering, 'I bled for Khayelitsha as if it were my own.'

These men sounded sincere, and it was hard not to be persuaded by their defences, though harder still to understand why, given all this, they would resent the commission so bitterly. The process was carefully picking out and examining their difficulties: the dearth of detectives, the dilapidated vehicles, the risks associated with every patrol. If anything, it seemed their conclusions would veer towards better resources and fewer, more strategic, tasks for the police.

Major-General Jeremy Veary, one of the province's most senior and respected policemen, an ex-liberation fighter from the Cape Flats turned top detective, scoffed at the idea that antipathy to the commission lay in high-level politics. The DA-ANC feud was a red herring, he said. Rank and file didn't pay attention to any of that, and it didn't filter down. But the men and women working in Khayelitsha's stations, and beyond, saw the commission as a personal attack on their performance. They were the ones always mopping up the mess created by society's broader dysfunction, not creating it. And so, he said, they had withdrawn into a laager and opposed it.

It was this 'laager mentality', a potent 'internal solidarity', that several experts before the commission drew attention to as a core element of police culture. It was found in police forces around the world, and, as it could easily abet corruption, it posed a problem everywhere. New York University criminologist Jerome Skolnick has argued that '... the constant risk of danger that officers face, their designated authority and capacity to use force against citizens and the pressure to perform their duties effectively and efficiently generates "a working personality" characterised by suspiciousness, internal solidarity, social isolation and conservatism'. Experts at the commission claimed this culture was especially pronounced in the South African police.

Dr Liza Grobler, a criminologist specialising in police corruption, characterised SAPS culture as 'an us-versus-them mentality, police against society'. She said this fed 'the blue code of silence: "don't talk, don't report your friends"'. Gareth Newham, a researcher at the Institute for Security Studies, argued that internal solidarity arose out of policing on the beat, particularly a dangerous one, where policemen needed to trust each other and cooperate closely. It was not seen in a negative light by policemen, but as an indication of 'group solidarity, empathy and support for colleagues in difficult circumstances'. But from the outside it was sinister, a culture that suppressed internal criticism and refused to cooperate with internal investigations, and forced individuals to overlook the misconduct of their colleagues. It was maintained with implicit and explicit threats. 'It can be dangerous,' said Grobler. 'Police have died reporting corrupt colleagues.'

And about Angy, one policeman, who had held a senior management position in one of the Khayelitsha stations throughout her time campaigning, had been honest enough to tell me, 'She was more vocal and more militant than the other activists – she made a lot of accusations.' He didn't think she'd been a destructive presence, but 'in her eyes, the police were the enemy. That's my take. She made it clear. A lot of police officers smiled inwardly when she got involved in the very thing she accused us of causing.'

Chapter Thirteen

The case in Court 17 resumed and now focused on the ambulance staff who had attended to Rowan. We knew that after leaving the scene at Blueberry Hill, the ambulance carrying Rowan du Preez sped down the N2, the major arterial highway into the centre of the city, with sirens screeching. At a short distance from Mfuleni, it stopped on the verge of the highway to pick up paramedics. Mohammed Abdullah got inside and found the ambulance was a mess and the patient was critical.[40] The kit bag on the floor was in disarray; there wasn't enough room for his partner, who was left behind.

Abdullah had qualified as a paramedic two years earlier and had seen many burn victims. In the townships and the shacklands, fire was a constant hazard. Paraffin stoves could explode; bootleg electricity connections could spark; embers could be blown from open fires used for cooking or heating. In neighbourhoods made of wood and tin, small fires quickly became huge blazes. One thing Abdullah knew about burn victims was that they needed all your attention.

The man was conscious, which was good. He could protect his own airway, which was very good, though not likely to be the case for long. The man wouldn't answers his questions about his medical history but that was okay, because the medications Abdullah gave him didn't have contraindications. He did not answer when Abdullah said, 'Sir, can you move your leg? Sir, can you rotate your leg out?' Neither could he check eye-movement because he believed the man's eyelids were burnt shut. 'Can you stick your tongue out?' he asked. The man did not answer but his mouth was open a crack and when Abdullah put in a flat wooden paddle he saw a tongue coated in soot. Abdullah fitted an oxygen mask on his patient to counteract carbon-monoxide poisoning but the man swiped at it, moaning, 'No, give me water.' He wet the man's lips. Next he tried to insert a drip into the back of the man's hand but the man pulled his hand away.

'Please do not move your hand, sir,' he said, but the man just moaned.

'No! Give me water.'

They could not give him water. That was what the drip was for. He tried to insert the drip higher up on the man's arm but encountered too much resistance. The groin was the next place he would usually try but whatever the man had been wearing before – tracksuit pants or shorts or some other garment made of synthetic fibre – it had fused to his body in a solid film which the needle could not penetrate. He moved to the neck but couldn't find a vein.

In the end they put the needle into a bone near the man's shoulder. The man screamed '*Jou ma se poes!*' many times.

Before they got to the hospital Abdullah did a mortality calculation: 100% for the surface area which was burnt, 30% for the burns inside. The man would certainly die.

❖ ❖ ❖

The testimony of seven medical witnesses took up the majority of the trial-within-the-trial. The emergency had been called in by the police at 01.21 am and their ambulance had been dispatched immediately from Elsies River Day Hospital, taking exactly 11 minutes to arrive. Martha Pieterse, an ambulance assistant, and Andrew Swarts, the ambulance driver for the Metro Emergency Medical Services, were the first on the scene and loaded Rowan into the ambulance. They had radioed for a paramedic, but as that stretch of road was hard to find it was decided to collect the paramedics on the highway en route to Groote Schuur Hospital rather than risk their getting lost in the dark scrub near Mfuleni. Mohammed Abdullah treated Rowan from the collection point until he arrived at Groote Schuur Hospital, at which point Dr Jessica Bernon took over.

These four medical staff had direct dealings with Rowan and their evidence – and the notes they took at the time, as well as the autopsy results – were crucial in determining whether Rowan was able to make the statement the police attributed to him. This question had two components: was he physically able to speak, and was he coherent? Three expert witnesses would be called to help the court come to an answer.

Arguments for both physical ability and cognitive function ultimately revolved around Rowan's physical condition. For issues of physical capacity, the experts dwelt on injury to his lips, tongue, vocal cords and throat, and for coherency, on his level of inebriation and the more diffuse effects that shock or pain might have had on his mental state. The statement the police were attributing to Rowan was several lines of dialogue, complete with a series of actions and including his exact address. This had been made on two occasions. King argued that Rowan would've found it difficult to talk, and, crucially, almost impossible to follow one train of thought and relate a cogent narrative. The state's position was entirely defensive: the testimony of the ambulance staff and the evidence of the coroner supported their story.

The first witness was Martha Pieterse. She had been an ambulance assistant in the Metro Emergency Medical Services for nine years when she arrived on the scene with the ambulance driver, Andrew Swarts. They, of all the people who had dealt with Rowan at the height of his injuries, had no agenda in court. Another doctor had dealt with him at hospital, but only after pain medication and liquids had been administered.

Pieterse explained that once all three of them were in the ambulance, she had performed a standard test used by the emergency services called the Glasgow Coma Scale (GCS). Originally designed for rapidly assessing levels of consciousness following a head injury it was now widely applied by emergency services to patients suffering various traumas. The GCS had three components: a test for eye opening (max four points), verbal responses (max five points), and motor responses (max six points). These were assessed to give an aggregate score out of 15, with three indicating the patient was deeply unconscious and 15 that they were fully awake and responsive. A high GCS score would be good for the state, as it would show a medical opinion from the time of Rowan's brutal assault that suggested he was aware of what he was saying and that he meant to say it.

In the ambulance Pieterse gave Rowan full marks for each test. In court, she explained her rationale. His eyes were closed when they approached and he didn't appear able to blink, but the lids could be peeled back revealing corneas that appeared undamaged: 4/4. While he did not answer their questions, she felt he could clearly hear what they were saying and so scored him 5/5 for verbal responses. His high score for motor response Pieterse derived from his requests for water, which she felt indicated that he knew what was happening around him.

But in her evidence she said, 'We tried to speak to him, he couldn't speak to us, that was why I wrote "male patient unknown". I asked for medical history but nobody could give me one, as no one knew him.' And she explained that the whole time she was with him he didn't say anything except 'water, water, water'.

'So he couldn't speak?' Henney asked her.

'No.'

He asked her again, leaning in, serious, 'This is why you're here.

This is what's important to us. Could he speak?'

Again, Pieterse said, 'He couldn't speak. He wasn't in a state to speak.'

She didn't know how the police arrived at the name Rowan. For 'address' she wrote, 'Male patient unknown', because the police didn't give her any other information.

When King said, 'No questions,' Palesa was taken aback. Perhaps he had noticed what King had not, that there was a crucial question which Pieterse still needed to be asked: 'Did you actually ask Rowan du Preez any questions?' Palesa argued that Pieterse's statement that Rowan couldn't talk was ambiguous. It was an assumption. Maybe she got the name from the police who had not volunteered any other information about the victim. Maybe because Rowan looked in pretty bad shape, she didn't ask him anything else. King argued for a different interpretation. When their divergent interpretations became apparent, not long after Pieterse testified, King lodged a formal application to recall her 'in the interests of justice'. Henney refused.

Mohammed Abdullah had been a paramedic for four years when he delivered his testimony. A man in his mid-twenties, with hair cut short and gelled up in the centre, his delivery was sincere, and self-consciously professional. He made a point of emphasising that he was also a lecturer. At the time of the incident he had two years experience and a bachelor's degree in emergency medical care from the Cape Peninsula University of Technology. He was hardly a veteran, but he had perhaps 20 minutes of crucial first-hand experience of Rowan's state before they arrived at the hospital. His cross-examination did not need to be tense. But when King probed his rationale for the high score he gave Rowan on the GCS, Abdullah became visibly defensive: his professional judgement was at stake.

King made Abdullah run through his reasons for his scoring. These included that Rowan had physically pulled the needle out of his arm when they tried to put in a drip; that he tried to remove the oxygen mask when they put it on him; that he pushed the wooden tongue depressor away with his tongue; and that he had asked for water. This latter implied that Rowan understood that he had been burnt. To Abdullah, these indicated good motor response and an awareness of what was going on around him. He had asked Rowan to open his eyes but Rowan hadn't. Abdullah said it was because they were burnt shut. Not wanting to disadvantage him for this reason, he scored him full marks.

King asked what Abdullah meant by 'responsive behaviour'. The paramedic said he asked Rowan several questions: 'Can you feel this? Can you move this? Can you keep this still?' Rowan hadn't answered. Later, Abdullah also asked him to blink his eyes, and to rotate out his legs, to which Rowan either didn't respond or to which he said, 'give me water'. Abdullah said he never established Rowan name's and when King pushed him on this, gave an impassioned defence of his priorities at the time. A name was only there to 'lend a personal air to the treatment', he said. It was not essential information. 'He responded to pain so I didn't feel it important to know his name. I felt it was important to know what to do and to do it.'

Next on the witness stand was Dr Izelle Moller, a trim, neat woman with a sharp brown bob. She completed the postmortem report and had worked at the Department of Forensic Pathology at the University of Cape Town since October 2010. In 2011 she had completed a diploma in forensic medicine. She cleared up one matter.[41] The vocal cords showed evidence of damage, but through laceration, and not due to heat. This accorded with what the paramedic had said. At the hospital, doctors had failed to intubate several times, which would have repeatedly jammed the tube against the vocal cords.

The rest of her evidence left more room for debate. Both the tongue and the trachea were still moist, and Moller did not find the tongue to be swollen, though it was covered in soot. The pharyngeal wall showed corrugations typical of 'heat shrinkage', a clear sign that it was badly burnt. The upper respiratory tract also showed signs of heat damage, and so did the oesophagus. Her findings on carbon-monoxide poisoning – which would have deprived his brain of oxygen – were inconclusive. While she did send blood for testing, the specimen was deemed 'unsuitable for analysis'. According to the Cape Town laboratory which analysed a sample of Rowan's blood taken at his death, in other words, 18 hours after he was found on Blueberry Hill, he had a concentration of 0.01 grams of alcohol per 100 millilitres.

The state's sole expert witness was Dr Estie Meyer, an ear, nose and throat specialist who had been practising at Groote Schuur Hospital since 2012. She had not examined Rowan herself, but had compiled a report based on the pathologist's autopsy and, crucially, the GCS from the paramedic. 'In order to talk you need three things,' Meyer explained. 'Your brain needs to formalise what you want to say. Then the message goes via your cranial nerves to the end organs. Then, for speech, you need your vocal cords, you need your tongue, and you need lips. Those are the main structures you need to speak so that people can hear you. Anatomically,' Meyer concluded, 'there was no reason he couldn't speak.' His tongue was not damaged – which surprised her – and the vocal cords had probably only been damaged by intubation. While the pharynx was corrugated from burns, this part of the throat was not used for speech; and, lastly, his brain was functioning.

Aside from lack of injury to spine or brain, her main source of evidence about his brain functioning was the GCS score, as 15/15 can only be given to a patient who was 'talking sense'. Running through his behaviour and the rationale Abdullah used to score it, she conceded the 15 was too high, and it should have been several points lower, which would have changed her assessment.

❖ ❖ ❖

The defence's first expert witness was David Klatzow, something of a celebrity expert witness, who described himself, on the website for his forensic consultancy, as 'pre-eminent amongst South Africa's few forensic experts'. He had considerable expertise in pyroforensics, the study of the chemistry of fire, and in the calculation of blood alcohol levels, and his evidence on these topics had been accepted by numerous courts. Klatzow had conducted an experiment with tyres of different sizes to ascertain how long they would burn, in order to calculate a rough timeline between the attack and the police or ambulance arriving. The value lay in establishing an estimate of how long Rowan would have been in the heat, which might affect his degree of injury, and how long his body had been reacting to his injuries.

Klatzow explained the latter was particularly important when it came to understanding how his body would have been 'compensating' for his injuries. The most probable reaction was medical shock, which progressed from mild to severe. The effect this shock might have had on Rowan was important: shock reduced the ability of the body to pump blood to the tissues, and so to deliver oxygen to the 'end organs' (such as heart, liver and brain). This process was known as 'perfusion'. 'Compensatory mechanisms may kick in to maintain blood pressure, but poor perfusion will result in generalised problems with virtually every organ system,' Klatzow explained. These systems wouldn't shut down immediately but would slow down progressively. For example, as the brain was deprived of oxygen cognitive function reduced, which was why patients in shock appeared more and more confused.

From the moment of Rowan being set alight to his discovery by the police, Klatzow's experiment gave an approximate time range of between 13 minutes and an hour, with a median of about 30 minutes. It did not seem precise enough to be helpful as a timeline, but drew attention to how long Rowan must have been alight – at least a quarter of an hour. And Klatzow, later, would link this to the autopsy findings: that having to breathe in the middle of the inferno had led to the charring of his mouth, lips and nose. In this time, gas would also have entered his mouth and been sufficiently hot to damage the pharynx and the upper part of the oesophagus. It was physically impossible, Klatzow said, for the hot gas to selectively damage deeper structures and not do some damage to the tongue. But as the autopsy had not sent a section of the tongue tissue for testing there could be no categorical answer either way.

Klatzow explained the significance of Rowan's blood alcohol level – 0.01 grams – at the time of his death. For each standard serving of alcohol the body absorbs about 0.02 grams into the blood stream (with peak at full absorption after 40-45 minutes). The average person sobers up at a rate of 0.02 fewer grams in the bloodstream per hour. If Rowan, uninjured, had had 0.01 grams of alcohol in his blood at 8.30 pm on Sunday night, it would have meant that 18 hours before – when he was found by the police – he would have had a peak drunkenness of 0.36. That was a level at which blood alcohol concentration starts to become fatal. 'You become incoherent, comatose, stuporous.' However, the back calculation was difficult to do in Rowan's case – his metabolism was not functioning properly, and while his body tried to stay alive it would have shut down processes like alcohol metabolism in order to concentrate on getting blood to vital organs. The breaking down of alcohol in the blood stream would have slowed, so it was possible he had not had that high a level of blood alcohol concentration but that his body had metabolised less alcohol, slower. Reduced metabolism was in fact a feature of shock.

Klatzow's argument presented a clear bind for the state: the less severe Rowan's shock, the more drunk Rowan would have been when he spoke to the policemen, and both conditions would have affected his cognitive functioning.

The seriousness of this dilemma was obvious from how deeply

unnerved Palesa was by Klatzow's testimony. Within a few exchanges, his manner of questioning prompted King to say, 'M'Lord, may the prosecutor desist from doing what he is doing, showing his disgust by walking around and throwing his arms around and making comments?'

Klatzow was not intimidated. A large-faced man, his head topped by a mop of dark hair turning to silver, his mouth turned down at the sides and eyebrows that reached up in the centre, gave him the expression of a guilty child being scolded. But in practice, his manner communicated the opposite: Klatzow talked like a man failing to suffer a fool, in fact, like a man enumerating a fool's many failings. I didn't know if Klatzow's science was foolproof, but Palesa became increasingly incoherent as he tried to tackle it, eventually attacking with questions that verged on gibberish.

'I like it when you say [damage to the oesophagus but not the tongue] would involve the suspension of the laws of physics. You see, nature sometimes outplays us!' Palesa, unembarrassed by this line of reasoning, repeated it, each time with less sense, in the face of Klatzow's appeals for clarity. 'And I put it to you: you talk about the mechanical functions of heat and the physical movement of it, but you cannot rule the nature as it works when things happen, can you?' And: 'When nature happens, all things happen, there is no explanation to such a thing when they happen and there is an investigation, isn't it?' It was as if, unable to go around Klatzow's argument by proving it was irrelevant, or through it by proving it was faulty, Palesa had decided to head in the opposite direction away from logic. When Klatzow did not concede, Palesa did not give up and continued with an equally unsuccessful assault on the shock and alcohol argument.

In the end Palesa took a final stab at the issue of damage to the tongue and respiratory tract, again putting it to Klatzow that either his inference was wrong because it disputed first-hand findings, or he had to accept that the 'paradox' of a damaged pharynx but undamaged tongue was inexplicable.

Klatzow, whose patience had long since worn out, did not waver: 'The laws of physics do not change. Not for this prosecutor, not for anybody!'

Unruffled by Palesa's cross-examination, King was smooth and self-assured as he returned to the blood alcohol question in his re-examination.

'It seems my learned friend has seen where I'm going to. Let's take it on the story as presented by the prosecutor. The person stopped drinking 26 hours before. Would you find any alcohol in his blood?'

'No, I don't think so. In fact, on that version he would have been fit to fly an aircraft – twelve hours between bottle and throttle for pilots.'

'You see, there's two deductions from that: either the blood alcohol result is completely wrong, or the witnesses aren't correct. Do you agree?'

'Well, those are two inferences and I'm not in a position to comment on that.'

If things were not going badly enough for the state already, the defence could hardly have fronted a more experienced trauma expert than Elmin Steyn. She had literally written the textbook with which Rowan's doctor in the Groote Schuur Trauma Unit had been trained.[42] Speaking with a relaxed authority, Steyn explained she was a specialist surgeon with sub-specialisation in trauma surgery. Having qualified as a surgeon in 1988, she had 26 years of experience. As a newly qualified doctor she'd worked in government hospitals near Pretoria, spending one year in the poor, deprived township of Kalefong, and the Ga-Rankuwa Training Hospital which served a large semi-rural area. As a consultant in Tygerberg Hospital, the largest public hospital in the province and second largest in the country, she ran the Trauma Unit. Since 1997 she'd worked in private practice, in charge of the Emergency Department and the Trauma Unit in the Chris Barnard Memorial Hospital, run by the company Netcare.

During her early career in Ga-Rankuwa in the late 1980s and early 1990s, the country was embroiled in political violence and she saw many necklacing victims. Then South Africa became a democracy and 'for a long time it wasn't something prevalent'. But it had not gone away, and in recent years she was again treating necklacing victims at Tygerberg Hospital.

When a burn victim came in Steyn would be in charge of the team that did the initial treatment. Afterwards she would be responsible for the patient in intensive care and perform some of the surgery, if skin grafts were needed.

A patient with Rowan's injuries speaking in full sentences was, Steyn explained, 'unlikely'. Patients with severe injuries usually only said 'single words, perhaps the most essential words'. Her severely injured patients often said 'Help'. They might say 'water', but longer, coherent phrases were uncommon.

Several factors conspired against their powers of explanation. Their severe stress, due to pain, anxiety and fear, would trigger high levels of adrenaline in the blood. The heartbeat would race, breathing would be more rapid, and the patient would become extremely thirsty with the throat drying out. Steyn noted a fast heart rate and fast breathing rate – 26 breaths per minute – in the Triage Report. Like Klatzow she also assumed – from the other injuries noted in the postmortem – that the tongue would have been damaged, and would also say that the results were inconclusive if there hadn't been a microscopic examination of the tissue. Her assessment of the pathologist's report was grim: the deep corrugation was evidence that the tissue was 'cooked'. That there was little smoke in the lungs did not mean there was not smoke damage. 'You will see from any burns textbook that it is not immediately apparent, you don't need to see a lot of smoke in the lungs to have the lung damaged.'

She didn't think that eleven minutes earlier – when the police first dealt with him – the situation would have been much different. She disagreed with Palesa's interpretation of the fact that the ambulance staff had been unable to get his name from Rowan as insignificant given their priorities at the time. Having a patient's name, Steyn said, was not simply to lend 'a personal air' to the treatment, as Abdullah explained, but was included in the training as a way of assessing speech, breathing and brain functioning. She went further, saying that patients with injuries like Rowan's could moan, scream and say words 'linked to survival', like 'water', without having 'enough oxygen in the brain to formulate logical speech'. And speech competes with their ability to breathe, 'so somebody who is desperately needing oxygen would probably rather breathe fast than speak'.

She said that – based on the same observations as Abdullah's – she would have given Rowan 9 out of 15 on the GCS, 'which is a reflection of significant, depressed level of consciousness'.[43]

After this routing of Abdullah's testimony, King said, 'A person with significant depressed level of consciousness, is he able to string a history of events together and enunciate them to explain to someone what happened?'

'By definition not.'

With Steyn, Palesa was calmer in his method of cross-examination than he had been with Klatzow, but just as stubborn. Palesa's primary tactic was to try to discredit Steyn. You didn't deal with him directly, Palesa told Steyn repeatedly, you're 'revising' and 'underscoring' the GCS, second-guessing capable people who treated him themselves. Abdullah – 'who is a lecturer' – had given him a higher score. He consistently characterised the evidence on which he wanted to rely, namely, Abdullah's GCS, a few observations and comments from the ICU, as 'a more rational pre-hospital reading'. He found Steyn's assessment merely 'a book understanding'. When she did not concede in this choice of wording, he suggested she was a biased witness.

Palesa's defence of Abdullah's GCS seemed to lead to testimony which further discredited it. He was impassioned as he described all the impressive things Rowan had done. He cited how Rowan moved the mask away from his face, even though his eyes were closed; he'd pulled the needle out when they'd tried to administer pain medication, which Abdullah had argued showed evidence of 'proprioception' and awareness of pain.

Steyn, with more experience in the trauma ward than Abdullah, disagreed. With full thickness burns, Rowan's nerve endings had been burnt away, and he wouldn't have felt the needle sharply. Indeed his actions showed something else: confusion.[44]

'To assess the motor parts of the Glasgow Coma Scale the person has to respond on command. So if he is told don't remove the mask, then he should not remove the mask or if he is told lift up your arm, he should lift up his arm.' In fact, she said, Abdullah's observations were evidence he wasn't cooperating with the people trying to save his life, which meant he couldn't have understood what was really going on.

Steyn gave Palesa an explanation for the differences in interpretation. The environment in the ambulance would have been chaotic, highly stressful, and by 'over scoring' Rowan's responses they were improving his chances of getting more attention at the hospital instead of being completely written off. 'The problem here is the interpretation of the information and I can understand why our scoring assessment is different.'

But Palesa dug in his heels when it came to Rowan swearing. When Steyn argued that it was common for people with brain injuries or under the influence of drugs or alcohol, in other words, people in depressed states of consciousness, to shout out filth, Palesa argued that Rowan's cry of '*Jou ma se poes!*' showed his lucidity and reason. These were words, Palesa argued, that were not directly linked to immediate survival. Even sober people used those words, what's more, he went on, in 'certain areas' you would hear it all the time.

Henney intervened at this point: 'You say that they say it like 'good morning' on the Cape Flats. Is that what you are saying?'

'It is like saying "good morning", exactly.'

Henney was not baiting Palesa. 'Ja, okay,' he said, and let Palesa continue.

'What about those instances?'

'I am saying that is inappropriate behaviour when somebody is trying to help you.' Steyn explained that it was, in fact, a symptom of a consciousness gone awry, one in which the normal controls could not rein in behaviour.

But both Henney and Palesa resisted this explanation. Henney too began to suggest she was avoiding the simplest explanation: he was an unsophisticated person responding to pain.

Swearing, Henney lectured Steyn, 'is a manner of speaking for a lot of people when they react to something uncomfortable or something that annoys them. A normal manner of speaking. Depending on what kind of person you are dealing with,' Henney went on, over her objections, 'and where you come from.'

Two theories about the manners of the poor were developing in what was now a three-way exchange between Henney, Steyn and Palesa. Steyn's thesis, drawn from decades working in the trauma wards of large public hospitals, was that the poor would act like the rich. If they were dying and they understood that medical staff were trying to save them, they would assist them. They might swear but they would respond to commands, or issue their own. Henney and Palesa, on the other hand, argued that there was a class of unsophisticated people, people from rough neighbourhoods, who swore constantly and could not help but react with aggression. In Palesa's narrative, Steyn couldn't comment on the 'normal behaviour' of 'the man on the street', and Henney concurred.

Palesa found another way to insinuate that Steyn was a biased expert: her comments on Rowan's rate of breath. Referring to a text book, he threw down a gauntlet: the normal range of breath per minute for a young man was 12–20. By saying that Rowan's rate, as measured in the ambulance, of 26 breaths was worrying she had blown this symptom out of proportion. Theatrically, he himself did a demonstration of talking and breathing at 26 breaths in a minute.

Steyn again was adamant. It was 'certainly very abnormal', and in any case, this issue was not about the number of breaths per se, but about what rapid breathing indicated in an injured person. It was about a body that had an elevated need for oxygen, driven by some injury that could not be seen or evaluated in the ambulance. 'The patient is not in an intensive care unit, they are not measuring the blood pressure, the oxygen levels, the carbon monoxide levels, the carbon dioxide levels: we are using the rate of breathing as a marker for all the other problems that the patient has.'

For the rest of the cross-examination Palesa, his tone aggressive, continued to raise the same defeated, and defeatable objections, at times misrepresenting her previous evidence in order to so. ('We spoke at great length on that subject,' Steyn pleaded, 'and that sentence is taken out of context.') It was like watching a toddler hammer a wooden block, relentlessly, imprecisely, into a hole it was not shaped to fit.

At the end Palesa again put the scenario to her of the policemen asking Rowan for his name and getting a story about his murder, and asked Steyn if she was saying that Rowan was confused at the time.

'I could only say in my experience and in my opinion and after looking at the information that I was given,' Steyn said carefully, 'but I think that it's highly unlikely that this person could have given an extensive explanation or declaration to two sets of people at that stage.'

Without backing down, Steyn gave Palesa further disclaimers, 'I wasn't there', 'it would be rare', 'it could be possible' and he cut her off at that point.

'So it could be possible.'

'But it would be very unlikely.'

The last witness was Dr Jessica Kate Bernon, a junior doctor, then in her first job since finishing her community service year. She had attended Rowan in the Groote Schuur Trauma Unit. She was called at Palesa's special request.

'When I saw him, he wasn't answering questions. He was able to talk, but he wasn't answering questions,' she told the court. 'He was confused.' They had asked him his name and he'd been unable to respond. However, he had responded to one request on command – to squeeze her hand – and he had opened his eyes. By then he had liquids, intubation, and painkillers, and this might have improved his condition, though he was immediately slated for 'humane' treatment. In other words, no one expected him to live. Bernon wavered but eventually said that she thought he hadn't been in shock, because his blood pressure – at 124/86 – wasn't abnormal, and his respiratory rate was high but not extraordinarily high. Bernon admitted that they hadn't been able to check for a more reliable symptom. This would have meant placing a catheter in the groin to see whether urine production had stopped but the injuries to his groin were too severe.[45] Bernon also confirmed that there was another possible cause for his raised breathing rate and confusion: extreme pain.

In argument, King drew together the various ways in which the medical and forensic experts had cast doubt on the statements of the police witnesses, as well as the manner in which the hearsay statement had been recorded. He also argued that the testimony of Martha Pieterse, and to a large extent that of Abdullah too (who had also failed to get coherent answers from Rowan), was 'mutually destructive' to the state's case. In essence: how could Rowan give a long and complicated story to the police one moment, and be unable to provide his name to the ambulance staff the next? In Wilhelm's account she arrived at almost the same moment as the ambulance, yet the ambulance people could not even get Rowan's name out of him.

King accepted that Rowan could speak, but argued that he could not have been both lucid and coherent, given his level of injury. So there were legitimate doubts that Rowan was sober during the incident.

Palesa took a narrower strategy: that of discrediting the unfavourable expert witnesses. Steyn got the brunt of this. Her evidence was repeatedly mischaracterised and random examples and inconsequential comments were used as evidence of her bias. Palesa, for example, read out Steyn's testimony on why she considered it serious that Rowan could not provide his name to medical staff: '"If I asked you what is your name and you can't tell me your name I would assume that you've had a stroke." This patient did not have a stroke!' Palesa cried out, shaking his head at her dishonesty.

'She says: "I would assume that you've had a stroke or you are drunk or you have a head injury." There are *no* injuries to the brain as per the pathological findings.'

He selected testimony from his preferred witnesses on an equally tenuous basis. Bernon said Rowan smelt of petrol, he argued, not of alcohol, and that he was alert, therefore he was not drunk. Besides, his family said he only drank five litres of beer and shared it with many people, so Klatzow's calculation could be dismissed. Throughout, Palesa relied heavily on the testimony of the family.

While not having engaged much with the medical evidence during testimony, Henney seemed to agree with Palesa. Both Henney and Palesa criticised Steyn for maintaining it was likely that Rowan was in shock, despite Dr Bernon's report that his blood pressure was not highly abnormal. 'If a lay person like me can notice that,' he said, 'then there is something wrong.' To underline this he repeated his favourite criticism of Steyn's testimony – namely that she'd had a different opinion about the meaning of Rowan's symptoms than the state's witnesses.

'So you say her evidence was not entirely objective?' asked Henney. 'Is that what you are saying?'

'Correct, M'Lord,' Palesa replied.

'Not based on medical science?'

'Correct, M'Lord.'

'Are you talking about the evidence where she says that a person who utters swear words, the swear words that people would usually utter on the Cape Flats when they are in distress, that when a person utters such a swear word such a person would not be of lucid mind? Are you talking about that?'

'Correct, M'Lord.'

At the close of the hearsay trial arguments, Henney took a post-ponement of just under a week in order review the evidence. When court resumed on 4 June, a wet Wednesday morning, he was brief: the evidence was admitted, and he would reserve his reasons until the end of the trial.

Chapter Fourteen

The High Court is separated from the Houses of Parliament by about 150 metres of public park. It was built on the site of the food gardens planted by the first white settlers to colonise the Cape. A long tree-lined avenue runs through this park and on any given morning injects a few minutes of something majestic into the ordinary day of its pedestrians. The avenue has a constant bustle of office workers, lawyers, cleaners, clerks, labourers, students and tourists passing through, some walking with great purpose, others stopping to nestle in one another's arms for hours at a time on the adjacent lawns. At noon every day a cannon sounds from the hill above the city centre. Pigeons take flight in chaotic unison, and once I saw a schoolboy grab his chest and shout, 'Uff! They got me!' while dying theatrically on the path behind a statue of Cecil John Rhodes.

Among the people strolling on that avenue or relaxing on the stone benches under the arbour, were two policemen from Blue Downs station, who testified during the hearsay trial. The first was Colonel Riaan Redelinghuys, head of detectives at the station, and a policeman whose career stretched back into the dark era of apartheid policing. Rumour had it he'd been in the Presidential Guard for FW de Klerk, the last apartheid president. After the democratic transition, he'd moved into a specialised Organised Crime Unit, where he rose to a senior position in the Western Cape.[46] But by

2002 he was on trial, charged with perjury, racketeering and living off the proceeds of the crimes committed by his wife, Paulina. She had, while out on bail for stealing from an attorney's practice and while her husband was paying off her debts for this theft, run a scam taking 'down payments' for houses she falsely claimed were about to be foreclosed on by the banks. Redelinghuys had used her profits to deposit tens of thousands of rands at a time into various bank accounts and their home loan. He had also put a down payment on a holiday flat in Mossel Bay as well as a deposit on a Land Rover Freelander. Despite this financial activity, Redelinghuys's lawyer argued that his client had been naive, and thought Paulina was reformed and her courier business, which was only a few months old, was making excellent returns. The judge acquitted him.

Then, there was none other than Anele Patrick Tshicila, who went by the name Andile, and was also known as Ta Ager. Tshicila was in Crime Intelligence, a police department reformulated in the democratic state out of the loathed apartheid Security Branch.[47]

Ostensibly, the state had called these witnesses for the purpose of establishing Angy's motive, though they served another purpose too: dispelling doubts about what had gone on at Blue Downs Police Station.

❖ ❖ ❖

Redelinghuys came to court nattily dressed in a charcoal-grey suit and blue tie with a geometric print. With his thick blond hair – beginning to turn grey – and his slightly nervous smile, he looked more like an estate agent than a policeman. He had joined Blue Downs station in February 2012, some six months before the television theft, as head of detectives with command over 40 men. Though a native Afrikaans speaker he chose to save the court time by answering questions in English. As a consequence his sentences often lacked grammatical concord and were heavily accented, but his responses were clear and relevant – a rare treat in this trial.

Redelinghuys explained that he first became involved when Angy launched a 101 Complaint[48] on 15 August 2012, the day after the television theft, which Station Commander Damoyi had referred to him. The complaint covered both a service delivery gripe (against duty officer Tchangani) and a specific allegation against one of the detectives, named 'Ta Ager' or 'Andile' by the complainant.

Angy and Redelinghuys met that afternoon at one of the Khayelitsha police stations. She was accompanied by Dustin Kramer, then her colleague at the SJC, and she reported her version of events at the station and her allegations against Ta Ager. These allegations confused Redelinghuys. He did not have a Ta Ager or Andile on his staff. Nor was there a Nissan Almera – the type of car Ta Ager had been seen driving away with Rowan in – among his vehicles. With the registration number Angy had taken down, he opened a file and began investigating.

Soon he found out that 'Ta Ager' was Andile Tshicila, an officer at the Crime Intelligence unit housed adjacent to the Blue Downs Police Station, whose ownership of the Almera was hidden through a proxy company because of the clandestine nature of their work.

Next Redelinghuys's investigation concerned Tchangani. Angy's complaint claimed he refused to open the case and posed as the station commander. As Tchangani had witnessed part of the dust-up between Angy and Tshicila, Redelinghuys wanted his take on it. The story Tchangani gave him was that Tshicila had come in with an 'unknown black male', informed him that he had 'caught' the man, and was putting him in the holding cells. Redelinghuys got two more statements, one from Captain Volschenk, who had eventually given Isaac the case number, and another from Constable Mbali, who was the cell guard at that time. These provided a basic outline: Rowan had been brought to the station following a community assault; and then Angy, Isaac and their party had tried to open a case against him but had been unable to until Captain Volschenk came on duty. Redelinghuys also took a statement from Mzinyathi, the man who phoned Tshicila at the station and heard his alleged admission.

The last person he took a statement from was Tshicila himself. He stated that he had been trying to protect Rowan from irate 'unknown males', so he'd taken him to the police station. He mentioned receiving phone calls from an unknown person asking about Rowan but said he told the caller he didn't know anything about a stolen television set. Tshicila didn't paint Rowan as an innocent victim: he had told Tchangani to arrest him as soon as the housebreaking and theft charge was finalised.

The same day that Redelinghuys took Tshicila's statement, Rowan was indeed 're-arrested' for the TV theft when he came to fulfil his existing bail conditions. Redelinghuys called Angy and told her the outcome of his investigation. Tchangani was going to disciplined: he would be charged on three counts for his behaviour behind the Community Service Centre desk, as well as allowing Rowan to be held in the cells without a proper arrest statement.

But Tchangani was one of Station Commander Damoyi's men and Tshicila wasn't, and that's where Redelinghuys's authority ran out, he explained to Angy. He'd have to hand over her affidavits and the statements to Tshicila's superior, a Lieutenant Maree, for him to investigate. 'It is the common practice, M'Lord, that you only investigate cases against members of your unit or station and Sergeant Tshicila was not at Blue Downs Police Station.' A week later Redelinghuys handed on the documents and Damoyi closed the file on the complaint.

Redelinghuys then reached what was presumably the point of his testimony for the state. Rowan's bail for the TV theft case was opposed and he was sent to Pollsmoor Prison for about two months.

On 9 October he was released. That day or the next Redelinghuys had his first contact with Angy Peter since the complaint had been finalised. 'She was very upset when she phoned me. She wanted to know why was Roy released and is back in the community.'

Then on 11 October, Redelinghuys noticed an albino male sitting in the corridor outside the detective's office. He introduced himself to Rowan, who confirmed that he was reporting for bail at the station. Redelinghuys did not tell the court what else Rowan said to him because it was hearsay. However Palesa wanted the hearsay included in the record because it implied that Rowan had come to tell Redelinghuys he was being threatened by Angy. Palesa also tried to get another piece of hearsay on the record, namely, that of Sergeant Mbali, who was never called to testify to this. At about this time the sergeant had also told Redelinghuys that Rowan was receiving threats from Angy Peter.

❖ ❖ ❖

Though Redelinghuys's evidence added little material to the state's case, William King, with no detectable animosity, still wrung several points out of him in a long and wide-ranging cross-examination. This must have been at least partially Palesa's intention: Redelinghuys was there to shield his underlings from having to testify, especially Constable Muthien, the investigating officer. Palesa had by this time officially 'washed his hands' of the investigating officer, and King considered it too much of a gamble to call him.

King soon asked Redelinghuys to help him make sense of the police docket concerning Rowan's murder.

King had asked for the docket three times. The first time was seven months before the trial began, when he requested a copy of the investigation diary, also known as the C-Section.[49] 'I was given a jumbled bunch of documents that it was impossible to put together,' he said. Unable to make sense of the documents, he launched a written request through the High Court for a second copy. The prosecutor obliged but it was only delivered shortly before the trial, and again it was an unusable mess.

'So we asked, finally, during the trial,' King explained to Redelinghuys, 'for a proper one. And you would think, third time around, someone would have taken the effort to present exactly what is correct.' But again King found an omission: the month of December. 'I started getting suspicious then, as would anybody, that someone is conniving and withholding. Now that's what I want you to answer.'

He gave Redelinghuys some examples. There were two pages marked C3 and one was marked 14 October and the other 27 December. King couldn't find page A47 but Redelinghuys said it was there, but on page C9. King pointed out C5 – the first C5 – referred to a search warrant on A46, but A46 was in fact Constable Wilhelm's statement.

'Colonel, what I'm trying to establish, is I don't believe that I've got this full C-Section docket. I suspect that there's pages missing. Can you comment on that?'

At first Redelinghuys said the sequence was not correct, and this had affected the numbering. Redelinghuys asked for time to go through the docket. After he had reordered the document, King pointed out that there was nothing in the docket for the whole of December 2012. Again Redelinghuys asked to reorder it and follow dates and sequences of events rather than the numbering system, which was clearly incorrect.

But this didn't solve all the problems and both men, as well as Henney, bent their heads over the pages and picked and puzzled. It went on for hours. Redelinghuys, head of detectives, and 30 years in the police; William King, a former magistrate with decades under his belt as a criminal lawyer; and Robert Henney, who worked his way up from prosecuting criminal cases in the lowest courts in the city to judging them in the highest, knew their way around a docket. Yet they could not put this one together.

At a certain point Redelinghuys remembered the prosecutor making a duplicate docket, which resolved some questions. But could not account for why no work was done that December. If there were two dockets, Muthien could have continued investigating while it was at court.

Redelinghuys said Muthien might have been on holiday. 'Or it might be someone's removed the pages,' King replied, 'because there's information that it doesn't want the defence to get.' Later King would say the illogical sequencing and omissions could only be explained 'if something's missing from this diary, or someone's been playing cards with the docket'.

Redelinghuys's face, shining and smiling, managed to communicate both shock at the state of the docket and amusement at King's paranoia. 'I don't know what playing cards means, M'Lord.'

'Changing them around, shuffling the deck. Adding, subtracting, putting them up your sleeve.'

By the end, Redelinghuys had reordered the C-Section into a better sequence, but all the problems with it – as well as the other sections – remained unanswered.

King moved on to other questions he had for Redelinghuys.

'Would you confirm that the police are not just interested in prosecuting a person,' he asked. 'They are interested in establishing the truth.'

'That is correct, M'Lord.'

Angy and Isaac's alibi had never even been checked, even though the police's docket contained numerous press clippings which gave details to their alibi. At one point, King read out from one such newspaper article:[50] '"Community members later heard that ... he appeared to have been burnt alive. 'We know Angy and Isaac were not involved in Rowan's murder,' the resident said. 'She was not there when Rowan was being beaten on the night of the murder. She lives in Mfuleni and we all know her around here. Two people were seen beating him and it was not [Peter and Mbadu].' " '

Why, King asked, was the alibi and defence set out in the article never investigated? There had been instructions in the docket for the investigating officer to look at that article. Yet 'no investigation whatsoever is carried out by the policemen on the ground relating to this. Can you explain that?'

'No.'

King then set out the various things which were not done, even after the director of public prosecutions had instructed they be investigated. He began with the vehicle, which was pointed out on the day the suspects were arrested. Police didn't impound the taxi. They had reason to believe it had transported Rowan. They knew exactly where it was. Eventually a month later it was impounded, a taxi which witnesses said had driven a struggling, bleeding Rowan, along with the people and materials needed for his murder. During that month it had been in constant use. That meant it carried more or less 18 people per trip, on dozens of trips a day, seven days a week. For forensic purposes, not ideal.

'Yet not one single policeman thought fit to have a look in the car to see if there were weapons, to see if there was petrol, to see if there were matches, to see if there blood splatters, to see if there was anything left of the deceased in that vehicle. Can you explain that?'

The investigating officer had not asked Desiree for a description of the attackers or what clothing they were wearing or what weapons they used. 'That is basic 101 detective work when you take a statement. Would you agree?' The obvious follow-up would have been to compare cell-phone records and to collect the phones. Only Angy's was collected. The others were collected several months later under direction from the director of public prosecutions.

Their houses were never searched and their neighbours were never questioned; there are no statements from the tavern owner or the man in the shack. According to the witnesses, Muthien changed the time he took the statements by several hours. Witnesses said statements contained things they never said and signatures which were not theirs.[51]

The newspaper article which contained Angy and Isaac's alibi was forwarded to a Major-General Mathope with an instruction that he should 'peruse the docket and give report by 31 October 2012'. That note came from one 'A H Lamoer, Lieutenant-General'.

'Who is Lamoer?' King asked Redelinghuys.

'He is commissioner of police in the Western Cape.' The highest post in the province, one of nine commissioners reporting only to the national commissioner herself.

The newspaper article and note had in turn been sent on 'for attention: the Branch Commander, Detective Services, Mfuleni'.

'Remind us who that is?'

'Redelinghuys. That is me, M'Lord.'

'It says, paragraph 1: "Herewith correspondence and newspaper articles. Read the alleged murder and kidnapping which allegedly happened at the policing precinct of Mfuleni SAPS. Investigating officer must report on 30 October 2012 at the office of Major-General Mathope, Sixth Floor."'

For a man operating in a police force that had chosen to re-adopt military titles in recent years – to reflect, at least, the reality of the culture, as well as the nature of the command structure – Redelinghuys's evasion of the importance of this letter was almost comic.

'Now I presume you can remember this correspondence?'

Redelinghuys frowned. 'I don't remember this one. I remember there *was* correspondence.'

'Well, we know that you were involved. Look at the last two pages of this bundle.' Redelinghuys had forwarded progress reports to Lamoer. Given all this, how the investigating officer's poor detective work could've gone under the radar was hard to fathom.

'Given your history with this matter, it would have shown that this is a case out of the ordinary. Would that not be fair comment?'

'This case was out of the ordinary. This is one out of the ordinary.'

'So you say it would be foolhardy to have a manipulated docket where the investigation of the docket and this case was under scrutiny from people like the DPP's [public prosecutor's] office?' asked Henney. 'Is that what you're saying?'

'It will be foolhardy – it will be suicidal for that police member, or whoever, to do that. It is correctly said: it's got media attention, it's got DPP attention, it got General Lamoer's attention... You don't play with your career like that.'

Redelinghuys's appeal was emotive, here and throughout his testimony.

Confronted with all the failures of the Blue Downs investigation of the case, Redelinghuys conceded and defended them in turn. However, when pressed he said, with disbelief, 'I cannot explain it.' He came across as the regretful superior, only finding out now about the derelictions of his subordinates. 'You are talking about things that I do not even know about.'

'If you had known about it, it would not have happened – put it that way, Colonel. Would that be fair?' King asked.

'I should have attended that crime scene that evening,' Redelinghuys said, as if he wanted to hang his head in shame.

But King was not really offering him a loophole, and pulled taut the argument he'd been trailing: 'The reasoning for the slack investigation, if we can call it slack, was that the police were probably not looking to find the truth. They had found the truth that they wanted. Do you understand what I am saying?'

'I understand, but I cannot agree with your statement.'

❖ ❖ ❖

The questions King was asking of Redelinghuys were serious: irregularities, suspicious derelictions and mysteries which suggested evidence had been fabricated. A huge amount would turn on this: when was incompetence unfortunate, and when was it sinister?

It was easy to trace parallels between the events unfolding in this court case and events unfolding at the Khayelitsha Commission. There a picture of true dysfunction was emerging from the testimonies. All the stations were understaffed when you looked at the size of the population they had to serve and the severity of the crimes they were expected to police. And the detective branches faced the worst of these shortages. While the commission determined a maximum acceptable detective-to-docket ratio to be 1:40 dockets, at most 1:50, the detectives testified that their men and women carried far more than this. Average ratios were closer to 1:79 (Harare), 1:67 (Site B), 1:127 (Lingelethu West). The impact these workloads had on the quality of investigations was obvious. Harare Police Station had a conviction rate of 3.3% for its murder dockets. And this was only the dockets that made it to court – less than a quarter of all the murder cases opened. Understaffing was compounded by employee absenteeism, itself underpinned by burnout, low morale, and trauma.

Police said that in the midst of the poverty and violence of Khayelitsha, it was impossible to do their jobs well. Could anyone fault them for failing in an impossible situation? In its most sophisticated form, their defenders argued it was inappropriate to untangle their responsibilities from the complex history of these neighbourhoods, or to isolate any individuals who were responsible in a morass of compounded failures of other government departments and social institutions.

When I first heard them, these excuses had instinctive appeal: the reality was confusing, their jobs were hard, and it wasn't clear how that situation could be any different.

But part of what was so extraordinary about what happened at Lookout Hill was that the commissioners and their evidence leader didn't let up. After more than a year of poring over the police documents, they knew the three stations intimately, as if they were people, with unique habits and flaws. They parsed the policemen's defences and demolished their weaker excuses, and they did it with the police's own inspection reports and meeting minutes and correspondence, with research reports, and a dose of complaints from other government departments.

Watching the commissioners roll back the station commanders' excuses, I was genuinely taken aback: an object lesson in how warped my sense of accountability had become. In the years before the commission, people in power had repeatedly been exposed as having broken laws. Their response was, who cares? And that was the end of the story. People in public service who failed to do their jobs, retorted, so what? And that was the end of the story. Mountains of evidence of corruption or dereliction were exposed by journalists or red-flagged by opposition parties but no one lost their jobs or saw their day in court. And so the citizenry's expectations shifted. In establishing something as truthful in the public discourse, the facts were not nearly as important as the reaction to the facts; and the reaction, time and time again had shown that none of these transgressions really mattered. To live through the Zuma years was to live through a great queasy equivalency, an assault on truth and rules that was atmospheric as much as acute.

In Court 17, I felt myself sucked in by the dispiriting familiarity of Redelinghuys's defence of his station, a narrative that mined the overlap between realistic expectations and disgraceful results. His blue eyes were plaintive, as he delivered a refrain of 'well, it shouldn't have been that way, but it was – and that's bad, but not suspicious, which is to say, not at all unusual'.

King countered that negligence in the police was matched only by fierce respect for hierarchy. There had been enough consistent oversight on the case from the police and prosecutors. So if the investigating officer ignored instructions or failed to investigate, he did it with political cover.

❖ ❖ ❖

King also spent a lot of time questioning Redelinghuys about decisions and actions taken in the wake of Rowan's murder – decisions and actions for which Redelinghuys was responsible.

According to Redelinghuys, after Kock and Barnardo called the Ops room about Rowan, Redelinghuys got a call at 1.30 am informing him of an attempted murder. He was the senior duty officer on stand-by for the whole of the Kuilsriver Cluster that week, which included Blue Downs, Kleinvlei and Kuilsriver. Redelinghuys said he was simply told there had been an attempted murder, a burning, on Blueberry Hill, which he knew to be in the Kleinvlei jurisdiction. The Mfuleni Ops room would next have called the Mfuleni detective duty officer – Captain Jonker – if he hadn't already been informed. Protocol determined that he should have attended the murder scene, rather than Redelinghuys.

At about 6 am on the morning of Rowan's abduction, Desiree woke up her father and they walked to Blue Downs Police Station, some 45 minutes away. By John Ndevu's estimate it was 7.30 am when they asked at the service desk if there was information about an albino boy, their son, who'd been assaulted and kidnapped the night before. John Ndevu's and Desiree's accounts differ from here on, but they have this in common: no one knew anything at the police station. They were taken in a van by Warrant Officer Baartman, who made a detour to an unrelated murder scene, a stabbing on Gusha Street, also located in Bardale.

At the crime scene, Baartman left them in the van while he sought out one of his superiors. John Ndevu struck up a conversation with an unidentified policeman. According to Desiree, 'One gentlemen spoke with my father, in Afrikaans. And I climbed out the car, and I said to him, "Wait, sir, my father doesn't understand Afrikaans so nicely. You can tell me." And he asked who I am, and I said to him, "I'm Rowan's aunty, and I'm as good as his mother, as I brought him up."' This policeman told them that Rowan had been necklaced the night before.

Soon afterwards they went with Warrant Officer Baartman and the investigating officer Muthien back to the police station and then to Angy's house to arrest her. In this time, no police officer asked them what had happened or what they had seen. As neither Ndevu nor Desiree made statements until about 2 pm, how did Muthien know to arrest Angy and Isaac? At that point no one had read Barnardo's statement, and the witnesses hadn't declared what they knew. This issue was never resolved and right then it wasn't King's main objective.

Redelinghuys arrived at the Gusha Street scene at around 6.45 am. It was busy. Being a 'serious violent crime' it had required the presence of an overall commander – Redelinghuys – as well as the duty detective, Captain Coetzee. Captain Jonker and Constable Muthien, the investigating officer who would then be assigned Rowan's case, were also there, and there was at least one other policeman, the one who broke the news of Rowan's death to Ndevu.

Using the investigation diary, King pointed out that the first entry was by Warrant Officer Baartman. Baartman came on duty at 6 am, and he would've collected the new dockets and taken them to the crime office in another part of the station. There he would've read through their A1 at least – the initial summary, which in this case was Barnardo's statement – before handing them to his superior, Captain Coetzee. Coetzee, Redelinghuys conceded, should have scanned through the A1s at the beginning of the shift.

'I received the case docket on 14/10 at 06:00,' Baartman wrote in the diary. 'I informed Captain Jonker and Constable Muthien about the case of attempted murder. It happened about 1:15 at Bardale squatter camp.'

What made this strange was that the information didn't transfer to Muthien or Jonker. Possibly Baartman didn't know the individuals concerned, or the background of Angy's complaint or her adversarial relationship with Damoyi and Redelinghuys. But why was the basic information not given to the family? Not long after Baartman read the docket he was told by John Ndevu and Desiree that their albino son had gone missing in Mfuleni. Baartman also drove them to Gusha Street. And in all that time he never mentioned the necklaced albino.

King, in essence, did not believe that if Barnardo's A1 statement existed at 2 am, Redelinghuys and the other senior officer would be unaware of the necklacing and the victim until the next morning. King couldn't believe that no one had called Redelinghuys and said, 'Here is a big case, here are problems.' Or told him about Angy and her husband and Rowan. 'Can you explain that?'

'No, M'Lord,' said Redelinghuys.

'Of course, another explanation for you not being informed is that no one knew who the victim was and no one knew that Angy and her husband were involved at that time.' King was referring to when Barnardo and Kock discovered Rowan on Blueberry Hill.

'I can't give a comment on that.'

At this point King's cross-examination felt truly laboured. Of course, these policemen could've, should've, might've read the A1 that should, if Barnardo was telling the truth, have been in the docket, and could've, should've, might've joined the dots between Rowan's identity, and Angy's, and the ruckus two months previously about the stolen television set. But Redelinghuys simply conceded that it would have made sense for the police officer to inform the others about the context, but no one had. In the early morning all he knew was that someone had been burnt on Blueberry Hill, and it wasn't until after 8 am that he knew it was Rowan. He gave ground to King, he was calm and apologetic, and he appeared sincere.

'Let us continue with what Captain Jonker records: "5. Scene photos outstanding. 6. Statement of victim outstanding". Let us just pause there. Captain Jonker at 8.23 envisaged that the victim could make a statement. Would that be fair comment reading what is written there?'

'Yes, M'Lord.'

'Now I would like you to read out the next entry because it concerns you.'

Jonkers' handwriting was poor, so Redelinghuys read the entry slowly. But King was not impatient; in fact, he seemed almost jovial, which was odd because the cross-examination had not yielded any major coups.

'"Obtain states…"'

As Redelinghuys stumbled, King helped him on: 'Statement.'

'"Statement from Lieutenant-Colonel Redelinghuys. He" something "inform…"'

'Mentions.'

'Mentioned?'

'Your guess is as good as mine.'

'Yes, okay: "He mentioned – informed ops about the attack on the…"'

'The victim.'

'"On the victim after he got a call from an informer".'

Redelinghuys stammered, rushing to explain, but King cut him off. No matter the explanation he would later give – this informer hadn't actually told him any names. The idea that he was completely ignorant about Rowan's death that evening was looking a little worn.

❖ ❖ ❖

Near the end of Redelinghuys's cross-examination King did another unexpected swerve into new territory. He handed Redelinghuys the docket of the case against Rowan for stealing Angy and Isaac's television set.

He asked Redelinghuys what was the first question asked of an arrested person. 'What is your address?' Redelinghuys explained that not only did the police need to confirm the address for their own records, but it was important that the suspect supplied it correctly lest their lie be used against them when the judge made a ruling on bail.

Redelinghuys didn't see where this was going. As if to prove there was no error, he ran through the many times – in that docket alone – Rowan had provided that address of 24514 Minister Street, Bardale Village to both the police and the court.

But King then said that this was not the address contained in the Barnardo, Wilhelm or Kock statements. These were the three policemen who stood next to Rowan du Preez as he was lying on his back and asked him for his name. King's eyes glittered as he moved in: 'Either Rowan du Preez told them wrongly, or the police got it wrong when they were told what to say. These three policemen all say Rowan du Preez said his address was 24541.' King waited for Redelinghuys to reply, but Redelinghuys kept on staring at the docket. 'That is not his address.'

'No,' Redelinghuys conceded, 'there is a difference between 1 and 4, and 4 and 1.'[52]

King let the matter drop but returned to it, obliquely, at the close of Klatzow's evidence-in-chief. Begging leave to address 'one final issue' which 'may or may not play a significant role later', King asked the forensic expert, 'You say you were in academia, you were a lecturer at some stage?'

'I was, M'Lord.'

'Have you ever marked student papers?'

'Not only did I have to mark papers but I had to mark their projects. Happily that is no more.'

'Where you find two students who give you the same wrong answer, what is your conclusion?'

'Well, the one inference that you can start to investigate rather significantly, particularly if they are sitting close to each other, is that they might have been copying from each other.'

Later in the trial King would add the final piece of his theory: that the number 24541 was not merely a mistake made by either Rowan or the police officers. It did appear elsewhere in the murder docket, but only in John Ndevu's statement, not in anything Rowan had previously given to the police.

Barnardo's statement, King argued, didn't exist when the docket was first opened. This was why the policemen who'd seen the docket that morning couldn't tell John Ndevu and Desiree anything about their son. Instead, it had been written at a later date, when the police had copied the address from one of the eyewitness statements. Kock's and Wilhelm's statements had been copied from Barnardo's, repeating the mistake.

This was, of course, conjecture. King didn't have a single shred of proof, and Henney dismissed the theory for this reason. It was baseless, he said, and irrelevant too. At the time King brought it up with Redelinghuys, he was prevented from questioning Redelinghuys further, as Henney deemed the questioning unfair. ('He might be the commanding officer, but I do not think he has got all the magical powers to understand whether a deceased would have given the wrong address at the scene.')

King might not have had 'facts' to prove the statement was doctored, but there was still the original fact: that on Blueberry Hill Rowan 'told' the police the wrong address. Twice. And the state couldn't explain it, except if they argued he'd been confused in the moment. Nor could they argue that they made the error because how would they have all made the same mistake, in three different statements?

Palesa gave it all a wide berth.

❖ ❖ ❖

When Redelinghuys had been tried for perjury, racketeering and profiting off the proceeds of crime, he'd been represented by William Booth, a top criminal defence lawyer in Cape Town who was something of a household name. He was famous for representing people accused of terrible crimes who seemed almost certainly guilty. Often he represented these people with great success. On more than one occasion, Henney mistakenly referred to King as Booth, and I wondered if the link in his mind, went beyond the fact that they were both white men called William.

The judgment from Redelinghuys's fraud and racketeering trial told a story of elaborate cons, marital woe and financial madness. But it was also a story where the circumstantial evidence for Redelinghuys's guilt was substantial. Reading it, I felt huge curiosity about this top detective who had been able to convince a judge that he just didn't know what was going on.

❖ ❖ ❖

Learning that Sergeant Andile Tshicila would testify was something of a thrill. He was the villain of the defence's narrative, a man whose entry into the story brought with it conspiracy and violence. For the state he was an ordinary cop maligned by Angy in her attempt to avoid prison. Yet in person he looked like an archetypal nerd: he wore a sleeveless red jersey which clashed with his patterned shirt, blue jeans and glasses. On the stand he spoke strangely, softly, somewhat like a child. When I approached for him an interview during an adjournment he declined with a handshake that was limp and moist.

184

Once Tshicila began testifying, Angy very obtrusively thrust a note at King. He stood up and requested a bathroom break for her. As soon as it was granted, she ran out, in tears, the door banging behind her. Tshicila had, incredibly, smiled at the scene. The pint-sized interpreter was sent out to investigate. 'Yoh, she's really crying. You can hear it from the corridor!'

After an hour Angy came back, still tearful, and King spoke to her before the judge returned. 'It's ludicrous that he's been called. But you must keep yourself in control and let me do my job.' Angy said nothing and wiped her eyes. 'Let's get him,' said King.

In dribs and drabs, Palesa got Tshicila to tell his version of events. His relationship with Rowan was not that of fence to thief, he explained, but of handler to informant. Rowan had been officially registered as one of his recruits. He had been on the books only a year and few months before he was de-registered, also by Tshicila, for being 'scarce'. Tshicila said he had struggled to contact him several times, eventually calling Rowan's grandfather, pretending to be a friend. (The official record contradicted this. It revealed that Rowan was de-registered because he faced criminal charges.) After de-registration Rowan remained in the grey zone: 'a contact'.

Roy – as Tshicila called him – had phoned him on Sunday 11 August, the day after Angy and Isaac's TV had gone missing, to say he had 'some stuff' for him. This was their code for information. Tshicila didn't leave immediately – he was at church – but Rowan wouldn't stop phoning him, and eventually he relented.

He went on to confirm much of the story that had already been told by the state witnesses, and that would also be recounted in Angy's and Isaac's testimony. But his version had a few important differences. He claimed Rowan never said, 'I have the TV.' Instead, he used the code words, 'I've got some stuff for you.' Tshicila had opened his boot to take out a diary, not receive stolen goods. His explanation for never making an affidavit about the incident was plausible – as an officer in Crime Intelligence he was supposed to avoid appearing in court at all costs, where he'd be obliged to disclose his sources.

When the time came, King's cross-examination of Tshicila was exceptional not just for its speed, but for the cold anger that animated it. While King might have been impatient with previous witnesses or frustrated when losing a battle with Henney, it always seemed as if these emotions rose out of his assessment of the game. With Tshicila, the anger seemed personal. His questions were rapid-fire, crisp, and generally short.

'So were you criminally charged,' he began, 'for being a thief?'

Immediately he was forced to withdraw and rephrase it.

'Were you charged criminally?'

'No, never.'

'Were you warned you were a suspect in a theft charge?'

'No, I was never warned.'

'Your reputation as conveyed to me and my instructions are that you are an extremely dangerous man. What do you say about that?'

'I have no knowledge of that.'

'Accused 1 and 2 took their family and fled from Mfuleni when they found out about your reputation. Two days after this incident, that Monday, they fled Mfuleni because they were so scared of you.'

At this Tshicila smiled slightly, as if trying not to. 'I have no knowledge of what has been spoken about.'

For most of his testimony, after being warned that he might incriminate himself, Tshicila declined to answer questions about the theft of the TV, and King focused instead on events in the police station. Tshicila repeatedly maintained he left him in the crime administration room as Rowan was, in his eyes, a victim and not a perpetrator. King then cited the statement that Tshicila made to Redelinghuys. He read out two lines:

'"I suspected that they were the victims of this housebreaking Roy was telling me earlier. I then put Roy at the holding cells and informed Captain Tchangani." Okay. I must put it to you that statement makes a mockery of what you've said previously that this was a victim of a crime. You don't put victims of crimes in cells, as you yourself say. Can you comment on that?'

'I won't dispute what is being said. I will say the way it happened or the manner that it happened, it was to protect him, nothing else.'

'Then why lie to this court now and say you knew nothing about him being put in the cells?' The pint-sized interpreter, in a turban and skinny jeans, appeared to take on King's vehemence as she translated. Tshicila smiled slightly, perhaps at her, perhaps at some other thought that played in his mind. I forgot, was his reply, it was a long time ago.

Moving on to how the station dealt with the complaint against him, it emerged that after Redelinghuys forwarded the complaint to his superior, the process stalled and Tshicila never attended a disciplinary hearing and was never charged. When Henney asked him why he had never been charged, Tshicila said it was Damoyi, the station commander of Mfuleni, who had closed the inquiry on the grounds that the complainants, Angy and Isaac, were too afraid to continue. The records King read out to him told a different story.

A letter by a Captain Dlepu, who represented Tshicila in the departmental inquiry, read: 'It is my humble submission that no further disciplinary action can be taken against Sergeant Tshicila, my reasons being… The complainant witness in this case Rowan du Preez (alias Roy) has been murdered as per Mfuleni CAS 417/10/2012. He is the person who originally alleged that he sold a stolen TV to Sergeant Tshicila and that they have a corrupt relationship and he was the only person who could have testified to this fact.'[54]

I thought about Nathaniel's statement: 'I suspect that Anele was involved.'

'You see,' said King, 'I want to put to you that you are a prime suspect in the murder. You had motive. Do you agree that you had a motive?'

'That is a lie.'

'Well, let's examine that. If you had been convicted you would have lost your job, am I correct?'

'I don't know.'

'If you had been charged in a criminal court, you are a policeman, you are a part of a corrupt relationship and you stole, you would go to jail for a very long time, is that correct?'

'I have no knowledge of that.' Tshicila jutted out his bottom lip, as if King was being absurd.

'Well, as a policeman do you know that there is zero tolerance by the courts for corrupt policemen at the moment?'

'I know that.'

'That is the motive. Do you understand that now?'

❖ ❖ ❖

There was one more thing to cover, when it came to the police testimony. It was considered by Henney to be largely irrelevant to the case, but I found it interesting.

Before concluding with Redelinghuys, King asked to put one last set of questions to him. He was apologetic about it because they didn't directly concern Redelinghuys. 'This is because we are not having the benefit of the investigating officer and this relates to the three subsequent charges.'

Ah, I thought, Angy's other charges. I had been wondering if the defence would risk bringing those up.

On about 4 April 2013 a man walked into the Mfuleni Police Station with a harrowing tale. He gave his name as Thabo Menziwe, and listed an address in Bardale, 22629 Intenetya Street.

Menziwe said he had been walking past Bardale Primary School in the early evening when a taxi pulled up and abducted him. Inside the vehicle were Angy Peter and two other men. They asked him where the TV Roy had given him was and, when he denied that he knew anything about it, they slapped him. The taxi drove to an Engen petrol station where Angy bought petrol. They then drove around and the men continued to punch and slap the terrified Menziwe.

Eventually they dragged him out of the taxi onto Monwabisi Beach. They took a tyre and a five-litre jerry can of petrol. Angy poured petrol over the tyre. Realising he was about to be burnt alive, Menziwe pushed Angy and as she fell over he ran away and escaped.

Warrant Officer Edward Balie was assigned the case after Menziwe laid a charge at the Mfuleni Police Station. Balie organised an arrest warrant for Angy Peter, and went to her house where he took a statement from Isaac. He searched the house for Angy but she wasn't there and couldn't be found for the rest of the weekend. On the Monday Joshua Greeff, Angy's attorney, arrived at the station with Angy, who handed herself over. Greeff presented her alibi to Balie, a statement from her manager, Lesley Liddle, who claimed to have been with Angy at the time.

Angy's explanation was that an extra room had been added to her shack and she returned home from the health clinic, having suffered from an asthma attack the day before, with a small baby, to find the room unfinished. She and Isaac had argued, and her manager, Liddle, put her up at a B&B for the night.

Balie set out to investigate. He went to the Engen garage and got their video footage but it didn't show (or entirely rule out) Angy buying petrol. Next, he questioned the B&B owner who corroborated Angy's story. This, of course, presented an alternative version for Balie, but now he couldn't track down the complainant.

Officer Balie was perhaps that rare policeman: a persistent detective. On 5 April he went to the address the complainant had given and found no one there. He called Menziwe's phone but got voicemail. He left a message. Menziwe never called back. Balie returned to the address a few times, but never found Menziwe home. Neighbours said they had never met a Thabo Menziwe.

Officer Balie didn't stop there. He visited two separate government offices – Home Affairs and the Department of Labour – and ran the complainant's name. Neither had any record of such a man.

By November 2013 there had been no progress: Angy had an alibi and the complainant was awol. A prosecutor struck down the case.

The Menziwe case was neither the first nor the last. In August 2013, another charge was laid against Angy at Site B Police Station, Khayelitsha for a strikingly similar crime. Again she, with accomplices, had allegedly abducted a man, a Zokolo Toto, questioned him about the TV, and tried to necklace him on Monwabisi Beach. This time she had forgotten the petrol and again the victim managed to escape.

He'd laid a charge, and Angy was arrested and spent the weekend in custody at the station. Again, she had a full alibi. She had been at work the whole day, to which her colleagues attested, except for a trip she'd taken to buy groceries at Pick n Pay. The store was fitted with CCTV cameras, she pointed out, and they could corroborate her story by requesting the footage. (Despite an instruction from the director of public prosecutions to do so, the footage was never obtained.)

The complainant in this matter also disappeared without trace. It was unclear whether the case was still being investigated.

Then there was a different charge in between the two alleged attempted necklacings. In this instance Angy was arrested by detectives from Lingelethu Police Station in Khayelitsha on 31 May on charges of kidnapping a baby. Angy was detained for seven hours and when Greeff arrived he demanded the complainant produce proof that the baby existed. He insisted that a birth certificate, or even a witness who could testify to the fact would be sufficient. When neither could be produced, Angy was released pending further investigation.

'And the complainant in that case is it, is gone?' asked Redelinghuys.

'Gone, no trace. I start getting suspicious,' said King.

Redelinghuys laughed, as if shocked. 'I start getting worried what happens to the complainants!'

❖ ❖ ❖

More of this story came out later in Angy's testimony. On 13 December, two weeks after she and Isaac had been released from Pollsmoor, the flying squad descended on her house at midnight for a drug raid. Angy was taken to Blue Downs Police Station under suspicion of drug dealing, but no charges were laid.

After the baby-kidnapping charge the police had come to the house where she was staying and called her children into the yard. They had asked each child's name and date of birth, and then demanded to see their birth certificates. They searched the house for the baby. After Angy was released from the kidnapping charge, she was placed under house arrest in her 'safe house' in Khayelitsha, which had been set up by Amnesty International and the SJC. It was a safe house no longer as she had to disclose its address to the police.

'Why was it necessary to have a safe house?' King had asked her.

'M'Lord, I started the war with the police, I couldn't handle it.'

Angy was told she was under house arrest and waited at the house for the police to return. 'They said I should not leave the house at Site B without an order from them. They never came back. I stayed there for two days and they never returned back. I then went on with my life.'

After the attempted necklacing case opened in Site B, Angy was granted bail on condition that she did not 'place my foot in Khayelitsha'.

'Who asked for that? Who asked that you would not be allowed in Khayelitsha? Who insisted on that condition?' King asked.

'It was the prosecutor. He said I was dangerous.'

'And what happened with the case?'

'It was withdrawn.'

Once again, the complainant who had lodged the case did not want to cooperate with the police, and ran away when they came to gather more information.

After this third arrest, the SJC staged a protest outside a church hall in Langa, where Riah Phiyega, the national commissioner of police, was addressing 300 policewomen. When she found out that 15 activists were waiting to speak to her outside she refused to leave the hall. The SJC waited outside for five hours, waving 'Hands off Angy' boards and singing protest songs.

Eventually, a message was sent to Phiyega that the protestors would not leave until she came out. She left the building and Isaac addressed her and her delegation. He explained the harassment they believed Angy was undergoing, and that she was in custody that weekend.

Phiyega promised that Provincial Commissioner Arno Lamoer would meet with them. When he failed to respond to their request, they walked into Lamoer's office and refused to leave. Their sit-in lasted five days before Lamoer, his legal advisor, and the provincial head of detectives agreed to meet with several senior members of the SJC.

Lamoer promised to look into their concerns. No more was heard from him but the arrests stopped and Angy reported a drop in police surveillance. In October 2013, she laid a complaint with the Independent Police Investigative Directorate, which the SJC leaders knew 'was unlikely to yield any results' but felt was 'important to have on record'.[53] The directorate never responded.

❖ ❖ ❖

The problem with presenting these arrests as evidence that Angy was being harassed in a case where the judge disliked inference, seemed to me ill advised. It took matters far beyond the interests of Tshicila and the grudges of the Blue Downs cops.

I wavered about the credibility of Angy's conspiracy defence. Its major weakness was its complexity, the way it, to paraphrase Gobodo-Madikizela, required so many people who did not usually do things together to cooperate. On some days it seemed simpler to say she must have committed the murder if only because her guilt required fewer assumptions and was therefore more likely to be true. But in the next instant I would think: But how can you explain everything that doesn't add up in the trial, let alone all the inconceivable matters outside the trial? I would then try to trace motivations and lines of command and my conviction would waver again. In one moment it would suddenly seem ridiculous, so extraordinarily vengeful, indeed *belaglik*, that Angy's harangues and complaints, or even the Khayelitsha Commission itself, could have produced such a vicious, complex response.

Chapter Fifteen

Do you think I care I don't so go straight to hell you are more than welcome there – Angy Peter's WhatsApp status, 18 June 2014.

The defence presented its case through June and July, the middle of a wet and cold winter, until the mid-year recess. I had to be in Johannesburg on an assignment, and I missed Angy's and Isaac's testimony. When proceedings resumed in August, I returned to court to find the pint-sized interpreter swaddled in such big scarves and coats she almost disappeared. One of the accused, Azola Dayimani, was concluding his testimony.

I had read the press coverage and, later, the court record, of Isaac's testimony, and by these accounts it hadn't been particularly eventful. In his evidence-in-chief he'd recounted the events surrounding the theft of the TV and the subsequent complaint. King had presented the affidavit Isaac made at the time of the theft case which confirmed that his version had remained consistent. Isaac also mentioned the mock-drowning which had happened in his yard, attributing the assault to Ta Topz, 'who was very furious'. He claimed he'd asked Ta Topz to stop as the assault was unwarranted, and told him to take the matter elsewhere if he had to continue. He stated that Angy had not been present for the assault.

Isaac had incurred censure over his failure to give his alibi to the investigating officer at the time of his arrest. His testimony was unclear and contradictory at first. In his evidence, he said he'd told the investigating officer that he would not divulge his alibi until he had spoken with his lawyer. In cross-examination he said the investigating officer had never requested it. He had only been asked if he knew 'a taxi man'.

Prosecutor Palesa blamed Isaac for his failure to state this rather than the police for failing to elicit it. He first called this a 'slight' change, then 'a major change', then a 'dramatic' change. After being asked to clarify, Isaac decided that he had never been asked for his alibi. This could have been refuted by investigating officer Muthien had he taken the stand.

Asked if he had been targeted as part of a police conspiracy, Isaac admitted 'no qualms' between him and the police prior to the murder. His work had never touched on criminal justice issues. Rather, he had been implicated by the police – opportunistically, because he was present when Angy was arrested – in order to strengthen their case against his wife. 'Angy was pregnant and it was impossible for her to [commit the crime] alone, meaning there had to be other people involved.' The police hadn't asked the children for his whereabouts that morning or asked Angy where he was when they spoke to her on the phone. Instead, they'd seen Angy give him her wallet as she was put into the police car, and then decided to arrest him.

Palesa moved on to the other accused, Azola and Chris. In their case, he argued, 'Your defence then falls apart: you cannot [explain] why Accused 3 and 4 are involved in this case.'

'I would say that they are victims of the police in this matter.'

'How is Accused 4 connected to Accused 1?'

'That is what I am asking myself.' Isaac's words exuded the same bewilderment I'd encountered from Angy the first time I met her and asked about Rowan's last hours. 'I also had hoped to get some reasons here in court.'

Palesa only seemed to have scored two valuable points in his cross-examination: he had called attention to Isaac's vacillation about whether he'd explicitly refused to give his alibi, or had never been asked; and he had pointed out that if the police were taking out information from dockets to fabricate Rowan's statement, they could easily have found Isaac's name in the documents on the TV theft case. A fair point, but it was a separate docket: King had only alleged that they took the addresses from the witness statements that morning. Neither victory seemed detrimental to Isaac's alibi, or explained the other irregularities in the docket.

But Palesa did prove to be a rather audacious practitioner of legal judo: he repeatedly tried to use the weakness of his own case against the defence.

'You see, the difficulty I have,' he said to Isaac at one point, 'was that they could have used better means to implicate you and Accused 1!' Better, he said, than 'using witnesses that were drunkards or an old man', and Desiree Jack, about whom 'there was an allegation that she was not mentally all there'.

This would crop up again, the idea (originally Henney's) that if the police had wanted to frame anyone, they would have gone about it more effectively.

It wasn't a surprise that Isaac appeared to have fared well. He gave his side of the story clearly and calmly. Angy I found – in my own conversations with her – to be an unreliable narrator. She had poor recall of details, even about events that had taken place within a week of speaking to her. Her version of any story was often confusing. Most anecdotes, in fact, she related in a non-linear way, with a frustrating tendency to cast herself at the centre of events, even when it was to her detriment. Add to that her allergic reaction to authority, and I wouldn't have been too surprised if her testimony was a disaster for the defence. Reading the record later, this was and wasn't borne out.

Her evidence-in-chief had gone smoothly enough, with King

leading her through the events before the TV theft, as well as her activist work, and the reaction she'd had from the police, and the media attention she attracted.

'Were you in contact with the Mfuleni Police Station, the detectives and personnel during the lead-up to 2012?'

'Yes, lots of times. They knew me well because at times when they didn't want to open a case, maybe of a child who is the victim, I would sit there and disobey their orders.' If she refused to leave the station she believed they would eventually take her and the child to the Family Violence, Child Protection and Sexual Offences (FCS) Unit in Bellville.

'And how regularly do you have contact with them? Once a week, once a month, every day?'

'It would depend how many victims would want to open cases during that time.' She explained it was a reactive relationship: she would visit the station because she had been approached by one of her neighbours, usually because the police had refused to open their case.

Angy talked about falling out with Rowan in early 2012, when he'd been arrested for the robbery and murder of the Somalian shop owner, and had phoned her from his cell in George. During that phone call he had told her he was being 'used' by a person who was 'quite powerful'. He wanted Angy to arrange for a police detective to see him – one that she trusted. But she was collecting testimonies for the Khayelitsha Commission at the time. 'And while there are detectives that I trust, because I was quite busy, I did not get time to do as he requested. So I failed Rowan in that manner.'

King took her through her version of the theft and the events that followed. Angy described how, after Isaac had opened the case, they had been unable to get the case number from Tchangani.

'What did you think would happen if you didn't get a case number?'

'According to my experience they were going to deny our presence there.'

'And what would happen with Rowan?'

'They were going to set him free.'

'And your TV set?'

'We were not going to get the TV back.'

'And Andile Tshicila, would anything happen to him?'

'Nothing was going to happen, because as we speak now, nothing happened.'

Angy described how she followed up on her promise to her neighbours to pursue the matter through the police's own mechanisms, first with her 101 complaint, which Station Commander Damoyi had referred to Redelinghuys. Then when the complaint was not making progress, she had tried to directly approach senior police officers. 'As the court can see that Damoyi didn't want to listen to me. I would call [Police Commissioner Lieutenant-General] Lamoer's office and I would not get straight answers from the office and after I could not get any attention from any one of them, I then called IPID [the Independent Police Investigative Directorate]'.

'Now what were you attempting to achieve by phoning these people, what did you want?'

'I wanted this Ta Ager to be arrested. I wanted to stop this corruption from the police. I wanted proper criminal justice.'

But when IPID had finally sent a representative Angy had been unhappy with how the officer handled the matter. She was annoyed and alarmed when the woman from IPID did not take any notes while she relayed her complaints. After their conversation, in front of Angy, the woman phoned the Blue Downs station commander and told him to deal with the complaint in-house.

Henney interrupted here. 'You can make it shorter, Mr King.'

Angy described how she warned Redelinghuys that she was afraid of Ta Ager, and also that she wanted him to face justice. 'I told him should Rowan be convicted then this Ta Ager character should also be convicted, and that this Rowan was not a problem but Ta Ager was a problem, and I told him about my fear.'

'When Tshicila gave evidence in court I noticed that you asked the court for a break,' King said, referring to Angy bursting out the court room in tears. 'Why?'

'M'Lord, this Ta Ager character stole my TV. I had to take my children out of school because of him and it didn't end there. I believe that he is the person that killed Rowan but the state did nothing about that until this day. I went to all the legal sections that could help me in this and the only thing I got were empty promises and a bunch of lies. The same state that didn't want to assist me called this Andile character as a witness, yet while he was still a suspect in the case of my TV, he was not called and he was not asked anything.'

Palesa made some good arguments in the course of his cross-examination. His best work was in recasting Angy's own account of events in a more menacing light. In his hands her search for her TV on the morning after the theft looked increasingly like a brewing mob attack. She had gone to Rowan with a suspicion that he was responsible, and she had pursued that suspicion herself, rather than through a police investigation. Later, she had – at best – let a mob form in her yard and left Rowan in its midst.

'You see, mobs, they accuse a person, they conduct their own investigations, they don't go to the police. Is that not how they operate?'

Palesa also, with pomp and flourish in his words, delivered an argument that he said 'neutralised' Angy's alibi. Quite simply, it went like this: if the police had gone to arrest Angy right after they found Rowan, they would have found her at home with her children as, according to Desiree, she had already returned home from the necklacing, in the taxi playing loud music.

Palesa made quite a fuss about how 'I read through, I analysed this. If one looks at the evidence of the witnesses, the evidence that the ambulance arrived ...' He went through his various points of triangulation: Desiree's sighting of the returning Quantum, and when

Asavela said the tavern closed. And he drew on the 'very scientific' opinion of Klatzow 'that was called by the defence to show us a tyre burns on average 20 to 30 minutes'.

But while this deflected criticism of the police's failure to act on the information they said they had in the early hours of that Sunday morning, it didn't disprove Angy's alibi. Angy countered that Desiree was a dishonest person.

Palesa also tried to recast Angy's assertion that she was widely known to the dozens of police who worked at Mfuleni station, and beyond, as pure arrogance. 'Every police officer at Mfuleni, and maybe also Kleinvlei – you would expect them to know you? Is that what you're saying?'

It was unclear to me why the defence spent so much time trying to defend these assertions. Barnardo, Kock and Wilhelm didn't need to know who Angy was to play the role the defence alleged they had. All Kock needed to know was that the victim was Rowan. Once she radioed that information to her superiors, they would have arranged the rest, including the statement from Wilhelm, made five months later.

Angy made a plausible case for her general notoriety, by stating that she was well known to the Khayelitsha station commanders because she continually made complaints at their stations, and they met each week with the Blue Downs station commanders and sometimes other senior staff, as they were part of the same 'cluster', an administrative division of eight stations in the same area. 'Therefore my name would then be mentioned on those meetings because of the complaints that I have lodged.' Angy also gave a range of reasons why the Blue Downs police officers on Rowan's murder scene would have known of her, insisting she was a regular presence in the station, even if she didn't remember meeting them herself.

As far as I could tell these were the threatening questions Palesa put to her. Angy's testimony didn't appear to have been a disaster, but neither was it an unblemished triumph. She was often hard to follow, and would tell her version of events in a way that was unstructured and often confusing. Worse than that, she was frequently combative. She didn't hesitate in telling the prosecutor, or even Henney, that their questions were poorly put. 'I want you to ask the question clearer if you want to know how did it happen,' she said to Palesa at one point.

And she complained to Henney, 'What is confusing me, M'Lord, is the state is asking me questions. He would say things and not state everything and also generalise. That is what is creating a problem.' At several points, when she was in a corner, she would deflect responsibility for answering the question to King or Isaac.

On her fourth day, Palesa asked her why she'd wanted to know why Tshicila hadn't been cross-examined on whether he'd given weapons to Rowan or his friends. At the time the prosecutor could not recall her words on the record so she adamantly denied saying anything of the sort. ('What is said by the state now was never uttered by me, I never said that.') The next day Palesa had found the reference in her evidence-in-chief. Her reaction was, 'M'Lord, during the state's cross-examination yesterday if he did not mention the word "the day before yesterday", I would have responded.' This seemed dishonest and obstructive, over something that was not a cornerstone of her defence. Nor did her reaction cover her in glory and it gave Palesa the leeway to say she was an evasive witness.

But Palesa's performance was equally, if not more, confusing and often aimlessly hostile. Pages and pages and pages of the record were taken up with Palesa pursuing an argument, incoherently, with frequent re-phrasing at the behest of the judge, the witness, and the defence counsel, only to have it declared an unfair question.

But perhaps this did have a logic. In the process, Palesa made so many allegations and smears, unconnected to his questions, unsubstantiated, and often retracted or dropped mid-way, that you were dazed by his repetition and rudeness. This tended to leave his accusations lingering in the mind.

Later Palesa told Angy, 'We will argue, Ma'am, and you may comment, all these matters show the audacity that you had, the impunity which you operate with. There is no firm basis to argue that the police concocted this evidence to suppress your involvement in the commission. What is your comment?'

'It is sad, M'Lord, because the state does not stay with the police. The police are capable of anything. That I was going to demonstrate at the commission of inquiry. That is why I had collected evidence against the police, because there's many things that the state is not aware of.'

❖ ❖ ❖

Chris Dina, 27, was a truck assistant at Coca-Cola. Most days he spent inside a warehouse in Athlone loading trucks. Chris regularly fell asleep in court. Angy said it was because, having to spend his days at the trial, he worked a late shift.

Azola, also 27 at the time of the trial, drove the Khayelitsha-to-Kuilsriver route for a Site C taxi boss called Mama Sasa. Azola had grown up somewhere in the Eastern Cape, but had to drop out of school in Grade 8 because of his epileptic fits. He'd looked for work in Cape Town and had lived in Bardale with his wife and four children since 2007. He was a devout Christian and said he never went to shebeens because he was teetotal. To make up the income he lost being in court he spent his weekends driving a taxi to the Eastern Cape and back, a return journey of just over 2 300 km.

In many ways they conformed to the profile of vigilantes – not because they were young and misbehaved, but because they were working men, managing to make a living in low-wage, long-hour jobs. They earned just enough to buy goods on credit at punishingly high interest rates – goods that conferred respectability: a TV, a small fridge, furniture. They were men who might come home to discover that the goods they were still paying off had been looted by tsotsis. They were men who might be mugged on their way to the train station as they commuted to work, men who understood their role as breadwinners and protectors in neighbourhoods where jobs were scarce, wages low, and violence ubiquitous.

Azola, though he was pious and effeminate, was in a category of even higher suspicion. He was a taxi driver. And taxi drivers were profiled as potential vigilantes.

It was possible that their defence was false and Angy's true: perhaps they were involved, the real culprits.

Luckily for them there was little evidence tying them to the murder: not a shred of forensic evidence, no eyewitness accounts at the murder scene, and no specific mention in Rowan's hearsay declaration. Not that this was emphasised in their lawyer's performance. Ndlovu, the second legal-aid counsel they were assigned, was not very active in the case. Perhaps feeling that King had already covered the important ground, his cross-examinations were usually brief. He had been silent during the hearsay trial too. Perhaps this was because he believed the hearsay statement was no threat to his clients, but he had not contributed to any of the cross-examination of the medical witnesses. And while he had briefly questioned the police officers Barnardo and Kock, he had not asked any questions of Wilhelm, even though her version of Rowan's hearsay statement was the one that came closest to implicating his clients as 'two other men'. Most disturbingly, he'd declined to cross-examine Redelinghuys, even though much of his client's defence rested on how prejudicial their arrests had been and how poor the investigation.

Ndlovu was also dangerously complacent about the threat of the hearsay statement. If Henney placed enough weight on it, it could lead to a murder conviction for Angy and Isaac, and the state was arguing for a common purpose[55] conviction for Azola and Chris.

In the course of Palesa's cross-examination of Azola it became clear that Ndlovu had let some important issues slip by in his short cross-examinations. For the first time the court heard that there was corroboration that the taxi was parked elsewhere. Yet Ndlovu hadn't asked any of the eyewitnesses if they had fabricated their accusations. Nor had he questioned Desiree about her simple description of a man 'with a big tummy'. This was the man she later argued was Azola.

'Desiree don't know me, and it's impossible for her, not knowing me, to come to point me out in court and say I am a man with a big tummy,' Azola spluttered in court. 'She doesn't know me.'

'What is wrong with that, that she came and identified you as the person with the big tummy?'

'Firstly, I don't have a big tummy. There are many black persons with big tummies. Others are even fatter or bigger than me.'

Azola was, in fact, rather lean. So a fair point, I thought. Azola's alibi was that on the night Rowan was murdered he was at home, ill with diarrhoea, and he spent the evening watching Nollywood films with his sister. His taxi – the one that the witnesses said was used to kidnap Rowan – spent all that night similarly indisposed. It was parked in Site B, Khayelitsha, as he had lent it to a friend to make use of that weekend. He hadn't gone to the doctor for his stomach bug, but had prepared a natural remedy himself. There were consequently no doctor's records to corroborate his story. But his boss, Mama Sasa, confirmed he was off work. He called her on the Friday morning to explain he was ill and she had told him to find a friend to cover his route for the days he wouldn't be driving.

His testimony was bolstered by the appearance of another witness called Monde Cofa. Cofa's surprising cameo almost certainly fell in the category of 'too little, too late'.

Cofa was a 27-year-old taxi driver who lived in Khayelitsha. He'd known Azola since 2003, when they were both teenagers from the Eastern Cape trying to make a living in the city. He got to know him better through the taxi business, though they had never worked for the same boss. In 2012 his taxi was undergoing repairs after an accident. The way he put it, the repairs took a year. So he made his living by filling in for other drivers when they were sick or wanted time off. Cofa had already done this for Azola on a few occasions that year – enough times for him to be familiar with Azola's route from Khayelitsha to Kuilsriver.

On the day before Rowan's murder he'd collected the taxi's keys from Azola's house. He'd let himself into the house, and peeped into the bedroom behind the room divider, where Azola lay ill in bed. Azola didn't get up. He told Monde Cofa where the money for petrol was stashed in the taxi. Cofa scooped up the keys from a table in the living room on his way out.

Later that day he and Azola spoke on the phone. Azola told him where to take the day's cash, and to drive the taxi home, rather than bring it back to him. He still felt ill, and would be down the whole weekend. They didn't speak the next day, Saturday, the day of Rowan's attack, and Cofa didn't return to Mfuleni. All the drivers knocked off early on Sunday. The owner of the taxi collected it from him at about 8 pm and took it back to Azola's house. (This would have been about an hour before Sergeant Lesley Freeman arrived to arrest Azola and when Desiree said she saw the taxi.) On the Sunday evening, Azola was feeling better and expected to pick up his route again on the Monday morning.

On the Monday morning, Cofa got a call from Azola's boss to say he should take the taxi as Azola wouldn't be working. Cofa said he only learnt from Mama Sasa after the shift that Azola had been arrested. Her explanation for Azola's arrest was that he'd 'slapped a young man there in Mfuleni'. Azola's arrest, Cofa pointed out, fixed the memory of that weekend in his mind.

He drove the taxi for the rest of the week. On the Thursday he heard through the taxi-rank rumour mill that the vehicle had been used to commit a crime. That day Mama Sasa told him he'd have to return the taxi to her the next day for that reason. He didn't ask any questions. Nor did Monde Cofa question Azola about the incident until late the following year.

Cofa's appearance in court was the first time these events had been heard. Palesa's cross-examination was conducted with tempered disdain. 'But didn't you say,' he asked Cofa, 'hey, brother, but I've heard you've been arrested because of this taxi they say that you used? But you remember that weekend – you were sick and the taxi was in my possession? You didn't speak about that?'

'I become upset very easily and very quickly,' said Monde Cofa. 'When I heard about this I became very upset and I just decided I am not going to talk. I am not going to talk about this at all. I am just going to keep it to myself.'

'You see up until now we've never received information about you and/or your possession of the taxi.'

I thought of all the times King had accused Palesa of 'conducting a trial by ambush'. But Palesa hardly seemed bothered by Cofa, whose story Ndlovu had never mentioned before.

'You wouldn't just sit in custody,' said Palesa, encouraging Cofa to think through what would have happened if the tables were turned between him and Azola, 'trying to get out on bail knowing that there is somebody else actually who had the car?'

'Yes, that is correct.'

'Don't you find it strange that Azola has done that?'

'No, that surprises me.'

'It is shocking, isn't it?'

'Yes.'

'It does not make sense, does it?'

'No.'

Monde Cofa claimed he had been intensely upset by Azola's incarceration and wanted to 'rescue' him. And yet he hadn't, and Ndlovu had never mentioned his existence before. In the recess

Barbara Maregele, who was covering the trial for the news agency GroundUp, said she'd heard him, sheepishly, giving another account of why he hadn't come forward earlier. He'd heard the police were on the hunt for taxi drivers, and he was afraid any taxi driver might do.

❖ ❖ ❖

Chris's alibi was that on the night of Rowan's murder he was at a different tavern, Boetie's Tavern, in a different part of Mfuleni with two friends. The shebeen had closed at midnight and he'd spent about 45 minutes walking back to his shack, where he'd fallen asleep immediately. Before his arrest he had not known any of his co-accused, nor Rara, Desiree or John Ndevu. But he was well acquainted with Rowan and, at one point, he and Asavela had been in love. According to Chris, he had given his alibi to the investigating officer but the police had not followed up.

Neither Chris or Azola were claiming to have been of specific interest to the police. The most powerful reason they could provide for why they'd been implicated in Rowan's murder was the wrath of Asavela. This provided Palesa with a set of truly thorny questions for them. If Asavela implicated them only because she felt rejected, Palesa asked them both, then why would she implicate Angy and Isaac? And why would Desiree have supported Asavela's assertions? And why would Rara? And if this whole case came about because the police had it in for Angy, why bundle you up in it too?

Chris said, plainly, he didn't know the reasons. He believed Asavela had been 'unable to accept it' during their recent break-up. And it was she who had given his name to John Ndevu, and she who was 'in cahoots' with Desiree Jack. Desiree Jack and Ndevu were 'bitter because of the death of Rowan and they are just happy for anybody to be arrested'. As for Rara? Well, he, Asavela and Rowan were inseparable before the murder, they were 'always going around together'.

Azola also said his troubles stemmed from Asavela. 'I had, sometime I had a problem with Asavela. Asavela at some time phoned Angy and asked for my number.' He told Angy not to give Asavela his number.

'I asked Asavela' – presumably the next time he drove her on SJC business – 'why does she want my number?' She could get him fired from his gig with the SJC, he warned her. She replied, 'Aren't you a man?' From then on Asavela did not want to speak to him. Azola continued to reject her, and believed this was what made her bitter.

When it came to John Ndevu, Azola said he was 'aggrieved because the police did not do a proper job in searching or looking for the persons who murdered his son. Now he is taking out his anger on any person the police mention or bring forth.' Azola continued in similar vein: Desiree was a bitter person, who agreed with whatever evidence was put in front of her.

Chris and Azola were not fundamentally bad witnesses. Their stories were consistent, and their alibis had not been disproved. But though their allegations against the family and the police were similar to Angy's and Isaac's, when they were delivered through Ndlovu's straightforward questioning, and their own nonchalant tone, rather than King's intricate constructions, or Angy's and Isaac's earnest explanations, they seemed flat and contrived. They seemed the kind of things a dozen guilty people in courts would say on any one day alone.

❖ ❖ ❖

As the defence's case drew to a close, King started complaining about something new, and Henney blanched visibly. King and Greeff's fees were seriously in arrears, and King had begun to openly state in court that they might have to pull out of the case. In private, Joel Bregman was receiving 'difficult' emails from him. While fundrais-ing for civil litigation had been bread-and-butter for many of the

Khayelitsha-based organisations, a criminal trial was an entirely different story. It was far harder to predict the outcome for donors, and a criminal trial advanced nothing but one person's innocence or guilt. A guilty verdict was a possibility that always lurked in a prospective donor's mind. If King and Greeff pulled out over payment that would leave Angy and Isaac at the mercy of legal aid which might mean the trial would have to begin again. This was not something Henney, or anyone else, wanted.

This pressure from the lawyers came at a time when Angy and Isaac's relationship with the SJC could not have been worse. From the things I'd heard Angy say, something had gone awry in their relationship. There were comments in April about the Khayelitsha Commission, which she now viewed, in line with other cynical observers, as a doomed talk shop. 'They are getting victory, and I am getting victimised. They are getting all the credit and I am getting this horrible life. That is comrades for you,' Angy lamented. In June, she reached another level of bitterness, when she told me on the phone, that 'issues with the SJC' were making her feel 'a little bad, maybe'. When I asked her to explain why she felt this way, resentment and claims of abandonment poured out. She was a founding member of the SJC, yet in court only junior members, latecomers to the movement, were present on the benches. Bar one or two people, senior leadership had abandoned her. 'I built that organisation!' she said, over and over again. 'They got the glory of the [Khayelitsha] commission of inquiry. Now they won't even give me the time of day.' Her colleagues were avoiding her, she said: 'I don't even get a simple phone call!' When they wanted to know what was happening in court, they read GroundUp or they called her lawyer. 'If they had a way to dump me in the desert, they would do so.'

When their members had been the victims of crimes, the TAC and the SJC had protested loudly on the court steps, toyi-toying and demanding justice. Now that two of their members were accused of committing a crime, they were in a more awkward position. They had to respect the court and the process, and be seen to do so. But that didn't explain why senior members of the organisation were not lending Angy solidarity by sitting on the gallery benches. It created an impression about her standing in the organisation – and it wasn't a good one. I started to ask myself if they were hedging their support because they were no longer sure she was innocent. I don't believe I was the only person in court to draw those conclusions.

But even from the little I knew, her feeling of abandonment wasn't entirely fair. The organisation had arranged them safe houses, counselling, various expenses, a muted but consistent media output attesting their innocence, eye-wateringly expensive legal representation, as well as a private investigator to look into Angy's third arrest. They had protested to gain the attention of the national police commissioner and held a sit-in at the provincial commissioner's office. It was almost because of the level of support they'd received in 2013, that the lack of solidarity in court in 2014 seemed so odd.

There was one senior employee in court regularly, Joel Bregman. And behind the scenes he was furiously fundraising, though it would emerge later that these details were largely hidden from Angy and Isaac, lest they discover how hopeless the situation seemed at times. Joel was also the organisation's spokesperson. He was the man I was directed to if I wanted information from SJC employees. He was professional, ethical, and scrupulous, and so for my purposes, useless. He wouldn't explain the disjuncture between their press releases and the court's empty benches.

Later I discovered that beneath Angy's comments was a growing row between her and SJC member Dustin Kramer, who was responsible for monitoring her and Isaac's household expenses. The SJC had been covering these expenses since the latter part of 2013. The receipts the couple brought were inadequate for the organisation's bookkeeping, and Dustin was increasingly short with them about it. In May, these arguments had taken a darker turn. Dustin had reviewed their bookkeeper's files, and become concerned about the receipts Angy had supplied for her counselling sessions. They were generic cash receipts, without a practitioner's logo. In fact they were identical to the receipts the couple submitted for the court transport and food. When asked for a proper receipt, Angy and Isaac provided a letter from a psychiatrist with the amounts they had paid and what was still owed. The letter did not reassure anyone. Joel called the psychiatrist's rooms and established that they had never been there.

Angy and Isaac denied forgery, despite the SJC's documentation of the events. In correspondence to me, Dustin, Phumeza Mlungwana, the General Secretary of the SJC, and Joel said, 'It hurt tremendously … it was a difficult situation for everyone, we felt a lot of hurt at being lied to in such a way, after having put so much into trying to protect them and having put ourselves and the SJC at such risk while trying to get us through this crisis.' When Zackie Achmat, founder of the TAC, spoke to me about it months later, he was seething and less than diplomatic. It was 'a crime against the organisation', one that undermined all the work they'd done to support her through the trial, and it reduced her to 'a nasty person' in his eyes.

By September Isaac and Angy had officially resigned. In August there remained the matter of King's and Greeff's increasingly urgent demands to be paid for the fees in arrears, which amounted to hundreds of thousands of rands. The SJC was deep in financial crisis, and the trial continued to drag on with no end in sight, racking up bills of more than R100 000 a week. Yet, in the end, the SJC agreed to be wholly liable for settling all costs relating to the main trial, including those which would be incurred in the future.

That, effectively, was the end of personal forms of solidarity from several members of the SJC leadership.

Chapter Sixteen

The defence's case closed after Azola testified, but there was still more evidence for the court to consider. During Chris's testimony, Judge Henney had declared that he intended calling witnesses himself, namely, the investigating officer, Stanley Muthien, and the arresting officer, Lesley Freeman.

King and Henney had a fairly amiable discussion about this. King raised the possibility that it might be seen as benefiting the state's case to call Muthien. Henney said if that was the impression he would not do it, but cautioned King 'it can go both ways. In actual fact, Muthien might actually come and sink the state case, in respect of the witnesses'.

'Yes,' said King.

Henney explained his thinking. The main issues at stake were why the witnesses had recanted their statements to the investigating officer, both adding and subtracting details such as suspects, abductions and murder weapons. 'If Muthien sticks to his guns and said, "No, this is what was said," then, obviously, the state has some difficulty.'

'Yes.'

'Even so with Freeman,' said Henney, 'in respect of that.'

King came round. 'Look, M'Lord, I am sure that Muthien is going to assist the defence case probably more than the state case. So let me not try to dissuade the court from seeing that justice is done, if I might leave it at that.'

And so at the beginning of August the investigating officer was finally put on the stand.

❖ ❖ ❖

In court Constable Muthien often wore a suede jacket with a sheep's-wool collar, a blue tie patterned like an early Windows screensaver, and the sour aura of deep depression. A thick-set man, he had an overhanging forehead, big jowls and a head of glossy black curls. But it was the dark rings under his eyes which dominated his face. Even on the first day he looked exhausted and when Palesa asked him how he felt, sitting in the audience benches before testifying, he mumbled something about pills.

He was still stationed at Blue Downs where he'd been since 2011. He joined the SAPS in 2004, and had started out in the detective branch yet had not received any training in detection methods during his first ten years on the job. His training in detective practice – known as 'The Rock' – had happened at Hammanskraal in 2014. This was some two years after he investigated Rowan's murder. Even then, he had only completed the theory component, not the practical. In 2007 he had done a stint in Crime Intelligence, where he worked on tracing suspects and where his tenure would have overlapped with that of Tshicila, though he claimed not to have met him.

He had not been in continuous service. In 2008 he had resigned from the police and tried 'something', returning to SAPS and Blue Downs in 2011. Under cross-examination King tried to discover if this 'something' was a stint at undercover work which would provide a strong Crime Intelligence connection. Ultimately, Muthien confessed to something more prosaic and revealing: he left the police to study mechanical engineering at a Cape Town technikon but failed the third year for reasons he didn't disclose. Having failed as a constable and as a would-be engineer, he returned, in defeat, to police work. And here, it became obvious as he testified, he had continued to fail ever since.

On the stand, Muthien was a figure of dejection. His two positions were hunched or slouched, and he was inert and self-pitying in reply to the questions the judge and the lawyers put to him. During cross-examination he stared at his lap or the docket, occasionally raising his head slowly to regard King. At moments he mumbled so badly he was inaudible. As far as the docket was concerned, Muthien made no sense of it. He had no recall of the investigation, the record which he had put together and tended to for the 18 months it took to get to trial, and to which almost all of King's questions related. When King referred to a document Muthien's fingers scurried through the docket's pages trying to find the appropriate reference in the jumbled mess before him. Even when he didn't need to refer to the written matter, he flipped backwards and forwards through the paperwork, as if he had to check that the defence wasn't lying about the existence of a particular statement or departmental record. Even Henney lost his patience at times: 'Just accept that it is the housebreaking docket!' he'd snap.

In addition, Muthien's body, as well as his mind, appeared to revolt against being put on the stand. At the start of his second day, a Tuesday, Muthien complained he had a sore throat. He'd been booked off sick from work that day and the next, and Henney let him off testifying, saying his voice would need to recover as he was going to do a lot of talking.

On the Thursday, the trial was again postponed as Muthien was still ill. Henney demanded a sick note from a doctor, the merit of which was greeted with a fair amount of scepticism by the assembled lawyers and accused. 'If he's unable to come and it's a genuine sick certificate,' Henney said, 'then there's not much one can do.'

King was particularly displeased. 'M'Lord, one of my clients at the moment is a Khayelitsha doctor charged with fraud in exactly this type of situation.'

'Yes, it's happened many a times,' said Henney. 'I've asked the prosecutor, "Please, get the doctor to come and testify," and the doctor said, "I've never seen this person." The receptionist issues these certificates.'

The sick note arrived in due course and Henney announced that Muthien had been diagnosed with pharyngitis.

King asked to see the note. 'I just want to make sure it's not my client who signed it.' He wasn't impressed. 'They've spelled it "faringitis".'

The next Monday Muthien managed a full day, but then on the following Wednesday morning, at around 11.30, Muthien told an usher he had a headache and it was hard for him to continue. Henney stood the matter down until 2 pm to give him time to recover. Muthien only testified for the last two hours of the day. This was the day when the discrepancies between his version and the witnesses became apparent.

He was not well enough to attend court the following day, and provided a doctor's note that diagnosed him with a migraine and high blood pressure and booked him off for two days to recover.

When this was announced Angy marched up to King. 'It's been nine months! I can't take this nonsense any more. Do you know how much it costs me to get here every day? R100. It's better to go to Pollsmoor than to keep going up and down like this!' King spoke in low, soothing tones in reply. 'Tell Henney to prosecute me,' she told him. 'Or keep me in Pollsmoor. This is complete nonsense! Muthien has been sick almost every day.'

It was the following week, Monday 25 August, the third week the court dealt with Muthien's testimony, that he returned, seemingly fortified by tablets to keep his blood pressure under control. He said it was the first time he had ever suffered from hypertension. I might not have believed everything Muthien said, but I had no doubt at that point that testifying was indeed making him physically ill.

❖ ❖ ❖

From the start of Muthien's testimony, he had repeatedly claimed that he could barely remember what he had or hadn't done in the course of investigating the case. Luckily King was on hand to remind him: he had not followed up on any of the first prosecutor's most basic instructions, such as getting a statement from Thobile, who was repeatedly mentioned as an eyewitness in Roger's statement. He had not spoken to the owner of the tavern where the assault started, or to the person who lived in the shack in the crèche where the assault continued.

When asked why he had not kept the notes made by the three police witnesses taking down Rowan's statement, Muthien answered that it was not his custom to keep such evidence. He had not asked for the notes, and the three police officers had never mentioned them either.

'To be honest from when I was a detective we never gather those notes,' he told King, which only served to quicken the advocate's pace.

'But you are not a detective, are you?'

'Come again?'

'You are not a detective?'

'Is that a question?'

'Yes: are you a detective?'

'I am working in the detective environment.'

'But you are not a qualified detective.'

As King went laboriously through Muthien's investigation, he would finger through the documents, then look up with dark-ringed eyes and say, 'Perhaps.' Or 'I cannot really recall.' Or 'it might be so.' But before that he would probably say, 'I don't understand the question.'

Now you might think that a witness who repeatedly said 'I don't know' would produce the worst, the most tedious kind of cross-examination. But you would be wrong because there was one worse fate: the cross-examination that produced the dominant refrain, 'I don't understand the question.' This only prolonged the torture because although it provided Muthien a little respite from the uncomfortable questions coming from the defence, King would then subject the court to several reformulations of the same question. And then it would be put in almost identical words by Judge Henney, who had to be obeyed. Inevitably this resulted in: 'I don't know.'

This was only one of the tortures inflicted on the court by Muthien, and it paled in comparison to his evasions around the docket. Early on Muthien was instructed to read it thoroughly, to take it home and rearrange it. Yet, in the third week of his testimony, he was in a state of almost constant confusion. Back on the stand after his week of hypertension, Muthien continued to fumble, grope, and splutter in his exchanges with King.

At noon one day Muthien asked for more time with the docket. Henney agreed. It was 'senseless' to continue without the docket in order, because all the questions that would be asked of Muthien would relate to his investigation. Henney surrendered his office so that Muthien could order the paperwork. But even with the help of the usher and a two-hour tea break, Muthien still could not reconstruct it. He complained that the 'time was too little' and the job too great.

'Look, we have gone through this exercise when Lieutenant-Colonel Redelinghuys was here,' said Henney in despair.

Redelinghuys had already reordered the C-Section – though to no one's satisfaction – and there was still the rest of the docket. 'Exactly, M'Lord,' said King.

'And it was also a tedious process.'

'It is going to be even worse now, M'Lord. You said, "Mr King, wait until Muthien if he ever comes gives evidence, then ask him these questions." And I was, in fact. I withheld asking Redelinghuys those questions for exactly this reason.'

Henney told King to proceed with cross-examination anyway that afternoon and see how Muthien fared. Unsurprisingly this exercise went poorly and Muthien's memory again failed him. Near the end of the day he was sent home with the docket and asked to familiarise himself with the case he had presided over. But in court the next day, Muthien said he had still not read it. On the way back to the station, he explained, his police car had broken down. The fault had been beyond the skills of the police mechanic and Muthien had waited from the late afternoon until after 8 pm on the side of the road for the towing service. 'I came round about 9 o'clock home and I was so exhausted and so tired.'

They proceeded anyway but Muthien shook his head in response to King's questions and pleaded for more time to read the docket. 'I requested time so that I can apply my mind to what really…' he mumbled on, ' …and then the rest of the questions…' and then became inaudible again.

'Unfortunately for you, Mr Muthien,' said Henney, 'from where I am sitting we have no more time for that. Do you understand that? We have postponed this matter because you were sick. It comes to a point now that we cannot give you any more time.' Muthien would just 'have to make do'. And so for two more days they trekked through the thicket of Muthien's incomprehension.

The docket discussion was exceedingly sensitive because 'the only other person that could have made that mess' was sitting on the left of the front bench. For lengthy periods at least one copy had been with the prosecutor. And Palesa was not enjoying various accusations that documents had been manipulated. Towards the close of Muthien's cross-examination, the proceedings were repeatedly derailed by fights between Palesa – defended by Henney – and King, who stopped trying to veil his allegations. These, in turn, seemed bitter and senseless allegations of a conspiracy.

The most serious of these occurred when King accused Muthien of 'dis-arranging' the file he had taken home. Palesa defended Muthien and King responded with a take-no-prisoners attitude.

'I put it to you that it was purposefully done to mislead the defence, repeatedly purposefully done by either you – or the state.'

'We object and we are objecting with a very serious concern!' said Palesa, high pitched and outraged. 'To say now that we have denied them information is completely incorrect and a mere allegation without basis.' Henney ordered King to retract it; King fudged his reply; Henney flew off the handle; King persisted, repeatedly returning to one theme: would the defence ever get an explanation for the state of the docket? Henney turned the heat on Muthien: 'Do you know why these documents were given to them in such an order? Are you able to answer the question?'

Muthien talked as if he had a head injury, and was clinging to a semblance of presence and consciousness. 'I need to sit down and then I can give my answer, but I cannot at this moment in time. I don't want to give an answer, then it is maybe something else.'

At moments like this the mix of tedium and paranoia and frustration in the court made every minute heavy. We were in the bitter end days of nine months of acrimony, of Henney saying King was putting irrelevant information on the record and King complaining that he wasn't getting answers to the simple problems. Nine months of questions that either shouldn't have been asked or shouldn't have been evaded. Someone had to be punished for what felt like so much wasted time. The worst side of everyone came to court each day. Henney didn't protect Muthien as he had the previous witnesses and King throttled the investigating officer like a dog's chew toy and got nowhere for it. His patience, in turn, wore thin with Henney and Palesa too, and Henney paid him the same favour.

Soon, they descended to bickering again.

'Do not argue with me on those points.'

'No, no, I am making a point now … this is not argument, M'Lord.'

'You are arguing it. I am telling you: you are arguing it.'

'M'Lord, I am making a submission.'

'No, I am telling you: you are arguing it, sir.'

When, on the last day, King put it to Muthien that the docket had been manipulated, Henney asked what the point of that would be.

'To hide documents, to add documents, to extract documents. We do not know and that is the problem: we never will know because we cannot get an order!'

Muthien had by that time physically broken the docket, by dropping it on its spine. During this cross-examination he asked at least twice if he could splash his face with water, lest he fall asleep.

❖ ❖ ❖

One of the main issues that the court wanted Muthien to address was the huge discrepancies between what the witnesses said they told him and what was contained in the statements he took the day after Rowan's murder. Muthien had the power to rescue the witnesses' credibility by saying that he had interpreted their stories, that he mixed them up, or that he misunderstood.

When King delved into Muthien's statement taking, it emerged that he did not take statements in the manner of a qualified detective. He did not read Wilhelm's statement back to her, or ask her any questions about it. He did not ask her if it was the truth or have her swear an oath on its contents. He maintained that he believed he had commissioned the document because 'I put a stamp on'.

'That is not commissioning,' Henney told him. 'What do you do every time when you come here to testify?'

'Get sworn.'

'You get sworn in to tell the truth, isn't that so? That is what we call commissioning. Not putting a rubber stamp on a piece of paper.'

Muthien explained he had learnt how to take statements, how 'one do it at station level'. But only the year before at his detective's course had he learnt how to do it 'the right way'.

'Mr Muthien,' said King, 'do I understand your evidence correctly: not one of the statements that you took as investigating officer in this docket was properly taken?'

'I don't understand what do you mean by properly taken?'

In the manner required by law, Henney told him.

'Okay, ja.'

When they reprised the topic later Muthien explained, 'If you come on station level and then you will see your colleagues do things different and that is how you adapt to it.' Getting animated for the first and only time in his testimony, he leant forward and said, 'If Advocate King can just do me a favour this afternoon … if it is possible go to any police station. Do not say anything; just observe when a person take a statement. Any police station. It don't need to be Mfuleni.'

Icily, King recapped that Muthien had been taught to do it the right way at basic training, but then copied his colleagues in doing it incorrectly at the station.

'You adapt to what you see,' said Muthien.

'Mr Muthien, I am just trying to establish what type of detective you are and it appears that you are the type that adapts to wrong things. Is that a fair comment?'

While this level of incompetence might have played well for the state, throughout his testimony Muthien repeated that his 'wrong' way was, at least, consistent. He did not edit or restructure or summarise the stories that people told when he took a statement. He wrote their statements down 'word for word', and there was 'nothing that I add or take away'. The statements contained only 'your exact words and I just put in. Then afterwards when I have done it, I give that statement to the person and then I ask the person to read through the statement and if the person is happy, then the person sign.'

'Your exact words' was not good news for Palesa. King ran through all the things the witnesses had denied they said or blamed on Muthien and he refused their versions. By the end of it, Palesa seemed saddled with a fairly large problem: either the investigating officer had altered the statements or the witnesses had lied in court. In his brief cross-examination of Muthien this would be the only issue he'd raise. And Muthien would not budge. He had taken them down verbatim. So, too, Muthien couldn't explain why the times were 'misrecorded' on their statements, or how it was decided to issue an arrest warrant for Angy Peter and Isaac Mbadu, without having been briefed fully by his superiors, taken the accuseds' statements, or read Barnardo's statement. Even Henney was perplexed at how Muthien, after having been assigned Rowan's case that morning, could so blithely have left his superiors without having been given any real information about the attack. How do you investigate a crime without any leads or suspects? he asked Muthien.

Apart from the issues with the eyewitness statements, there were a raft of other irregularities the court had wanted Muthien to explain. For example, that the director of public prosecutions had ordered Muthien to impound the taxi so as not to contaminate any DNA traces Rowan might have left, had he been in the taxi, yet Muthien had not done so for an entire month.

Though Muthien didn't answer that question, when Henney asked about the taxi Muthien said, 'What I think what happened here is that I was, the taxi or the registration number of the taxi was not known at that time.'

King pointed out that two of the witnesses said they had the number. 'You see, the argument will be, Mr Muthien, that you purposefully did not do it because that would have probably proved that Rowan was never in that taxi and you knew it.'

Muthien also could not explain why he had taken a witness (John Ndevu) to point out the suspects, especially as Nedvu told him he had not seen anything personally. Nor did he resolve why the methodical Captain Speed took photographs of all the wrong places, given that he and key witnesses, Desiree and John Ndevu, accompanied Speed on that exercise. Again and again, Muthien said, 'I just put stuff in the docket.' 'I had to submit, submit ... I didn't have time from A to Z to go through everything.' When asked why he hadn't held identity parades for the identification of Azola and Chris, Muthien told the court, 'I cannot act on myself with regards to certain instructions.' Muthien had expressed this already: he never took the initiative in an investigation. He only followed orders from his superiors.

Why, King asked, did he file Redelinghuys's statement in the docket, the one about his investigation into Tshicila? What was it meant to prove? Henney put pressure on Muthien and in response the investigating officer cycled absurdly through 'I cannot recall', 'I don't know', 'What is the question?' and 'I don't understand the question'.

'Had you followed up you would have discovered that Lieutenant-Colonel Redelinghuys had contemporaneous notes proving that Angy and Isaac weren't after Rowan at all,' said King, working up to greater speed and more hostility. 'They were after the policeman. And you never bothered to find out, and Lieutenant-Colonel Redelinghuys never bothered to give you that information.'

'What is the question?'

'Can you dispute that?'

'I don't know what to say.'

'What do you think the motive was for the murder as the investigating officer as you stand there?'

'Which murder?'

'This one!' yelled King.

'Of this accused in this matter,' droned Henney.

'What is it?' King asked, fast and impatient. 'What is the motive?'
Muthien threw dull, defiant silence back.

'Do you know why the accused,' Henney added, 'would have gone to the extent to place a tyre around the body of this person and set it alight?'

'No, I don't know,' said Muthien.

'If they didn't have a motive then they probably didn't do it,' said King. 'Can you dispute that?'

His refusal to acknowledge or hazard a reason why Redeling-huys's statement was in his docket, led King to a cutting summary of his work as a detective.

'Mr Muthien, I am going to argue in this matter that you never investigated this matter at all. You merely acted as a clerk.'

'I did investigate the matter. And in addition I cannot recall. I mean, this is way back.'

'Did you get the point that Mr King is trying to make?' asked the judge.

Muthien was sulky. 'That I didn't investigate.'

Henney phrased it in several ways, acknowledging – as Muthien asked him to – that as an investigating officer he had a heavy caseload.

'Then you take a statement, then you file a statement, then you make a subsequent entry about that statement in the investigating diary: that is what you did, isn't that so?'

'That is right, ja.' Each time Muthien agreed with how Henney characterised the work he did on the case but still he resisted the conclusion.

Why? Was this a last remnant of pride? Muthien appeared to be a crushed man. If he was supposed to be the fall guy for the failings of this case perhaps he was at some level resisting his destiny. He refused to help the state. He refused to confirm the witness's accounts of when the statements were taken. Nor would he let the defence characterise him as a secretary, a stooge. Or was this also a way of protecting his superiors? He couldn't admit to total passivity, or what he had or hadn't done would rebound on them.

Henny again: 'You were more a compiler of a docket than an investigating officer. That is the point that Mr King was making. Do you agree?'

'No, I wouldn't.'

Early in his testimony, Muthien, like Redelinghuys, maintained he could not remember the provincial commissioner's interest in the case.

'To be honest with you, I don't just investigate this case,' he told King. 'I investigate a lot of cases, so if I do not recall then I don't recall.'

Henney had picked up King's theme: 'The point is given that the police investigates thousands of cases, but it is uncommon for the provincial commissioner...' He gave up in the face of Muthien's blank expression and started again. 'How many dockets do you carry?'

'Up to date I got about 141 serious cases.'

And how many of those did the provincial commissioner write you a letter about, Henney asked? 'That is uncommon, not so? It is something one would remember?'

'If I maybe can just...' Muthien began examining the page again.

'No, no,' said Henney, 'sir, that is the point: that is something one can remember.'

'I really can't.'

That, perhaps, was where Muthien's testimony might as well have stopped. So much, particularly how so many mistakes had been made under so much oversight, would be left unexplained. He played his role within established codes of obedience, submission and rank. He was the downtrodden front-line grunt. He was the subordinate who didn't possess the faculties to think for himself or the words to defend his own behaviour. His poor diction and refusal to take the initiative were symptoms of the tribulations with which committed, senior staff like Redelinghuys had to deal.

This, at least, seemed to be how Henney received it.

❖ ❖ ❖

The other witness that Henney called was Sergeant Lesley Freeman, the arresting officer. In 2012 he'd been in the service for 12 years, and had spent that time in the VisPol at Mfuleni Police Station. Freeman described how Azola and Chris had been pointed out, and then arrested. He said only Desiree had accompanied him, and he had made her wait in the van. She had indicated from there that he had the right man.

Palesa had no questions. King had a field day pointing out all the discrepancies between Freeman's testimony and those of the eye-witnesses.

Henney made a point of checking Freeman's testimony with him: 'Three witnesses disagree with you: Rara, Ndevu and Desiree all say all three of them were there, positioned out of sight, but nearby to point out.' He ran through their different accounts, which in Desiree's case including going into Chris's house with Freeman.[56] 'So, are they making a mistake or are you?'

'Your Honour, if Rara had done the pointing out of the suspects or their houses, then I would have recorded his name. Desiree was the person who came herself to point out the residences. Her father was present at the beginning when I first met her, and he wanted to come with. Then I said no, he couldn't come with, because I wasn't told I would fetch her and her father. The order was only that I would fetch *a* witness who would point out the suspects.'

'And you are absolutely sure of that? You can remember?'

'I can remember.'

King, who must have been feeling confident, chirped from his seat, 'I can see why the state never called this witness.'

❖ ❖ ❖

On Monday 25 August, at the Khayelitsha Commission, journalists, observers, policemen and activists gathered at Lookout Hill in Khayelitsha, shuffling and chatting excitedly, with children casting occasional wistful looks at the snack tables.

O'Regan and Pikoli presented their executive summary together, taking turns to deliver their findings. 'It is clear to the commission that policing in Khayelitsha is profoundly challenging. Deep levels of poverty, poor levels of infrastructure and very high crime rates make Khayelitsha a particularly difficult place for SAPS to operate…[But] [t]he commission has concluded that there are inefficiencies at the three Khayelitsha police stations and at the Khayelitsha FCS Unit.'

In the final weeks of the commission, after it became clear that the proceedings hadn't been a witch hunt, more and more of the Khayelitsha rank and file had dropped in to listen to the proceedings. Some of them were present for its finale too. Western Cape Premier Hellen Zille also sat in the hall, listening as they read off the many serious failings of the three police stations. If she was trying not to look smug, she didn't manage.

'…The commission has also concluded that there is a breakdown in relations between the Khayelitsha community and the SAPS members stationed in Khayelitsha. In reaching this conclusion, it should be noted that the commission does not find that there is an *irretrievable* or *irreparable* breakdown, but a breakdown that is characterised by a significant level of distrust…'

Printed and bound, the commission's final report contained almost 600 A4 pages. Using diplomatic language, it pulled its punches but its 19 recommendations covered everything from building a new station in Khayelitsha to fundamentally shifting how the quality of policing was evaluated. Most of these recommendations had provincial or national implications for the police force. One township's commission had the power to change the face of policing in towns and cities across the country – assuming that the police leadership took the recommendations to heart. This was far from certain.

In the next few weeks the same researchers who'd initially written off the commission as a talk shop, started to use the commission's report to prop up their laptops for better desktop ergonomics. Quietly the commission and the report receded into the background. But I was left impressed by what the commission had already done. It had taken the script that Cape Town had for its townships and said this wasn't good enough. That script held that township poverty was so deep, the dysfunction manifested so enduring, that it wasn't really fair to hold the agents of the state to their mandates. Yet without shying away from complex social issues, the diffuse legacy of the past, or the complex interrelation between them, the commission had isolated problems and traced lines of responsibility, and maintained that even if the neighbourhoods' problems were far bigger than the police, the police could still be held to account. That was not something I, for one, had entirely believed at the start.

Chapter Seventeen

Prosecutor Palesa promised the court a short argument, one not 'entangled with theories we cannot back up', and I looked forward to it. Throughout the trial he had frequently said, 'Well, I'll save that for argument.' Rather than gathering the threads when dealing with a question or a contradiction the defence had thrown up, he would defer to later, to his argument. I was eager to hear how he'd finally address their challenges.

In the end I was disappointed. Palesa's argument that the conspiracy defence had been 'repelled' was no more sophisticated than that the police had denied it on the stand. He said the defence didn't have a smoking gun. He tap danced through his own case, relying on a witness's credibility even where their reliability had been shot to pieces. Then he would reverse the process for the next problem, all the while crudely winnowing out what was in his favour and scuttling, lightning quickly, over the problems. He would grab an unsullied but unimportant piece of evidence to counterbalance a tarnished and vital one. He would confidently claim an argument from statements that didn't quite cohere. Nothing made me more certain that the eyewitness evidence was compromised than the contortions Palesa went through to restore confidence in it.

His first move was to declare that he'd be relying on '*viva voce* evidence under oath *in facie curiae*'. In other words, dismissing the witness statements made before the trial and resting his argument solely on the testimony given in court – arguably, an admissible tactic for sidestepping the incongruence the statements raised, but not one which could resolve all the issues with which he had to deal.

Palesa made an example of Asavela, trying to leverage her fraught relationship with Angy as evidence of her reliability – she knew Angy well enough to identify her at night. He also argued that she should be seen as an independent witness. 'Counsel had argued along the line why other neighbours were not called, yet it takes away the fact that Asavela Zici herself is a neighbour of Accused 1 and 2.' Palesa didn't stop there. He said Desiree also counted as a neighbour, living just across the field. In a stunning tautology, he said, Asavela couldn't have been lying because that would've meant concealing the identity of the true perpetrators. In other words, it would've meant lying. 'The question is if in fact this commission of offences was committed by somebody else why then would she not point to these other people if in fact it was not these people?' Next, to neutralise Chris's accusations against Asavela, he conflated them with Azola's and then accused Chris of inconsistency.

Henney, getting mildly annoyed at Palesa, and putting him through his paces for the first time in the trial, told him to address the more serious threat, rather than the accusations of the suspects. This concerned the contradictions between Asavela's testimony and that of the other state witnesses. Palesa tried to turn this to his advantage: didn't it show how honest her testimony was, he argued, that she admitted when she bent the truth? Didn't it show how she didn't bear Angy and Isaac a grudge, that she didn't maintain she had seen them put Rowan in a taxi when she could've? He would often lead with a fair point (for example, that even if she lied about one thing it didn't mean she was dishonest on the whole) but clinch with something baffling, such as, 'Especially in view of the fact that she observed everything at a very close distance.' This introduced the incongruous idea that physical proximity to potentially imaginary events made them more likely to have happened.

Palesa conceded John Ndevu's evidence was unreliable. 'One has to admit the natural wear and tear that Mr Ndevu might have suffered due to his age and the time at which these offences occurred,' he admitted. Then he argued that this strengthened the credibility of other witnesses who had not claimed the Apollo light had been working that night. 'So it is a two way, it is a double-sided sword in that if you criticise Ndevu then you must accept the other witnesses on whose evidence then the pointing out comes from.'

Palesa's last ditch was to rely on 'probability' to bolster his witnesses' credibility. Because the state's version of events was more probable than that of the defence, their witnesses were less likely to be lying. The hearsay statement was crucial for this argument to work. Again Henney yanked him out of a shadowy corner. Probabilities don't matter unless you have credibility, he told him, because credibility was the basis of fact. 'That is how we deal with it in a criminal trial because you must prove beyond a reasonable doubt and not on a balance of probabilities. That is totally a wrong way to assess evidence in a criminal trial.' But Palesa continued, at heart, to rely on this argument.

When it came to the fact that the alibis of the accused had never been investigated, Palesa set up two circular chains of reasoning. The first was that Angy's alibi was rebutted by Rowan's hearsay statement and the evidence of Desiree Jack that she saw Angy in a taxi outside her home at around 1.30 am. Also, he argued that even if the alibis had been revealed at the bail hearing, the state had no obligation to investigate them because this would have been 'second guessing' the strong case they had put together since the arrest.

Finally, he was allowed to move on to the hearsay statement, where his argument gained confidence and smoothed out. Palesa traced the relationship between what the witnesses saw and Rowan's version of the murder. 'If one views them together in totality they fit and complete the state's case and the story then is completed in its entirety.' And as for motive: 'The accused are not as clean as they want the court to believe, we submit.' The other cases against Angy only proved she was suspected of committing similar crimes. 'We warned counsel not to present it!' Palesa did not talk about honour or pride, neither did he suggest any motive linked to the betrayal Angy might have felt towards Rowan. 'It all starts obviously with the theft. There was never peace regarding the television set.'

In his defence, Palesa did have two good points. The first – and the only place where he directly addressed one of the defence's arguments – was that if the police had extracted Angy's and Rowan's details from their paperwork in order to fabricate the hearsay statements, they could also have fabricated Isaac's name, because it was on the theft charge and the 101 complaint. Secondly, he argued – quite fairly – that the conspiracy argument was confusing. Who had actually done what? Their theory of conspiracy 'shifts around', he said, without identifying a 'static line of defence'. 'So there is no point on which they in fact rely, no single-static-constant-uniform point on which they can rely on to prove that the police would have concocted the evidence against them.'

Otherwise he made dubious leaps of logic. 'She [Angy] testified about meetings that she had at Khayelitsha with the hierarchy of SAPS.' After implying she hadn't proved she was known to senior policemen, he said, she was 'thereby also confirming in fact she never had direct dealings with these three police officers that came to testify in court'. And he concluded with his favourite card: no proof. 'She could nowhere establish a fact as to how the hierarchy of the province could have influenced these three witnesses.'

Minutes later he argued that those very 'contradictions', which Angy's defence had offered as proof of a conspiracy, in fact proved the opposite. They proved that nothing had been fabricated, because if evidence had been fabricated it would have been fabricated perfectly. 'This is not a perfect case where everything is A, B, C, D, E, F in sequence. We argue that the existence of certain contradictions, however minor they are, point out to the fact that this is not a concocted story. How can it be rehearsed when we have in fact the relatives of the deceased coming to complain about the conduct of the police themselves?'

❖ ❖ ❖

When it came to the defence, the highlight would be how King explained the police conspiracy.

While his attacks on individual pieces of evidence had always been clear, a larger, more coherent theory of conspiracy had only emerged in flashes, briefly gaining an outline and shape, before receding into the background again. Henney had clearly shown he would not accept idle accusations. It was unusual and, by custom more than by rule, improper for a judge to accept allegations against the criminal justice system he was a part of.

'I have been trying to understand what is not a concoction and what is. Where do you start? Where do you stop?'

Perhaps offering Henney a way to sidestep the difficulties of ruling against the state (and, implicitly, the police), King offered him an explanation that kept the cast of culpable characters small, and avoided implicating police in provincial and national management positions.

'M'Lord, this is not a case where the police abducted Rowan, beat him up, took him away and burnt him and then turned around and said, you will say that and you will say that and let us write this statement out.' Instead, he argued, the stitch-up originated in bias and motive, suggestion and revenge (when it reached the Ndevus). Bias was not pure concoction, it was 'a state of mind, a way of acting', that had infected the whole investigation.

Their motive, he argued, was political mileage. 'There was a commission. She [Angy] was collecting evidence [for the commission]. She was appearing on the TV and in the media. She was pursuing instances of corruption against the police.'

Bias. It was far too an innocuous word for what King was alleging had been done, and Henney regarded him sceptically as he played with it.

'But how did that [bias] pan out in this case?'

'Muthien,' said King. 'If you ask the question: why did Muthien not go and investigate the alibi? And you answer it by saying bias. It explains everything.'

'But is that not bias, but incompetence?'

'M'Lord, no. Bias.' Incompetence wouldn't wash when the case was being overseen by the experienced Captain Jonkers and Lieutenant-Colonel Redelinghuys, both of them aware that Lieutenant-General Lamoer was interested in the outcome.

'But this is exactly the contrary to your point,' said Henney. 'We have very good policemen in the Western Cape. Why would they make use of somebody like Muthien with all due respect to him?'

'Deliberately. They did not want the truth to come out.'

Henney shook his head. Convince me, he told King. 'I have yet to come across a policeman, an investigating officer that was so incompetent in almost thirty years that I have been doing this job.'

'I know – but do not let it rebound to the credit of the state, then.' It was not necessary for the police to do a good job at framing them, King argued. 'They had more than sufficient evidence. They had eyewitnesses.' The hearsay evidence was corroborated by three policemen. 'I am not trying to boast, but without a senior counsel defending them, their evidence would never have seen the light of day. The case, if you examine the state case before we started, it was a slam dunk. They were on their way to prison.'

King backed away from laying the conspiracy at the feet of the higher-ups of the police hierarchy. 'I'm not accusing Lieutenant-General Lamoer of concocting!' The police knew what was wanted without being asked, he argued. 'The police on the ground wanted to assist the police's general need and the police's general need at that stage was to discredit the SJC.

'It suited the police to have these two accused. These people in particular. It was manna from heaven.' Muthien had undertaken a filing service, not an investigation. 'How many cases have we come across – as prosecutors, as officers of the court – where that someone is out of their depth, and they are taken out and someone else is put in their place?'

King's argument against the eyewitnesses centred on John Ndevu, who he argued, had not been confused or mistaken, 'he was lying'.

'Well.'

'What other deduction can you draw when a witness comes to court and says: you see this large Apollo light at 30 or 40 metres away, that was shining so brightly I could identify them perfectly. This person did that, that one did that, that one did that – at the wrong place?'

'So are you saying he was lying because he was put up to it by the police?'

'M'Lord, you have to find out why he was lying and it has to be because of revenge. He believed they did it. That is the only and obvious deduction from that scenario. Why did John Ndevu implicate the accused when he had not done so in his two previous statements, he had not done so when he had spoken to the prosecutor at length and then had a sworn affidavit taken from him? It is not *maybe* or *mistaken* or *he got it wrong*. He was trying to mislead the court and if the court has another explanation, well, I am afraid I cannot find it. If you catch a person out on a lie of that magnitude then there is only one deduction: he wants the people found guilty and he will stoop to lying to do it.' And Ndevu, King argued, was the patriarch: he had influence over the whole family.

Eventually Henney made some concessions, while still resisting the broader implications, either for the rest of Ndevu's testimony or how it reflected on the other eyewitnesses.

'I agree with you, his evidence in that regard [the Apollo light] cannot be believed, it cannot be relied upon. There the state has grave difficulties.'

Even if the rest of John Ndevu's testimony was accepted, King argued, then the state was still in trouble because the eyewitnesses all contradicted each other and even themselves. 'Four different stories coming to the fore, four different stories that conflict with their previous statements, that conflict with each other, that conflict with their evidence-in-chief, with that of cross-examination and that conflict, especially, with what they told Muthien.'

As far as motive was concerned, there was hard evidence that Rowan was not Angy's target in her demand for police action. 'They accepted he was a black sheep of the community. They [are] trying to correct his ways, and then they find out that he was being used by a policeman to steal.' She hadn't wanted to open a case against him and neither had Isaac – even John Ndevu agreed about that. Angy was going after Ta Ager, and that was corroborated by the petition she'd launched, by the backlash she'd run from, taking her kids out of school and moving to a safe house.

In fact, the case against Ta Ager was a boon for the SJC's ambitions at the Khayelitsha Commission. 'They were looking for evidence that the police were not doing their job properly and here was a golden opportunity to prove that. In fact, they needed Rowan alive to complete the evidence for the commission.'

And not only was the state's theory of motive poor, but they had never excluded other suspects, Rowan's friends, Simphiwe 'Caras' Mdedi and Abongile 'Cheese' Khabiqueya, who he'd turned state witness on, or the unidentified man who'd driven to his grandfather's house to beat him up.

Or Tshicila himself. 'Remember, Mr Tshicila had a far better motive than a stolen TV. He was facing long-term imprisonment. He was facing being thrown out of the police because that loose cannon Rowan was running around with information ... that could sink Ta Ager.'

King rebutted Palesa's claim that you didn't need to follow up on other suspects if you already had one you were sure about. 'You don't have to find evidence that implicates them. You just have to exclude them.'

❖ ❖ ❖

During that morning's tea recess I overheard King telling Ndlovu how to defend his clients, which didn't bode well, as he would have to deliver his final argument once King stepped down. 'You argue they didn't know what their rights were. Their rights were never explained to them. They were undefended right up until you got involved.'

But when Ndlovu was called, he stood up, rearranged his robe and said, 'M'Lord, all the points have been covered as regards Accused 3 and 4.'

From his posture it was clear he was expecting to sit again. It was hard to describe how gobsmacking this moment was. It was perhaps the only point in my life when my mouth literally fell open. Ndlovu had basically gone with: Yeah, what the other guy said.

I swung my gaze to Chris and Azola, but they seemed quite relaxed.

Henney opened his mouth, closed it, and then said, in an obviously measured tone, 'The problem is Accused 3's alibis.' Ndlovu continued to look at him. 'You aren't saying that there is a fabrication or a conspiracy. You are saying [Accused] 3 was at home with his sister, and [Accused] 4 was at the shebeen.'

'Yes, M'Lord.'

'So, are you associating your clients with this defence?'

'The evidence of accused 3 and 4 is that Asavela has planted the seed of this matter.'

Again, Ndlovu seemed about to sit down.

'What do you say about Muthien using Desiree as an interpreter?' prompted Henney.

'That is unacceptable.'

'No. Explain how.' In this manner, Henney tried to walk him through the various ways in which the case against his clients differed from that against Angy and Isaac.

Ndlovu gave brief, unpersuasive responses. He hardly dealt with what would appear to be the greatest asset of his client's case, that there was not a shred of forensic evidence linking them to the murder, there was no direct motive, and the hearsay evidence did not implicate them.

❖ ❖ ❖

Palesa sniped at King's argument with more precision in his rebuttal. In a plaintive voice he cried out, 'Counsel submits a defence which is not based on fact! If she [Angy] was willing to have him back in society then why did she call Redelinghuys to say she was unhappy to have him out of jail?'

Overall, Muthien was his ultimate scapegoat. 'The fact that we have this type of investigating officer, it takes away all this suspicion! It takes away counsel's argument.'

'But,' Henney said, 'do you concede that this was not a proper investigation of this case?'

'Yes,' said Palesa, dwelling a few moments on the gravity of that. 'And it explains why I have a legitimate reason for not calling him. It explains why Desiree's statement does not make sense. It explains why the defence is licking his lips when he thinks about Muthien.'

'And it explains,' said Henney, 'why the SJC is up in arms about the police in this province!'

Closing his case, Palesa shook his head. 'I've always said that having to put forward Muthien was like having one hand tied behind your back in a boxing match.' He followed it with a chuckle, as if to say, Can you believe how unlucky we were?

❖ ❖ ❖

King's final argument was a convincing account of the holes in the state's arguments. But I worried about the gamble he had taken with 'bias'. Prejudice can ruin lives and even whole countries, but when policemen swear oaths on imaginary death-bed accusations then bias does not seem adequate. And bias cannot be manipulated and supervised as can intimidation or harassment, it can't be conducted so that an orchestra of policemen and witnesses sing the same tune.

King himself seemed to give this away, when he read a line from a profile of Thuli Madonsela, then the country's beleaguered public protector. 'To speak about corruption in high places is often subversive and always embarrassing,' King read. '"The machinery of state can be called upon to intimidate or even destroy and eliminate whistle-blowers." Angy Peter's case ticks all those boxes.'

Bias might have caused Lamoer not to probe too deeply into the case, or Redelinghuys to turn a blind eye to the problems in the investigation, but bias could not have fabricated Barnardo's pocket book. Bias couldn't get around the fact that the defence's case needed someone – or somebodies – who tied all the lies together, someone with access to the witnesses, control over Muthien, control over station resources, knowledge of the events that preceded Rowan's murder, knowledge of Angy's position in the community and the value of discrediting her, and enough influence over the whole Kuilsriver cluster to bring Kleinvlei station into line.

By giving Henney an out – a way to blame bias and incompetence and incomplete investigation instead – King might have dulled his argument.

And even though King countered Henney's objections, the pair didn't seem to ever overcome their greatest disagreement: about when a leap from a fact became conjecture, rather than a deduction. Because of this, King's theory of motive was weak, according to Henney. There was no proof that the police had it in for Angy Peter. There were only circumstances. For the judge nothing linked those circumstances to motive, though Angy, in her arrogance, might imagine it otherwise.

'It's at most theory that she was known to all and sundry in the police.'

'M'Lord,' said King in reply, 'then we need to ask, "It is reasonably possible?"'

'No. We need to ask, "Is it based on fact?"'

What was King to do with a conspiracy with no smoking gun? To have inferences, he pleaded, you needed all the facts. Out of this patchwork of what he knew and what he could observe of the state's actions and errors, he had to make do with deductions.

Where else can a theory of motive come from, I wondered, in a case with any mystery? I doubted, if this were a gang murder or a spousal one, if Henney would hold motive to such high standards. But then did courts ever admit that the state itself had motive to break the law?

While Palesa had delivered his argument King had scribbled on a piece of foolscap: 'I followed his argument with the blank uneasiness which one might feel in the presence of a logical lunatic.'

The quote came from Victor Serge, a leftist opponent to the Leninist regime writing in the American journal *Politics* in 1944, describing his encounter with a man called Konstantinov.

It was odd that King chose those words. Konstantinov was a

conspiracy theorist, and what Serge lamented was that his rambling contained truthful intimations of the fear and paranoia that would later take hold across the USSR: a mad, artless premonition of a nascent reality.

But in Court 17, I thought, it had always been King who was paranoid, twitchy, and delusional in Henney's eyes, even if the greater problems he gestured towards – police corruption and police harassment – were dimly perceived and tacitly acknowledged.

Chapter Eighteen

On the day of judgment we found the trial had been moved to Court 3, one of the colonial-era rooms near the foyer. These were rooms with high ceilings, with galleries for onlookers at a mezzanine level, cloaked in old, dark-stained oak against which everyone's shoes and briefcases, laptops and robes, files and phones clattered and shuffled.

The change of venue might have been because the National Prosecuting Authority was expecting media attention for the verdict, but there was only a quiet contingent from the city papers, just a few more bodies than the regulars. Rowan's family had been driven to court by the police and installed in the gallery. Palesa took a big sniff of the court room as he arranged his papers on the front bench. 'I love the smell of these old rooms!' he said. His manner was jaunty and confident. Ndlovu, on the other hand, said he was nervous and looked it.

The numbers one to four were stuck on the front panel of 'the Dungeon', the custom-built pen for the accused. From this stairs led straight down into the cells. Angy was dressed in a smart beige jacket over a teal blouse, her hair braided up into a high French-knot style. Isaac wore a pink shirt with no jacket, and greeted people – their lawyers, the Amnesty staff, friends – quietly.

'He can't,' I overheard King say to a man I didn't recognise. 'It's an impossibility for him not to acquit.' The man appeared to be the father of a young man in a suit who was work-shadowing Greeff.

'This case has consumed my life,' King continued. 'I've argued that this is a set-up. You can prove it beyond doubt.' He seemed to be urgently trying to convince the man, whose face yielded no sympathy.

The mood as we waited for Henney was edged with anxiety. People fidgeted and rearranged their buttocks, texted and bit their nails. When the usher finally flung open the door at the back of the judge's stage and called to us to rise, Henney came in, limping from a recent injury, his eyes darkly ringed, looking for the first time, frail, tired and nervous.

'I will proceed with reading out this judgment. This will take most of the day,' he stammered. And so he continued, faltering to correct grammatical errors. 'On the morning of 14 October police found the deceased in an open piece of field. He was still alive at that stage and it is common cause that he had burns all over his body…'

Laboriously, Henney recounted the murder, the arrest of the suspects, their alibis, and the details of Rowan's injuries and any facts which were not disputed, of which there were few. Then, he droned on through a summary of the state eyewitness testimony, which did, indeed, take the entire morning, and he read clear through the tea-break. Afterwards, without pause, he moved on to the testimony of Redelinghuys and Tshicila. By then it was 1 pm and Henney ordered lunch reduced to a 30-minute break. When the day had started there had been trepidation in the air, but as it progressed and as it became clear he would make no rulings on credibility until his conclusion, I felt a stultifying boredom set in.

When the proceedings began after lunch, King asked Henney to dismiss the translator so that the process might go faster. The faces of the family had remained blank throughout the judgment thus far, as had those of the accused, except for Azola and Chris who couldn't stay awake. But when Henney began explaining his ruling on the hearsay evidence the storm broke, backs straightened, and eyes cleared – this was the reasoning that the defence had been waiting for since the first weeks of the trial.

'The first witness who testified for the state regarding the statement the deceased made was Captain Kock. She came across as an honest witness.' 'Honest witness' and 'made a favourable impression on the court' would ring out like hammer blows as Henney dealt with each subsequent police officer.

Henney argued that as none of the police officers knew Angy and Isaac personally, or Rowan for that matter, they had no motive to falsify evidence. 'Accused 1 in her mind might have thought that she was so important that she would be known by all policemen at least in the Blue Downs area, but there was however no concrete evidence that Accused 1 was known to Kock, Barnardo or Wilhelm.' He would not mention the possibility of direction from a superior, or the fact that Kock and Wilhelm did not make their statements until weeks or months had passed. Nothing about their testimony drew his suspicion, or the fact that they had not kept their notes on the statement. The other station documentation that had gone missing was not mentioned.

Barnardo got the most impressive review. 'He was confident and very sure of himself. In my view, if one should take into account the way he testified, he was with respect a much better witness than his superior Kock. He was subjected just like Kock to tedious and drawn-out cross-examination by counsel in an attempt to discredit him as a witness.' King's attack on his pocket book – using the entry that was not chronologically placed – had been an utter failure. Henney used the argument that if Barnardo's pocket book was going to be fabricated, it would have been fabricated better, and it would not have contained the anomaly that King had pointed out. 'This allegation once again was without substance and nonsensical.'

Chandré Wilhelm was also absolved of any material contradiction or suspicion. The value of Wilhelm's tears became apparent as he continued. 'I also find the suggestion that this witness fabricated this evidence to falsely implicate the accused as far-fetched and without substance. She was deeply affected by this incident and had nightmares about it afterwards. She was clearly still distressed about it and broke down in court when she had to recall the events of that morning during cross-examination. It is therefore difficult to accept that she would unnecessarily adapt her evidence to what the deceased told her.'

Henney then swept away the last contradiction the defence had fought for: the wrong address, given on two separate occasions, which King had argued proved that the police had supplied it, rather than Rowan. 'This argument in my view is based on pure speculation and conjecture and lacks logic and rationality. Another simple explanation which might also be based on speculation is, that if the deceased's grandfather knew the address to be 24541 Minister Street, the deceased would in all probability also have known the house number in that sequence.' Yet King had argued that Rowan had given the right house number on previous occasions, all of them when dealing with the police, including bail hearings and arrest statements.

Henney still had all the medical evidence ahead of him before his final evaluation of the hearsay statement and the weight he would attach to it, as well as the eyewitnesses. But it was as good as irrelevant. He believed the police, without reservation. There was total silence in the court as he continued, a feeling that the onward march of his words was suffocating.

In his evaluation of the medical witnesses there was little discussion of the actual medical debates, and Henney made no distinction between physical ability to speak and mental lucidity. One by one he went through the witnesses whose testimony muddied the waters on Rowan's ability to speak and dismissed them for having no direct contact with the victim, or for being unclear.

Martha Pieterse, the only state witnesses who had denied that

Rowan was in a position to talk, was deemed inherently unreliable. 'Although this witness said he could not talk and he was not in a state to talk, she never said that she asked him questions and he could not answer. This aspect was not clarified.' Yet it was Henney who refused the defence the right to recall her later. 'This witness's evidence is therefore of little or no value either to ascertain the level of consciousness on the GCS of the deceased or his ability to talk. The court can therefore not safely rely on it. She was in any event a very poor and unimpressive witness.'

The paramedic Abdullah, who had nervously fought in the state's corner, made a favourable impression on the court. 'His evidence in my view was convincing and well-motivated. His evidence about the responsiveness as well as the level of consciousness, the court found convincing. It must be remembered that this witness actually dealt with the patient and had the opportunity to assess and evaluate him.'

Dr Bernon too got flying colours with little mention of her inexperience. As with Abdullah, 'She did not base her opinion about the condition of the deceased purely on her expertise but on her actual observation, interaction and treatment of the deceased.' Moller's findings were accepted without acknowledging that her findings on the tongue were ultimately inconclusive.

When it came to witnesses who had suggested that other witnesses might have drawn the wrong conclusions from their experiences, Henney dismissed them as not having had first-hand experience with Rowan. This idea was the dominant refrain of his analysis: that direct observation was somehow entirely distinct from, and entirely superior to, professional experience and one's skill at interpreting information. The opinions of Dr Meyer, the ENT specialist, who Moller herself had suggested should be called, was treated with circumspection as 'her evidence was not based on first-hand knowledge about the condition of the deceased, but on the various reports about the condition of the deceased. Her evidence just like that of the other experts was not about what she personally observed of the deceased.' This was the expert whose report was initially favourable to the state, but who said she would have reached very different conclusions if she'd known the basis for Abdullah's GCS score of Rowan.

Klatzow's whole attendance seemed the most irrelevant. His criticism of Moller and his alcohol calculation were entirely dismissed, and Henney mischaracterised his testimony on shock. Klatzow was dismissed in lengthier terms than any other witness, the most detailed being Henney's rejection of his method of back-calculation for alcohol.

This was the most specific of Henney's dismissals of a medical expert. Almost every other debate in the trial-within-the-trial was reduced to whether someone had 'first-hand dealings' with Rowan or not. In his judgment, Henney did not mention lucidity, he did not discuss the difference between being physically able to talk and being able to communicate a lucid series of statements. He did not examine what it meant to say a few words rather than tell a story, or the level of cognition needed to swear in pain, versus that needed to make sense. Neither did he mention the testimony on the effect of pain, let alone of shock, on cognition, or the difference in when Bernon saw Rowan – post fluid, post painkillers – and when the policemen would have found him. He did not acknowledge the errors in assessing consciousness made by Abdullah, which had affected so much of the other evidence, including Moller's report. In the end it sounded as if there had been no point in calling expert witnesses, at all.

Even Dr Steyn, who had quite literally written the text book Bernon studied, couldn't be relied on to look at the same markers as the ambulance and emergency staff and draw different conclusions.

The direct and circumstantial medical evidence 'fit logically in with the evidence of Kock, Barnardo and Wilhelm, who testified that the deceased said to them that "*Angie en haar man het dit gedoen*"'.

Lastly, Henney dealt with the safeguards imposed by the law of evidence on the admission of hearsay evidence.

One by one he gave the statements a flying pass, quoting law which essentially underscored that the statements should be admitted because they were so damning, because they could lead to the conviction of the accused. He further argued that the statements were reliable because they were put forward by credible witnesses. Their reliability was further strengthened because they supported the eyewitness evidence that Rowan had been abducted and put in a taxi. Again, he argued that their 'probative value' was greater precisely because there wasn't better evidence. Hearsay, because it might not be admitted by a court, was a poor choice to frame someone, therefore it was unlikely to be fabricated.

Lastly their good legal defence had counted against them. While hearsay was inherently prejudicial to the accused, Henney postulated, these accused had the benefit of a trial within a trial, had lawyers who attacked the credibility and reliability of the state witnesses, and had called expert witnesses themselves. 'Given these safeguards, in my view, the interest of justice justifies the admission of this evidence.'

This was all for the day, and his verdict would be delivered the following day. There was grave silence in the court. This was not what had been expected. King's face was dark with fury. Angy wrinkled her forehead, but looked sad rather than angry. Isaac's face was a mask. Chris's features had set in a murderous expression.

I left the courthouse to find the Ndevu family huddled together on the court steps with Palesa, waiting for their transport. Standing nearby was Isaac and I said goodbye to him and asked how he was feeling.

'Alright.' He paused. 'Although, things are not going so perfectly in court.'

'No,' I said, 'it doesn't seem like it.'

'But Henney still has to deal with our evidence.' Somehow Isaac remained optimistic. 'And with the evidence of the others.'

I greeted Angy as she joined us.

'So, you are back in town?' she said.

'Just for a few days.'

'Then you will be around to see us go to jail.'

I felt embarrassed as I made a non-committal response. She shrugged and continued down the steps. 'You heard what that judge said.'

Next, it was Joel Bregman from the JSC. 'Long day,' I said, hoping he'd linger.

'No,' he replied, walking on, 'a terrible day.'

When I got home I went straight to sleep even though it was late afternoon. It was the only way not to think about what was going to happen the next day. I was consumed with dread. When I woke up it was dark. I sat outside in the cold and phoned a friend who was a journalist in the 1980s. Through the states of emergency, she had worked on many difficult stories. 'I'm overwhelmed,' I told her. I explained that the story had grown larger than I expected, I could no longer find its the edges, and now I had nothing to grip onto.

Late in the morning of the second day, Henney approached his conclusion, and his assessment of the family's testimony. 'Mr John Ndevu, the grandfather of the deceased, came across as a very upstanding, humble and dignified person.' He accepted all his evidence. Elsewhere in his judgment Henney described Ndevu as 'half-blind' yet regarded his statement about the defunct Apollo light as 'mistaken', not a lie.

One of the points he held up as evidence of Ndevu's honesty[57] was that he had limited himself to what he had seen in Sipho Street. He did not 'try to mislead the court by trying to create the impression that he was a witness to everything that happened to the deceased'. This idea of a witness's credibility would recur in the judgment. Henny was of the opinion that even the Bardale witnesses could have fabricated a better story but hadn't which indicated they were not lying.

In Henny's eyes, Asavela and Desiree were cruelly maligned by the defence. Yet Asavela 'answered questions in meticulous detail when she was subjected to exhaustive and robust cross-examination'. Desiree also gave a detailed and convincing account of what she observed. Desiree was 'clear, concise and logical. [...] She was mocked – and in my view unjustifiably so – that she a 40-year-old woman who ran almost at the pace of a super-fit athlete. She had been running for her nephew's life.'

Henney repeatedly made the argument that the witnesses couldn't have influenced each other – even when Desiree translated for Asavela's statement. He based this on their slightly different accounts, and that they accused different people.[58]

In assessing Rara's evidence – again, 'clear', 'concise' and 'convincing' – he used the bizarre argument that Rara appeared honest because he could have lied more, and could have lied better.[59]

Freeman, who Henney himself called, turned out to be a pointless witness because 'too much was made about who pointed out Accused 3 and 4'. The issue of the pointing out was deemed 'irrelevant'. Of the contradiction between Freeman and Desiree, he said, 'I am inclined to believe the evidence of Desiree about this, rather than the version of Mr Freeman who it seems would not have a better memory of this event than Desiree.

'This is clearly a case where the individual witnesses observed an ongoing and continuous incident from different vantage points and at different times. This aspect will undoubtedly influence their evidence and their versions as to the exact nature as to what they observed and will logically be different.' Tshicila's evidence was largely dismissed as being irrelevant to the murder and assault case.

Muthien was ultimately the scapegoat who made this all possible. 'Muthien in my view was a very poor witness. He clearly was not a very conscientious police officer and should, with the greatest of respect, not be a detective. This he clearly illustrated when it emerged that he did not do much investigation work on his own initiative.' Henney continued to enumerate his many failings.

'Having said this, I did not get the impression that Mr Muthien was a dishonest witness who wilfully and deliberately failed to execute his duties.' Muthien's failure to investigate anything relevant to the case was the result of 'lack of experience' and 'inability to do his work'.

'Clearly, even if Muthien wanted to be part of a conspiracy, he would not have had the ability and knowledge to fabricate or concoct evidence against the accused.'

When he came to Isaac's and Angy's testimony, Henney made it clear what he thought of their entire defence. 'The defence of Accused 1 and Accused 2 tried to create an air of suspicion around everything in this case.' He felt 'a lot of unnecessary time and energy was wasted during this trial on nonsensical, baseless assertions. This was but a tactic used by Accused 1 and Accused 2 to divert the attention away from them.'

He returned to his favourite argument. 'I also find it very peculiar that the police management would not have concocted or fabricated evidence that could be proven much more easier in a court of law.' Why would they use, Henney argued, 'a partly blind old man', 'a rebellious, drunken teenager of bad character' and 'someone who was out to get them' out of revenge? (The reference here might have been to Desiree.) Why use hearsay evidence which was hard to admit as evidence?

'One would have expected that the police with all their resources and abilities to have concocted more solid evidence like fingerprints and forensic evidence which would be difficult to disprove.

'And secondly, the police in the Western Cape have access to the best detectives, not only in this province, but also in this country. Why would they make use, with the greatest of respect, of someone like Muthien, who is barely qualified and cannot even investigate a case properly or take proper statements from witnesses?'

Angy was characterised as 'an argumentative and evasive witness', as well as, he mentioned several times, 'arrogant'. 'When she was cross-examined by the prosecution [it] became apparent that she is filled with self-importance.' While the state's witnesses were excused their lies and distortions, anything confusing about Angy's story was taken as an example of dishonesty. Several of her responses were obviously mischaracterised.[60] 'Her version is rejected.'

Isaac too had been 'confusing', and had contradicted Angy about the events of 11 August. The only 'contradiction' Henney pointed out was a misunderstood instruction relayed through King about who knocked on Rowan's door at 2 am. Isaac's explanation for why he was caught up in the case – to strengthen the case against his pregnant wife, who could not have acted alone – was dismissed as 'strange' and 'not consistent' with the rest of his defence. The links in their defence to the aftermath of the TV theft were not addressed. Consequently, Henney argued, their defence made no sense.

The total effect of Chris's and Azola's weak defence – the questions not put to witnesses, the links not drawn between the circumstances of their arrests and the weaknesses in the investigation, the failure to put forward any argument to circumscribe their involvement in the assault – came together when Henney invoked common purpose, and rolled the assault charge into the murder count.

Ultimately, the state had not lost on a single point. It was as though King had not conducted a defence at all.

Henney arrived at his conclusion. 'After having critically appraised the totality of the evidence as presented by the state, I am convinced beyond reasonable doubt...'

By now he was no longer stumbling, he was on a roll, fast and fluent, and the rhythm of his words was more insistent than their meaning. In that harmony, I thought I saw the logic behind his logic, the world as Henney saw it: the four accused had insulted the criminal justice system.

'… [This] neatly ties in with the strong circumstantial evidence and the voice of the deceased fills in the gap between what the witnesses saw and what ultimately happened to him.'

They had thought they would show the system how it should really function.

'The accused, especially Accused 1 and Accused 2, clearly wanted to make a point.'

They had been arrogant, and their arrogance was their downfall.

'They wanted to voice their dissatisfaction with the police and the criminal justice system. They were not satisfied with the fact that the deceased – who had stolen their television and who was a known criminal – was released on bail.'

For while the police may have had failings, the courts had rescued the situation. They had provided justice, and in so doing had proved their value.

'In the result, therefore, this court finds all four accused guilty on count two of kidnapping and guilty on count three on a charge of premeditated murder. In my view, it can also be safely inferred from the facts that they acted with a common purpose to murder the deceased.'

The moral universe had been knocked off balance, but Henney himself had set it to rights.

The moment Henney finished King and Palesa leapt up to deal with the closing business. King talked about his clients' five children, who would lose not only both breadwinners but both parents too. He asked the state to extend bail until sentencing so that they could make arrangements for their children's care.

'Does the state object?' Henney asked.

'The state has no objection to bail being extended until sentencing,' said Palesa.

Henney stared at him with his jaw set. He had come to a crescendo of anger and righteousness at the end of the judgment and had not yet come down from it.

'Have you considered the legality of that, Mr Prosecutor?' Henney asked.

Palesa, who appeared taken aback by the judge's attitude, stammered. 'They were here every day. I can't ignore that. I can't ignore the fact that Accused 1 was angry with the other co-accused when they were late.' They had never broken their bail conditions, they were not considered a flight risk.

Henney was fuming, an anger radiating off him in waves, his tone nasal and sour. 'I'm going to reluctantly accede to your request, Mr Prosecutor, because no facts were put before this court that oppose it.' But Henney could not let it rest so easily. 'This case and this whole murder was based on disregard for the criminal justice system, where the deceased was a criminal who committed an offence against them and they took the law into their own hands. Those are the facts. The attitude of the prosecutor amazes me.'

Palesa got the message. 'My Lord, I must follow the law. What the law wants and what law prescribes. It might be wise to place it on record that consistent with the application of case law' – his voice now in an entirely different register – 'that we, in fact, oppose bail.'

King implored Henney to consider Angy and Isaac's case leniently. 'They have five children, they have attended court for three years, they have a fixed abode. Other than this crime, I respectfully admit they are model citizens. The interests of justice would not be affected if bail were granted.'

Henney stared at him coldly and turned to Palesa. 'Mr Prosecutor, your final word?' Palesa again extracted an argument to oppose the extension of bail. Henney called a recess.

Towards the end of Henney's judgment Angy had cried, but in the break she talked animatedly with the co-accused and with her lawyer, and made jokes with her friends in the gallery. When I walked past, Isaac tried to comfort me. 'Don't worry,' he said. 'Honestly, I was expecting it.' Someone else near the defence bench was saying to one of them: 'He's a vicious man. I'm telling you he's going to come back and oppose bail.'

And, indeed he did. Policemen stepped forward immediately and cuffed Angy and Isaac. With their hands behind their backs, they were marched down the steps from the Dungeon into the bowels of the building. From there they waited in holding cells before being thrown into vans which would take them to Pollsmoor. On the bumpy ride to prison, Isaac found himself next to a blind beggar who had been arrested for murder. The man said, 'I don't know why I'm here.'

PART FIVE: SENTENCE

Chapter Nineteen

**Diary notes kept by Angy Peter in Pollsmoor Prison.
02/10/2014**

*I went to High Court in Cape town with my co-accused thinking that justice
will be served.*

*It was before midday when Judge Hannies withdraw my bail and found
me guilty of murder everybody was surprised beside me I knew that will
happen because of his attitude toward me.*

I was sent to poolsmor with my co-accused without my medication.

*Back home I left my four minor children without saying goodbye it was
painful to think about my kids three girls were at school little Alexander was
at daycare centre.*

I arrive in Poolsmor femal prison with other female accused

*my heart was broken I acted like I don't care ruthless but deep inside
I hated life I cared so much about my kids when ever I think about them I felt
like beating someone.*

From court, Angy was taken in a police van to 'the Hanger' at Pollsmoor Prison to be processed for entry into the awaiting-trial section
(otherwise known as Remand). It was Angy's third time in Pollsmoor,
so she knew what to expect, and more importantly, what to say and
do to establish respect from the guards and other inmates. Prison
wardens recognised her from previous incarcerations. Hi Angy, they

259

said to her, why do you keep coming back? And when she explained she'd been found guilty, they'd shrug, Hey, that's life.

Her van arrived late at the prison. Sleeping provisions had already been dished out, and there was no spare bedding. But a '26 girl' recognised Angy and on her command blankets and a bed were ripped from another newcomer and given to Angy. Angy made no complaint to the 26, but said to the girl who'd lost her bedding, 'You can come and sleep with me.' They shared the blanket.

The next morning the women were searched, taken to admin, tested for HIV, and from there went to D Section, where the big cells were, with 48 bunks per cell but up to 100 inmates.

The '26 girl' was, Angy claims, a member of South Africa's pre-eminent prison gang, the Number.[61]

In South African prisons the Number wield a phenomenal level of power. To be a member, an *ndota*, is to command fear and control resources. To be a *frans*, a non-member, is to be a peasant, a grunt, a nobody. The Number gangs are a highly masculinised culture. *Ndota* itself means 'man'. Many of the rituals are constructed around rescuing men from femininity.[62] It was strange to encounter this mention of a female Number prisoner in Angy's story.

According to Angy, most of the women she met in Pollsmoor were there for shoplifting or fraud, though there were some cases of women accused of murder. A warden from Pollsmoor put it to me, 'Most of the women in prison are there because of their boyfriends – because they held the drugs or held the gun, or they bought the gun, or delivered the drugs, or they were just in the car while he did the deed.'

But a feminisation of violence seemed to be occurring in the city. According to gang researcher Don Pinnock, the more passive role of women in street gangs was changing. Since 2010 women had been forming female gangs that acted as adjuncts to male gangs, for example the Bad Girls to the Bad Boys, or the Vatos Babes to the Vatos Locos in Khayelitsha.[63]

Angy was put in cell 096. A week later she wrote in her diary about a failed attempt to organise a cell protest. In her words, '96 ppl one disfunctioning toilet one disfunctioning sink 46 single beds'.

On her first day she was adopted by a small gang of woman led by Phumeza, a self-proclaimed 28. Phumeza was in jail for helping her boyfriend hijack and kidnap a man from Somerset West. Despite this, Angy described Phumeza as 'quite soft'. She was the cell's resident preacher, and would often pray for Angy, who told her in turn that 'it was crap' and that Phumeza 'loved God too much'. That first day it was Phumeza, Portia, and Ncumisa who listened to Angy tell the story that every inmate tells: the story of their crime and trial. About this scene she later commented to me: 'I assume that they think I am just bullshitting.' Her story was, at least, different to most.

As she sat there telling her tale, the 26s in the cell wanted to break up the party. They began repeatedly telling Angy and her audience to go wash. Phumeza tried to calm matters, but the 26s swore at her. Angy stood up and said, 'I'm not going to wash.'

'Don't talk to me like that,' one of the women responded, 'you know I'm a 26.'

'Look here,' Angy said, 'I'm not interested in joining your stupid 26.' This, she said, made the 26s 'go mad'.

Phumeza and Ncumisa rushed to say she wasn't being serious.

'I mean it!' Angy shouted. 'Who said I didn't mean it? I mean it.' As they argued a space was cleared in the cell between the beds for the fight that was pending. Phumeza tried to make peace. Angy refused to apologise. Ncumisa began a physical fight with one of the 26s, with the others joining in. In the midst of that first row, Angy shouted, 'Who's got a problem with me?' To which the other three responded, 'It's *we*!'

Who's got a problem with *we*? A happy memory.

This was one of Angy's favourite stories from prison. She

partially recorded in her brief, fragmented diary: 'they welcomed me with warm hands Ncumisa offered to sleep with me they made [me] forgot about outside the prison'.

News about the life outside came from Joel Bregman of the SJC, who visited at the first opportunity. 'I wanted to cry,' Angy wrote, 'but usually I hold back my tears acted like am OK I avoided to talk about my kids but Joel told me they are fine I just made confusation short'.

Other than that the only thing that broke the boredom of prison, and relieved the dangers of ruminating on the world outside, was a fight.

Angy said that the fights between female prisoners could draw blood, break bones, and knock out teeth. Like the men they made weapons, she said, by putting a bar of soap into a pillow case and using it as a bludgeon. The fights were a constant – there was nothing else to do.

Angy had not thought of joining a prison gang on her first stints in jail. But it was, paradoxically, in seeking a way out of the monotony of these constant conflicts that she began to feel the limits of being a *frans*. 'There was this tension between the 28s and the 26s, but I was not familiar with how people became these stupid things.' Though she was confused by the gangs, she began to understand, through her conversations with her cellmates, that they were all trapped in the conflict. 'I realised we needed to do something more useful than fighting all day.' Why not, she asked herself, run education programmes in the cells instead? But Phumeza told her she couldn't run education if she wasn't a gang member. Still, Angy maintained, 'I'll do my things by forcing, but without putting my ethos aside. I'll run education anyway.' During her first attempt she was put in her place – physically – by 28s. 'They told me like, Angy, you can't. It's against the law.'

Then the situation in their section took a turn for the worse. Samantha Bailey, 'a big coloured woman', arrived. She was awaiting trial on multiple charges, including murder. According to Angy, Bailey made it known that she was a major drug dealer, a 'controlling gangster' and 'a very powerful woman', who ran the tik market for the whole of Kuilsriver, including Mfuleni. And Bailey came with money and favours that she could use while on the inside. 'She will just make a phone call and everything will be done in that moment.'

At the time Angy told me this story I had never heard of Samantha Bailey. It was two years later, when one of Bailey's cases finally went to trial, that I first found a press reference: Bailey was accused of ordering the execution of a drug dealer called Hendrik Hugo in January 2014. In 2013 the National Department of Public Prosecution had tried, and failed, to seize her house on the grounds that it was, to use laymen's terms, a vicious little drug den and major distribution point. According to the tabloid *Die Son*, she was the niece of Rashied Staggie, a former leader of the Hard Livings gang. Rashied's brother, Rashaad, also a gangster, was stoned and burnt alive by a mob of PAGAD (People Against Gangs and Drugs) vigilantes in 1995.

Bailey's arrival in Pollsmoor seemed to have prompted a furious escalation in conflict. She bought control over inmates and wardens with cash and food and drugs. Women began to compete for her favour, even going so far as tattooing 'MANTHA' on their toes as a sign of fealty. Bailey commanded her own gang. It was a sort-of 26s, and it fought for control with the cell's original 26s. 'So now it's like the cell is totally out of control. People beat each other, people break each other's teeth and people hurt each other. And I have no say, because I am not in any gang,' Angy lamented. There were, she said, 'three to five girls' who lost teeth. 'So I told myself, okay, if you can't beat them, join them.

'It was a Friday, if I'm not mistaken, that I decided to join a gang. I couldn't choose the 26s, because they were, like, complicated' – too deeply divided in their battle with Bailey, she explained. Also 'they believe in money and they sell each other for money, so it was like, more or less, worse'. She joined the 28s.

They had already made several overtures – 'because what they want is strong people in their gang' – which Angy had refused. Now, Portia, herself a 28, had provided the final persuasion. 'She's like, "Angy, you can become 28 if you want peace in this cell. You join the 28s then you put in your own laws. We can't support you if you aren't." So I told them, okay, fine.'

❖   ❖   ❖

A man who worked as a warden on the men's medium-security section of Pollsmoor for a decade and a female warden agreed to speak to me on condition of anonymity. They both waved away Angy's stories about the gangs in the women's section. 'In the women's section there are no gangs,' said the male warden, 'just broekies and rokkies.' Figuratively, slacks and skirts. 'The broekies are butches, they only fight over their women, the rokkies.' He was adamant: 'No woman in this country has ever held the Number.' He said the women were playing at imitating the gangs that their boyfriends had joined, speaking a *sabela* (gang language) that was diluted and incomplete. The women's section was more 'chilled' than the men's, he said, and not really violent.

I did wonder what his version of 'not really violent' meant. Of his own experience he told me, 'You work in a constantly violent environment. You are attacked and you have to use violence to assert authority.' He described himself as 'traumatised' by his job, and said that at one point the constant stress of his job had made him homicidal.

Criminologist Luke Lee Skywalker disagreed. He had interviewed female soldiers and hammerwomen (assassins) in the Cape's coloured street gangs who, in their time in prison, had passed through the

Number culture too. There was no debate for him about whether the Number operated in the women's prison, only technical questions about how an explicitly masculine and sexualised mythology handled the inclusion of women. Their accounts and knowledge was, he conceded, not as pure or as potent as the indoctrination that men serving long sentences received. However, he said, the phenomenon was indisputable. Angy's story was consistent with the stories he had heard from other female *ndotas*. The Number was a soft pulse that lay underneath the ostensibly gentler routines of women's Remand, he said. But as soon as there was an inciting event – such as the arrival of a violent and powerful inmate – that pulse began to hammer. Then, the Number grew 'fangs' and inmates were forced to choose sides: the gangs claimed more recruits.

The 28s bought drugs and alcohol from the 26s for the ceremony, and Bailey herself provided some ganja and tablets called 'bati'. The 28s 'judges' convened to decide if Angy was fit to join, and presided over her initiation, which involved administering a tattoo.

Angy realised they were 'desperate' to have her on their team. 'So I use that to my advantage of I'm not going to follow all the rules.' Angy agreed to smoke 'ganja, but nothing else, that's it'. They agreed that her first fight with the 26s, when she kicked a woman in the neck and she'd bled, would count as an initial bloodletting. Angy agreed to do another in the future, without any intention of complying. 'And there's this language of them that you need to learn,' – the *sabela* – 'so I was like, I don't have time for this nonsense.' And lastly there was the matter of the tattoo. She liked the idea because it cut out the chit-chat, the bravado. People just had to look at it and understood who you were and what you were capable of. But even here she had her own ideas.

According to convention she should have acquired a typical 28 tattoo: 'perfect killer' or 'silent killer'.

'It has to have something that says you are a killer. Or maybe a monster. Anything that would say on your behalf, "What the fuck are you looking at? I will kill you." Stuff like that. So to me it was like: uh-uh! I can't write that.'

She gave them another suggestion: WRONGFULLY ACCUSED. 'Of which we had a huge debate around it,' she said, rolling her eyes. Eventually they gave in. She could have the tattoo, but 'we have to write it in the wrong spelling': WRONG FULLY ACUSED.

They used a needle, a lighter and a rubber bracelet called a zombi. The stick and poke process took half an hour. Angy wasn't allowed to cry. She bled a little. Previously Angy had stolen a box of gloves from the clinic on one of her trips to pick up her HIV medication. 'I didn't want to infect the lady who was making the tattoo,' she explained.

'So after I gained my Number, then I start running education. Controlling the cell. Having sessions every morning. Because we spend lots of time doing nothing and that's where these fights come from, because people have nothing to do.' She ran classes on TB, which was rife in Pollsmoor, and HIV, human papillomavirus and other sexually transmitted diseases.

❖ ❖ ❖

Isaac kept his head down in prison, avoiding the gangs as much as possible, making friends without much discrimination across his cell. Of his close crew there was a young kid who had stolen a pair of sneakers from Zevenwacht Mall; Gerald, charged with fraud and with a growing following as a prison preacher; Kuwela, who said he'd been set up on a rape charge by his former girlfriend's new boyfriend; and Bong, awaiting trial for murdering an acquaintance after a pub brawl who was enigmatic on the subject of his guilt. Like Isaac, most people said they were innocent, though sometimes he'd listen to the Brick Gang's tales of mugging people in the township,

Imizamo Yethu. They did this by throwing bricks at their victims. They weren't ashamed to admit they were guilty of a gang-rape charge too. In Isaac's eyes Pollsmoor was a giant classroom full of eager students, grouped together according to their crime of preference – armed robbery, fraud, petty theft. And there was only one other curriculum: bad legal advice.

The first time he'd been to Pollsmoor, after the arrest for Rowan's murder, he'd felt huge relief at the intake when a warden had stepped forward and shouted out to the newcomers to divide themselves into gangsters and non-gangsters. The gangsters had been shepherded into a different section of the prison. Isaac thought he would be in a purely *frans* environment; he was wrong. This time, his second in the prison, he knew what to expect, but also that he could more or less avoid the gangsters. He was broad-chested, people expected a fighter; but also amicable. He didn't feel he needed to join a gang to get by. When I asked how he felt about Angy's gang membership, he shrugged and said, 'Hey, you do what you gotta do. You do what you need to survive.'

There were other horrors: the medical wards he had to pass through on his cleaning duties were full of living skeletons, prisoners with multidrug-resistant TB. Or there was the case of the man who had smuggled in drugs for the gangs and then couldn't excrete them from his anus – at least not on his own. Isaac could hear the screams through the walls. But his worst memory was of seeing his children.

It was an unexpected visit, his sister's idea. And he resented it because there were nights in Pollsmoor, he said, where he'd go to bed after an evening of talking and laughing with his friends, and his spirits would be high, and he'd carry that feeling into the next day. But he could also wake up and not know where he was, and when he remembered the feeling would crush him. 'And you never know which kind of day it will be. And you don't want to walk out to see your children when you're in that kind of mood.' He didn't want them to know he wasn't coping. The kids on the other side of the glass all asked questions at the same time. Why are you here? What did you do? When are you getting out?

'I kept on waiting for someone to come and apologise,' Isaac said, about both his times inside. 'To say this shouldn't have happened. Even when I got called to say I had a visitor, my heart always leapt – maybe this is the time a policeman will arrive to tell me it's all been a mistake! I thought, if they came and let me out, would I even lay a complaint? I felt like if I got out of there I would be so grateful I wouldn't even bother.' Sometimes he'd wonder, 'If I'd not joined the SJC, would this be happening? Would my life be better? But then I always thought the original decision to join the SJC had been one that was motivated by wanting to help my community. It wasn't like I'd decided to join a gang and that's what got me into trouble.'

Life felt full of so much that was undeserved and unforeseen. He'd think sometimes about something his father had told him when he was a teenager. 'This is life,' his father had said, 'the sadness, and the things that make you mad, and the bad luck. You learn. You can learn. You *have to* learn from everything.' His father was commenting on what had happened to Simon, Isaac's brother. One day Simon had run out of the house to watch a commotion in the street and been caught in the crossfire of a gang battle. He took a bullet in the leg.

'So I don't know what one learns by being shot,' Isaac told me. 'Maybe if you hear screams in the street then stay indoors! Or with this case – I don't know.' But he hoped one day he'd be able to tell a good story, and extract a lesson from it.

Chapter Twenty

I asked questions in Bardale before and after Angy and Isaac's conviction, and it was not, at first, very fruitful. With me on a few of these occasions was Masi Feni, a photographer who'd covered the trial periodically and who lived in a backyard shack in a different part of Mfuleni. Otherwise, my translator was Mluleki Sam, a community theatre director who lived in Site B in Khayelitsha. Mluleki had a talent for empathy and a well-timed joke, which proved to be invaluable.

I was lucky to meet Nomawethu Mbewu on one of my early visits. She was broad and garrulous with a mischievous sense of humour, and introduced me to many of the characters I'd heard about in court, usually by walking into their homes and teasing them mercilessly for several minutes. The first morning we met she strolled around her three-room shack, between sofas and huge cooking pots, in a fluffy fuchsia dressing gown debating whether to get involved. She had a deep, booming voice and seemed to like using it. Even so, she was at first hesitant about being quoted.

'Last time I was in the newspaper I ended up in jail for 30 days.'

'But you insulted a councillor!' I joked.

'Yoh. I didn't insult him! It was a vote of no confidence. If you are a councillor you must work!'

Nomawethu had been attending a training course in Durban in the week Rowan was murdered, but she had been around during the events preceding it, and for what came afterwards.

'This story. Ehh, I can't believe myself! I'm in the middle of it again.' She shook her head. 'Both Angy and Rowan were good people, though they lived in different ways.'

In the end, Nomawethu often accompanied us and remained steadfastly neutral, though on balance sceptical that Angy was guilty. 'He was sweet in that other way,' she said about Rowan. 'He wasn't a person you feared, when you look at him. He was a very nice guy, to be honest. He greeted people in the street. He was the victim, same as I would say Angy was also.' Although she also said, 'If it was me, at that time, I could have done it. When someone makes you a victim of crime they undermine your humanity, and then you want to take away theirs.'

Neutrality was not, however, the order of the day. Though I could find no one new who said they had seen anything on the night, there were plenty of people who had opinions about what had happened. These opinions seemed split between belief that Angy was innocent, and belief that she was guilty. And among those who thought she was guilty, there were, again, those who thought she had done them a favour, and those who thought it was wrong. The people we spoke to – who all lived within two or three streets of the Pink House or Angy's yard – were mostly friendly and receptive to questions. However, every now and then someone who had greeted us warmly would stiffen when I told them why we were there. One couple, who had been laughing and joking one minute, the next told us to leave.

There could be, of course, a hundred explanations for each cold shoulder, but there were two reasons that people were nervous. The first was that, as I was frequently told, John Ndevu was, well, not quite a sangoma, but a man who practised traditional Xhosa rites with herbs and appeals to supernatural intervention. The story I was told in this regard was that Rowan's funeral was held in Bardale, with the Bardale neighbours who had so resented Rowan's presence doing the cooking and contributing towards costs. Ta Topz himself had eulogised Rowan at the prayer session. At some point John Ndevu stood up and pronounced a curse on the people involved in his grandson's death. They would encounter trouble by the end of the year. And, indeed, though maybe not exactly on time, within a few months Angy had been arrested and Ta Topz was dead. Nobody was going to tell a white woman they believed in these things, but a lot of people brought up the subject of black magic.

The other explanation, the one people would not say aloud, also drew on the evidence of misfortune: Rowan was necklaced, Angy and Isaac were in jail, Ta Topz was dead, Asavela had been sent to the Eastern Cape, and John Ndevu was off a good plot in Mfuleni and back in a hokkie in Strand without electricity. Nomawethu reported being told cryptic things by policemen at Blue Downs Police Station about Angy's trial and how 'they'd sorted her out'. Which could just mean they'd successfully investigated the case, or it could not. In any event, it was a strange, dangerous business, so why get involved, even if that only meant answering some questions?

The Pink House had, in the period since the murder, been painted teal. The owner, when I spoke to him, said it was because pink was too feminine, but I wondered if it wasn't because he didn't appreciate the notoriety. He calmly told me about his diet plans and business troubles, but was quite sure he hadn't seen anything on the night. Angy and Isaac told me a different story. They'd asked him to testify because he'd said he'd seen the fight break out. But later he didn't want to have anything to do with the trial. He operated without a licence and, he told them, testifying for the defence was a sure-fire way to make sure his shebeen was on the VisPol's list of taverns to raid every weekend.

I did, however, find out things around the margins. Two people remembered the public meeting in the open field which had generated the petition that was handed to the Blue Downs Police Station.

This was the meeting at which, Asavela said, Angy exhorted people to burn criminals. Nomtha John said she'd only been at the meeting briefly, and it definitely hadn't been a straightforward vigilante rousing affair. In fact, she left because there was so much disagreement, and she couldn't stand the atmosphere. 'Some people were saying we should beat criminals, other people saying we shouldn't. There was no order.' Dimakaiso Khoathane, on the other hand, had been an active participant. She was involved in Bardale's political structures, a street committee of fluctuating membership. She also denied that the meeting had been a forum for Angy to rabble-rouse a necklacing. Instead she said that Angy hadn't called the meeting or even led it. She merely participated in the general debate, which included complaints about the police, as well as a discussion about whether Bardale residents would get employed in building state-subsidised houses in the neighbourhood. Khoathane remembered less disagreement than John. She was a strong believer in what she called 'the law of the sjambok'. She felt the tenor of the meeting and the drive behind the petition was to present an ultimatum to the police. This was that the police had to work with them or 'we are going to take our own actions and our own ways'. She denied that Angy had called for vigilante methods.

I received another curious denial, from Asavela herself. I had been warned of the high levels of fear in Bardale linked to the case. The prosecutor and a policeman from Blue Downs called Calitz, who drove the witnesses to court each day, said people in Bardale were scared because they'd been threatened by Angy. Asavela was in a witness-protection programme in the Eastern Cape because she had feared for her life. Palesa gave a vivid rendition of Asavela being 'rescued' by police in an armoured vehicle – a Casspir – from Bardale while an angry mob surrounded her house. Though this scene could hardly get more dramatic, he also said a sangoma had followed them the whole time they were in the neighbourhood. They'd bundled Asavela into the armoured vehicle and quickly left the area. Asavela 'was shaking, like a leaf. She was so, so afraid'.

I'd spoken to Asavela on one trip to Bardale. Angy and Isaac had been convicted and were in jail. I was told she had been back in the community for weeks, staying with her mother. I asked her mother about the incident with the Casspir, and the mob surrounding their house, and she'd looked at me as if I was mad. She hadn't heard about that, she said. Asavela herself denied it. I asked if Angy had ever threatened her and she said no. But Angy's friends had insulted her, she said. 'And they use strong words,' Nomawethu added. Asavela tolerated me for a few minutes but she was not talkative, and wouldn't make eye contact. From what she did say, it sounded as if the police had offered her a free trip to the Eastern Cape and she'd accepted it.

Other than that, she didn't recant anything.

'What did you think about these events at the time?' I asked.

'I thought it was sad,' she said, looking at me for the first time. 'I thought it was very sad.'

Of Rowan's friends, Roger corroborated, but did not elaborate on, the version of events presented in court. Rara was the only one to offer more. He took me to Blueberry Hill. I asked him, 'Were you angry at the time?'

He said, 'Rowan was like my brother. The night he was taken, I didn't sleep. It was almost past 6 am when I could close my eyes. Then, at 9, a policeman came to take my statement. He drove me to the station.' On the way they made a detour to show Rara the place where we were now standing: the site of Rowan's necklacing.

❖ ❖ ❖

I also made a trip to the nearby suburb of Eerste River. This was where the ambulance driver, Andrew Swarts, lived. Swarts had made two statements about his interaction with Rowan, both quite different.

He had not been called to testify. In September 2013, 11 months after the incident, Swarts made an affidavit. It was brief: he'd picked up the patient, who had been burnt with tyres, and then taken him to Groote Schuur. Then in 2014, in June, when the prosecutor was preparing for trial, Swarts made another statement, and it was, well, bizarre.

After describing Rowan's clearly badly burnt body, it read: 'I said to Martha Pieterse this person must be dead. To my absolute surprise, this person then suddenly spoke to me and told me he is not dead. I then rushed to hydrate this person.' Swarts described being unable to insert a drip, and was told he'd have to meet the paramedic en route. 'I then spoke to this person and asked him what has happened to him. He then told me that some people put two tyres on him and set him alight. I then asked him from where he is and he replied he is from Mannenberg. I then made a joke and asked him what he did that the people wanted to kill him. He then only laughed.'

During her testimony, his ambulance assistant, Martha Pieterse, suggested Swarts had been offered a bribe. However this couldn't be explored in court by anyone except Swarts himself, so it remained a mystery. In comments in the recess, Palesa and King sparred briefly about it, with Palesa suggesting he must have been approached by the defence, and King arguing the opposite. Palesa also suggested that Swarts was problematic. 'Way from the start I said there is something wrong about this guy. Right from the start I said I smell a rat somewhere!' he said.

On the face of things, it would have been difficult for Angy and Isaac to intimidate Swarts. For one, they didn't know his name and the EMS service would not have divulged it, let alone given out his contact details. But that information was all readily available in the police docket.

Calling on a favour, I was able to track down Swarts's address, and get his phone number from a neighbour.

Andrew Swarts, when he eventually answered his phone, could not be calmed down. I told him I was writing something about the criminal justice system. I just wanted to ask a few questions about his experience attending to a particular patient. I didn't mention the case directly, but he knew exactly what I was referring to.

'You know, this is very difficult,' he said.

I felt him shrinking from the phone.

'You know, this case, it was a big thing. It affected my work. I've decided I'm just going to keep quiet about that. They must sort it out themselves. I'm not going to say anything about that. I'm really not. There was a *groot dinges* [big thing] about this case, and it was all too traumatising.'

'You mean seeing the victim at the scene? Is that what traumatised you?'

'No! I mean the whole *dinges* afterwards. They must just sort it out between themselves. I gave my statement to the guy who put it all together, the case, the policeman.'

I asked if he stuck by those statements. Were they taken down correctly? He wouldn't answer.

'I decided to keep quiet about this and I'm going to stick with that. This *dinges*...'

He became increasingly incoherent.

I said, figuring I was losing him, 'There was an allegation in court that you were offered money, and the state says it was by the accused, and the defence says it was by the police, and I was really hoping you could clear up who had or hadn't put pressure on you?'

And that was when Andrew Swarts hung up on me.

❖ ❖ ❖

That wasn't the only funny business around this trial. In June 2014, when the defence case had just begun and Angy was on the stand,

Dustin Kramer, the Deputy General Secretary of the SJC, received a text message which read, 'Mr Kramer u have 3 days to force angy and Isaac to admit that they killed and murded [sic] rowan. That is if u still luv your job and u want to come to Khayelitsha hassle free.' Nothing came of this message. Dustin opened a case of intimidation with the police but the phone number was, to his knowledge, never traced.

Also, I met with curious resistance from officials when I mentioned the case. An example, perhaps minor, concerned the prosecutor who had tried to get Redelinghuys convicted for perjury and racketeering, a trial which had concluded over a decade earlier. We spoke first on the phone and he was amenable to an interview, if I went through the formalities with the National Prosecuting Authority. I sent a formal request to the press office. Although I never received an official response, the lawyer forwarded an email from the NPA's spokesperson, Eric Ntabazalila, about my request which was tantamount to granting the interview. The lawyer also confirmed that I was 'welcome to contact him'. But when I tried, a few weeks later, to arrange a meeting, I got a curt email: 'It is not correct to say that the NPA gave approval. I said that you are welcome to contact me. I thereafter had further discussions about this request with my seniors. Should you wish to obtain further information, you can contact Mr Eric Ntabazalila from our office. I have decided to no longer express any views in this matter.'

Needless to say the role of Mr Ntabazalila was to stonewall me. He ignored every request I sent to speak to any NPA employee about this case. No matter how many emails I sent or how fancy the letterheads I used, there was never an answer. NPA employees I contacted directly were warm at first but went cold when I outlined my intentions. They told me to go through Ntabazalila.

Perhaps this does not count as above-average obstruction, or suggest that it was about the sensitivity of the case. For example, even the city of Cape Town, when I asked for a simple set of statistics about fires, took my request directly to the mayoral committee, their highest decision-making body, then told me they could only consider my request if I provided a raft of information about the intended use, on letter-headed paper. And when I did this they still ignored all subsequent emails.

Clearly at all levels of government there were plenty of formal and informal sanctions for talking about something that powerful officials wanted suppressed, and there were no rewards for transparency.

❖ ❖ ❖

It was many months later that I was introduced to Malwandi Yentu, who had some interesting things to say about the night of Saturday, 12 August 2012. Malwandi had, with hindsight, been mentioned repeatedly during the trial, though not by name. King often lambasted the police for not speaking to two obvious witnesses: the owner of the Pink House, and the man who lived in the crèche, where Rara and Desiree both said they saw Rowan being beaten. Rara placed Isaac there. Desiree gave a lurid account of seeing all four of the accused beat Rowan in the crèche yard. Asavela said she'd seen Angy and Isaac at the gate to the crèche.

One day Mluleki and I went door to door on Khaya Walk in pursuit of anyone who had been part of the crowd that Rara, John Ndevu and Desiree said watched the assault or blocked their path as they ran in pursuit of Rowan. We had no luck: either people said they hadn't seen or heard anything at all that night, or they were newcomers. One woman said she knew who we should talk to, and took us several blocks away to the relatively well-to-do crèche owner's house. Here Malwandi, her son, quite calmly said he was happy to talk to us and he had a lot to talk about, in fact. He told us this story twice, once sitting in his lounge while his girlfriend had her hair braided and nodded in agreement at certain points, and a second time as we walked around the crèche.

At the time, Malwandi, acting as security guard for his mother, lived in a small room barely big enough to accommodate a bed and TV, separated from the single large room which was the crèche by a flimsy wall and a curtain. Malwandi and his girlfriend spent a lazy day at home watching TV that Saturday when Rowan was murdered. His friend Popo, one of the last of a stream of visitors, left them late in the evening. He was back in a few minutes to say there was a fight in Khaya Walk. 'Bras,' he said, 'Rowan is being beaten outside.'

They wondered if the fight had anything to do with the phone Rowan had presented to Malwandi the day before and which Malwandi had agreed to stash for him. Worried that this was the reason for the beating, they didn't dare venture outside.

But the noises of the fight, of a man crying, got louder, and then got closer, and came right up to the front door. At which point two huge men burst in with Rowan, already bloody, gripped between them. Malwandi didn't recognise the men. They had big stomachs, but it was fat that covered prodigious muscle, and they had *umkhemis*, belts impregnated with herbs and muti for protection in battle, strapped to their biceps. These they slapped as they shouted at Rowan, 'Come on, boy, your grandfather is no threat to us now!' To Malwandi the two men looked like professional heavies. They shouted, 'Where's the boss?' They also demanded to know where the plasma TV was. It became apparent that Rowan had told them that Malwandi was hiding it. As they confronted Malwandi, Rowan stripped off his ripped and bloody vest and flung it to the floor.

'Come on, Roy, tell them the truth, bra!' Malwandi said. 'Otherwise you're going to get beaten. Big time.'

With Malwandi's denials, the men realised that Rowan was misleading them and beat him again. Malwandi and his girlfriend begged Rowan to tell the men the truth. But Rowan broke free and dashed through the doorway covered by the curtain and into the crèche itself. This room was considerably larger than Malwandi's, with yellow bunnies painted on its plywood walls, blue streaks outlining them like malevolent afterimages. At the far end of this room was a kitchenette and Rowan scrambled towards it and grabbed a kettle. Turning on his pursuers he yelled, 'I'll burn you!' For a moment they hesitated until Rowan lunged towards a door on his left but it was locked. The men grabbed him again and marched him back into Malwandi's room and out the door into the yard.

Rowan kept calling Malwandi's name. 'How can you let me die in front of you?' he screamed. 'Why did I come to your house just to die in front of you?' The two men dragged him into the yard. At the gate they paused. Malwandi could see them shoving Rowan against the bars of the gates. Again Rowan shouted for help, and the men shouted for people to join them. But the streets were eerily quiet, 'as if by witchcraft', said Malwandi. Eventually the men disappeared with Rowan into the dark streets and the sounds of the beating faded. Later Malwandi had heard that Rowan was forced into a car, but before then he'd broken free and run to his own house for help.

The police spoke to Malwandi three weeks to a month after the incident. They came on several occasions, different policemen, different questions. They also spoke to people who knew Malwandi about what they thought he'd seen. They never took a statement. Malwandi hadn't known what to do with Rowan's bloody vest or the curtain that was also covered in blood. He told the police about these items but they never collected them and eventually he threw them away.

There was no way to reconcile Malwandi's story – observed in the light, at arm's length – with those of Rara and Desiree. If what Malwandi said was true then the police had – at the very least – deliberately suppressed eyewitness evidence that contradicted their case. They had also ignored items that could have held forensic evidence about Rowan's attackers. The story also suggested the men were professional assassins, perhaps the 'taxi drivers' that had been mentioned in the first press reports and in early statements by the eyewitnesses. The long thin bruises on Rowan's ribs – which the pathologist said probably were not caused by a golf club – could have been caused by the men slamming him against the gate. Yet Malwandi's story did not preclude any of the accused becoming involved at a later point, and it still seemed to revolve around a television set, although there was no mention that it was Angy's television set. And, indeed, I was told by William King that, post-verdict, only evidence which had the power to undoubtedly exonerate could help in court, and that this evidence didn't qualify.

Malwandi had also already, I learnt, refused to testify for the defence. Angy and Isaac heard he had seen something and, with strict instruction that he not tell them what it was, they asked him to be a defence witness. But somewhere in this conversation Malwandi had become suspicious of them. He told me they'd offered him money. They adamantly denied this. When he complained he couldn't afford the taxi fare to court, they had said that his expenses would be paid. It was also possible that he came to believe, as many of the young men who had been friends with Rowan did, that even if they had no direct evidence, Angy was responsible. They believed she could have pulled the strings from behind the scenes. And Rowan had been a friend of Malwandi's, someone who visited him often and made him laugh – and still visited him in nightmares where Rowan called out to be saved. Malwandi said he often wondered if there was anything he could have done to save his friend.

Malwandi was not the only one haunted by what happened that night. About a year after Rara and I had driven out to Blueberry Hill together, Mluleki and I visited him at his house. It had rained heavily in the morning and later on that afternoon a storm came in that lashed the Cape through the night. Nomawethu banged on his door but no one responded until a friend of Rara's arrived, and, impatient to smoke a pipe, slipped inside to rouse him.

When Rara emerged we stood with him in his sandy front yard, which was littered with a familiar array of detritus: a lone shoe, a torn cabbage leaf, orange netting. When we'd met the previous year he was well turned out in a tracksuit and a baseball cap and he looked about 16 years old. That day in July, albeit he had just woken up, his clothes were filthy. The beige jacket he wore was torn at both elbows with the stuffing spilling out and several buttons were missing. He looked much older. He said he was fixing phones for a living but business did not appear to be booming. While we talked several young men came in and out of his room to smoke tik.

Rara's answers to my questions were barely audible, quick and brief. He wouldn't meet my eyes and pretended not to notice that his elbow was getting soaked in a pool of rainwater that had collected on the lid of the rubbish bin he leant on. He seemed to steel himself before each response. It was confusing: everyone else who did not want to talk told us to go away. Rara did not. He submitted to being questioned, but evidently hated the process. Mluleki realised this too.

'Brother,' he said, 'what do you feel when you talk about Roy?'

Rara began to answer, but stopped. Two breathy barks of words came out and then he abruptly turned away, angry, and he seemed to stumble to the fence of the property just in front of us. Tears streamed down his face.

Mluleki tried to comfort him and Rara said, 'I really *loved* that guy. He was my *grootman*. I've tried and tried and tried to forget what happened to him and I just can't.'

Some justice, a little closure, the ability to believe their son, their friend, had mattered, that their own pain had mattered: I believed that was all that Rowan's friends and family wanted. We left Rara leaning against his fence, staring at a bled-out white sky and the sandy field beneath it, criss-crossed with dark tyre tracks, stretching towards Angy's house.

Chapter Twenty-One

Two months after the verdict, we reconvened in the old colonial court for the mitigation hearings.[64] I sat in the gallery, from where I could see Angy and Isaac's children enter, Alex riding piggyback on Thumi's back, Boontjie holding Hope's hand. King leant down to them and said, 'Hi, I'm mum and dad's lawyer.' Silence, then Boontjie piped up in an indistinct child's voice and King asked them to wait outside. From the Dungeon came the sounds of a scuffle and then Angy and Isaac came in, bumping and thumping, their hands cuffed and chained to their ankles. Angy looked up at the gallery and blew kisses, saluting her friends in a girlish voice. She had an almost-mohawk of thin red braids, and what appeared to be a tattoo on her forearm. Her friends were shy and scared alone but took up their space as a group, joking loudly about the proceedings. Rowan's family were in the minority in the gallery, painfully shy and ill at ease.

Social worker Judy Radloff presented reports on Azola and Chris. Radloff's report did not do either of them any favours. Most of the information about their personal circumstances 'could not be verified', but implied heavily that they were absent and irresponsible fathers. Radloff considered their defence 'an aggravating circumstance' which called for an even harsher sentence. About Azola: 'The fact that the accused refuses to take responsibility for these offences shows a lack of accountability.' And for Chris: 'Having shown a lack of remorse by minimising his involvement in these crimes is a clear sign of his untrustworthiness.' In her report they were the pictures of the stereotype, the Jims-come-to-Joburg (or in Cape Town's case, the Xhosas-come-to-Khayelitsha) who abandon their obligations in the village, and begin new ones in the city at which they fare no better. These are men who have failed to provide for their families, and failed in average ways, their crime evidence of their poor decision-making, their denial of guilt just one more example of their inability to take either control of or responsibility for their lives.

Ndlovu did take issue with the social worker's failure to explore the actual details of their family situation, which proved to be less damning than Radloff made out.[65] But it was King who pointed out that it was legally incorrect to call for them to be punished because they claimed they were innocent. This was one of their most basic rights in court. Mitigation was, in short, a brief mirror of their trial.

About Angy's and Isaac's situation, social worker Astrid Klaase was accurate and not unreasonably harsh. Klaase agreed with King's proposition that they were 'a loving, close-knit family'. Nolubabalo Zongolo, Angy's tenant, neighbour and friend, who had been caring for the children during their imprisonment, told the court she would not be able to continue looking after them, as she had two children of her own, was a single parent, and worked night shifts as a nurse. Likewise, no one from Angy's or Isaac's family had offered to take care of the children. Isaac's father – with whom Isaac was not on speaking terms – 'did not point-blank refuse' but said he wouldn't do it if it placed a burden on his wife.

❖ ❖ ❖

Phumeza Mlungwana, a Khayelitsha local who had been made the General Secretary of the SJC at the young age of 25, gave the longest mitigation testimony. She was attractive and articulate, and spoke with clarity and poise about the NGO's work. It was the first time there was real testimony about the work that the activists performed that did not come from Angy or Isaac. Phumeza spoke with conviction about how talented and committed an activist Angy was. For Isaac, too, she drew a picture of an activist who did his work well and with passion, and was, above all, a deeply amiable man. 'Isaac is a person that speaks his mind. He is very charismatic. He is a family man. I have never seen Isaac fight with anyone. He gets along with everyone at the office, he is, he is…'

'He is a good guy,' said King.

'He is a good guy,' said Phumeza, with a small smile.

Phumeza spoke at much greater length about Angy's work, described the cases she'd taken on, and sketched the strength and the importance of her leadership, and the breadth of her contact with police structures. She talked about the way Angy became the face not just of the commission, but of the organisation, as she was the primary community liaison for criminal justice issues and she recruited people. She was, in short, much better at defending Angy than Angy had been, and it was remarkable that someone from the SJC had not been called to fill these gaps before the judgment was handed down.

Zackie Achmat was in court on that day of mitigation in a show of solidarity for Phumeza, who was nervous about giving testimony. A few weeks later I was effectively summoned to meet with him and, against the wishes of both Phumeza and Dustin, he explained why Angy and Isaac no longer worked for the SJC. Zackie Achmat's motivation was ostensibly defensive: he feared the organisation being presented through Angy's eyes. But he was also still seething over the receipts fraud, and perhaps emboldened by her betrayal, or perhaps because the incident had retrospectively coloured everything that came before, he was unremitting in his condemnation.

Much of his comment was directed at asserting that she was always a bad activist. 'A good activist is someone who can channel anger,' Achmat told me, and she was not one of those. Sometimes confrontation was necessary, and sometimes 'it even has to be ugly' but that should be the last resort, 'and with her it's the first thing. And that's the difficulty.' It was a 'myth' that she had 'built' the criminal justice campaign. She was deliberately divisive and aggressive – even violent – as a colleague, she played favourites and sought out conflict, and liked to 'dress to the nines'. And most damning: she had been renegade, stepping outside her mandate, and had not reeled herself in when the organisation asked her to.

Achmat believed what a good activist had to do, and what he didn't believe Angy did, was 'get a grip on not acting out that anger, that fear, that depression'. Angy had 'seen so many horrible things in her life, and she's internalised them all'. He didn't see a fearless crusader but someone who sought out crisis and trauma because, he said, 'every time you look for it, and you help someone, it's as if you're overcoming it'. He recognised it, because it was a trap he'd been stuck in before. 'But the fact is, you're actually not overcoming it. You're taking more and more with you.'

These were allegations I addressed with Angy's colleagues and their reactions were mixed. Some of it they recognised, but not without qualification. Mandla Majola, who had always maintained that although Angy fell into the category of people 'who are sometimes not easy to manage', the benefits of employing her outweighed the challenges. She was hard working; executed her assignments 'to the dot' and went the extra mile to do so; had a phenomenal ability to connect with communities and bring people into the movement; and was, all in all, caring and committed. 'It is not easy to find someone like that,' said Mandla. Some allegations were vehemently denied by the people who were, according to Achmat, victims of Angy's aggression, who then rounded on Achmat, in turn. Someone who knew them both said, 'It's very Zackie. She was useful up until point X and after point X she was a liability. That's how Zackie works. It's ruthless and that's why he's been successful.'

'I think you have very many difficult activists,' Zackie Achmat said in that interview; 'I'm one.' In his own assessment he could be 'tough', 'difficult to work with', even 'horrible', especially when depressed. 'And I can't think of an activist that I know that I've worked with who's easy. But that's not the question. There has to be a limit. And the limit has to be enforced.'

Achmat was, nonetheless, sure that she was innocent, and the victim of something 'horrific' on the part of people within the police. But even though he maintained he wasn't blaming her, it sounded as if in parsing out just how much of a 'maverick' she was, she was, really, being blamed.

Tackling the police, Achmat said, was the most dangerous thing for an activist to do. You did it at 'enormous risk' to yourself and to the people on whose behalf you made complaints. 'You don't look for a fight with them.' But Angy didn't do things delicately, and she didn't vet her interventions with the organisation; instead she tried to fix them herself. And even when she operated within her mandate, 'she dealt with the police in a way that attracted extreme hostility'. Her manner created a 'very tense situation between her and the police. And I'm sure they wanted to take their revenge.'[66] Another SJC activist, over the course of the trial, had backtracked on an unequivocal belief that Angy was targeted in connection with political work and the crusade against corruption at Blue Downs. Perhaps, instead, it was merely revenge because of 'her way of going about things', he'd said. In other words, had she campaigned for the Khayelitsha Commission and lodged a corruption accusation against a policeman with more tact, the set-up would not have happened.

The interview with Zackie Achmat took place at the Ndifuna Ukwazi offices, where the SJC was temporarily based. From the beginning of 2014 the SJC's offices had been repeatedly ransacked.

To investigate these burglaries (though the SJC leadership remained sceptical that they were burglaries), police visited their offices and interrogated staff, and did so almost daily. Public-order police had arrived at private SJC meetings heavily armed and in armoured vehicles. Then in January 2015, the SJC offices were broken into and so thoroughly ransacked that they were unusable: tiles ripped off the walls and broken on the floor, doors ripped off their hinges, documents torn off shelves and dumped on the floor. Dustin, who believed the level of destruction indicated that the motive had not only been robbery, sent me photographs of the scene. Looking at them, I thought, yes, it was dangerous to campaign against the police, wasn't it?

When Phumeza described in court what the community lost by Angy's and Isaac's incarceration she spoke about the loss of a talented community mobiliser, about the fact that Mfuleni had no branches since Angy's had closed down, that the person who had filled Angy's position was simply 'not Angy'. In contrast, Azola's mother, when asked the same about her son, said that the community had lost a patient taxi driver. Chris's sister, Feziga, was even less effusive. Asked if the community would feel his absence, she was taciturn. Since they had lived together, she said, 'I never got any problems with him'.

❖ ❖ ❖

The bombshell moment came on the morning of the fourth day of mitigation. Henney walked in and effectively put a halt to mitigation, saying he wanted to propose that their sentence incorporate 'the possibility of restorative justice'. The SJC – hardly a neutral party – was put in charge of arranging a reconciliation process, which they wisely referred to NICRO, an NGO which worked with offenders. Ariana Smit at NICRO became the person to devise a series of victim-offender mediations and report back to court on the prospects for a non-custodial restorative justice sentence. Angy and Isaac were granted bail immediately.

This was, to say the least, unexpected. Non-custodial! After everything Henney had said in the judgment! It didn't make sense.

Henney's main justification was his concern for the children. And perhaps it was the testimony about family, or the request by Boontjies not to be separated from her siblings, or the appeal by Nolubabalo to reunite their children with the love of the parents, or the fact that the couple had no close relatives to step in, that persuaded him. All these points he referenced later.

But Angy's supporters speculated that his true motivation lay in a fight he'd had with King the day before this announcement. King had asked Phumeza to comment on a statement that began 'the court has found that Angy's and Isaac's television was stolen by Rowan'.

'Did I make such a finding?' Henney interjected.

From there followed hours of argument between the two men. It wasn't an interesting argument but it was, perhaps, a significant one. King brought up evidence from the record that Henney had made a ruling, early in the trial, that Rowan was a thief and liar. Henney countered that he had made that statement because he'd been – perhaps unintentionally – misled by the defence. The defence had said that the police docket contained evidence of a confession by Rowan to the crime. Henney explained his ruling was based on an assumption about Rowan's confession that he had later revised.[67] This meant that he changed his mind about the ruling although he did not formally inform the court.

'M'Lord, as a result of that,' King said, 'I never called a witness to prove it conclusively. M'Lord, that is going to be the grounds of appeal.' Those following this line of argument thought Henney was trying to prevent having his judgment overturned on a technicality which was why he raised the matter of restorative justice. As this held the prospect of a non-custodial sentence, Angy and Isaac would be able to spend the rest of their sentence in relative freedom, raising their children – but only as long as they admitted guilt, and asked for forgiveness. And with an admission of guilt, an appeal bid would be dead in the water.

❖ ❖ ❖

Ariana Smit, the social worker at NICRO who had been charged with overseeing the process and reporting to court, agreed to talk to me at her offices in the city, but declined to speak specifically about the case. 'The nub,' she said about restorative justice, 'is respect. Do unto others as you would have them do unto to you. It restores a sense of connection between human beings, but it also requires people to take responsibility for the crimes they've committed, in order to make it work.'

Ideally, she said, it would be driven by the victims, but usually, and unsurprisingly, offenders asked for restorative approaches. 'Previous cases we've done restorative work on are common robbery; it is popular in cases of shoplifting, for example, and culpable homicide, drunk drivers and so on.' She had never seen it used in a case of murder.

'What about a case,' I asked her, 'a hypothetical case, where the convicted parties steadfastly maintain their innocence, despite a harsh judgment and the prospect of jail?' Her eyes flicked down, involuntarily, to a folder in her desk – Angy's and Isaac's – and she said, 'Well, in a case like that, one would start to wonder if the convicted parties weren't in a state of denial.'

❖ ❖ ❖

I visited Angy and Isaac in Bardale, once they had settled back into their house. Isaac and Hope, with Alex on her back, came out to direct my car across the sandy field, and led me into their lounge, where we had a weary conversation. Angy, unusually, said almost nothing.

Isaac told me how surprised they were, though also pleased to be with their children. 'That is something that cannot be put into words.' But they felt deeply uneasy about the restorative justice process. It would involve a series of meetings between them and Rowan's family, they had been told. But Isaac couldn't imagine what he could say to the family if they asked him what happened that night. He seemed to be toying with a situation: could they simply say, 'I'm sorry for what happened to your son' and 'I'm sorry if anything I did hurt you'? But how could that feel like a proper apology to the family, he asked? And wouldn't they want to know the full truth?

'And what happens when I say, "I can't tell you what happened to Rowan because I was at home with my kids that night"?'

Angy wouldn't countenance an apology to the family. She said, 'They know. That family knows exactly what happened. So why should I go to say sorry, when they know?' She believed they had modified their statements for money, and that was what they wanted out of the process. She expected they wanted her and Isaac to pay compensation. When I asked Angy why she didn't go along with the apology, she said, 'Never. I would rather kill Judge Henney, get to go to jail for something I actually did, and then apologise to his family.'

Isaac was less adamant but ultimately, he told me, 'To have said over and over again in court that you are innocent, I can't just turn around and pretend I did it.'

'But what about your kids?' I asked.

'Well,' said Isaac, staring at his hands, 'that is the difficult thing. That is really the difficult thing.'

❖ ❖ ❖

At the end of April 2015, the court sat again for Smit's final report into the prospects for the restorative justice process. She did not give Henney the news he wanted: all four of the accused had refused to 'accept responsibility', and Rowan's family was still saying they were not willing to meet with Angy and Isaac. Smit spoke as someone who was genuinely trying to make a process of reconciliation work but she said, ultimately, 'It may be difficult finding a place to start.'

Additionally, Smit singled out Angy as having 'a medium risk of re-offending', while the others were all classed as low risk. According to Smit this was not only due to Angy's refusal to 'admit wrongdoing', but her 'broader attitudes to authority, justice'.

Angy had 'presented as a very angry person' on the two occasions she interviewed her, Smit said. 'There was little movement between the two periods in developing insight.' For that reason, she recommended that Angy be barred by the court from taking part in community work that touched on issues of justice lest 'things can spiral out of control and she puts herself in the wrong place at the wrong time'. Angy looked dejected, on the verge of tears.

❖ ❖ ❖

With the prospects for the restorative justice process extinguished, the court proceeded to sentencing. This was so damning that it seemed puzzling, again, that non-custodial terms had ever been on the table. Henney delivered his sentence fast, although occasionally he mumbled. His words, however, were so uncompromising that the translator – a new man, dressed from head to toe in shades of brown, with a preacher's delivery – grappled for the Xhosa equivalents. At one point he went off script, simply saying to the accused something that translated approximately as, 'The judge wishes he could put you to death.'

With incredulity I listened to Henney lay the grounds for his sentence. 'On the night of his death he was kidnapped and thereafter they proceeded to murder him by placing a tyre around his body filled with petrol and setting it alight. This was one of the most evil, inhumane and barbaric ways to kill a human being. This was also cruel, heartless and a cowardly act. No one, not even the worst criminal, deserved to die like this, and it deserves an appropriate punishment.' I thought about how much more relaxed his audience was this time. Everyone expected this. Angy, wearing her TAC 'HIV Positive' T-shirt, looked bored and cast wistful glances at her copy of Mzilikazi wa Afrika's book, *Nothing Left to Steal*. Isaac, in a yellow checked shirt, looked long-suffering. Azola and Chris had given up formal attire and wore hoodies. Chris had his headphones on during the break, listening to gospel to lift his spirits.

The restorative justice process had only served to add more fuel to Henney's portrayal of Angy. She was, he pointed out, the only one of the accused who would not even apologise to the family. (The others were prepared to say they were sorry for the loss the deceased family suffered, but not to admit guilt.)

Angy's case, Henney said, 'was far worse than the other three accused. Although the deceased was a criminal who was involved in crime, and society demands that criminals should be brought to justice, the accused were no better. She was a wolf in sheep's clothing. This case revealed the dark side of her character. She tried to mask her involvement in this by saying that due to her effort to support a commission of inquiry she had been the victim of a conspiracy. In fact, she came across as an evil person who would stop at nothing to stop from being punished for the acts which she had perpetrated.'

I wondered what the journalists attending the sentencing – for some, their first experience of the trial – made of it?

Henney continued, 'According to this court she played a leading role in committing the offence. The court has a moral, legal and constitutional duty not to let people take the law into their own hands. The finding is that this court impose a sentence of life imprisonment.'

Desiree Jack, who sat in the gallery, looking down, nodded slightly and wiped tears from her face.

And then Henney took another unexpected swerve: he gave them only ten years. While their crime usually warranted 25 years – life – he lessened the sentence on the grounds that Angy was the primary caregiver for four children who would be left destitute by her imprisonment. Ten years for the murder, three years for kidnapping, served concurrently. Ten years total, with a chance of parole.

King immediately asked for leave to appeal, and bail until the appeal was heard and it was, after a recess, granted. Angy and Isaac would go home that day, sign in daily at a police station until the appeal was heard, and report for the incarceration within 24 hours if it was unsuccessful.

A young journalist seated next to me said breathlessly, as we both watched Angy, 'My friend told me she wants to go back to jail. She met some woman there and she says they will help her.' The journalist got excited by the idea as she spoke. 'Maybe they will help her commit another murder!'

'Do you think,' I said, 'that maybe could've been bravado?'

'Ja,' she said, nodding, her eyes fixed on Angy, 'maybe it's a biiiiiggg ego.'

A few metres away Angy was complaining to King, and her voice was audible above the shuffling of people filing out of the court room. 'I knew we were going to Pollsmoor. He's been wasting our time. Making us go up and down, up and down.'

'Yoooh, she's angry, hey,' the journalist said, imitating her: '"making us go up and down"!' Afterwards she asked Angy for a comment, and came back saying, 'Actually, I think I like her!' She laughed. 'Shame, I think it must just be this brave face thing!'

Chapter Twenty-Two

August 2015, three months after the sentencing, marked almost a year since the release of the final report of the Khayelitsha Commission. It had been sent to the minister of police for his response. Yet neither the minister nor any of his subordinates had commented. Activists were increasingly vocal about the delay. Most of the final report's 20 recommendations were addressed to police management, and they encompassed reforms that would affect not just Khayelitsha, but potentially change policing in townships across the country. By June the Western Cape premier had received a response, not from the minister, but from National Commissioner Phiyega. Zille told the police that unless they informed her otherwise, by the end of July she would release it to the media.

On the ground in Khayelitsha, things were not as strained. While many of the recommendations were lost causes without national sign-off, the provincial police administration had decided to take a pro-active stance on those that fell within their purview. These were the recommendations that spoke to their relationship with civil society, and encouraged liaison with civic organisations. The intention was to address a number of social issues the commission had highlighted, among them vigilantism, shebeens, and youth gangs. To do so they created 'sub-forums', monthly meetings between designated police officers and the public, to which they specifically invited academics, activists, and community leaders. They had parachuted in a much-respected Major-General Johan Brand, an erect and trim Afrikaner with greying hair, to run the Khayelitsha Cluster and over-see the sub-forums. Brand was a serious appointment: a seasoned detective, he had almost three decades of experience at many of the country's most difficult stations, and a master's degree in public management. He made it clear that his door was open to anyone who wanted to work with the police.

One Saturday in early August, I attended an 'Anti-Crime Imbizo' held by Major-General Brand. The imbizos were public meet-ings which the police had been holding since preparations for the commission began. These were their first attempts at showing willingness to engage with the community, albeit somewhat crudely organised. (Their chosen method of announcing the imbizo was by driving through the streets of Khayelitsha broadcasting the meeting details by loudhailer.) The meeting took place at a school in Ikwezi Park, adjacent to Site C, one of Khayelitsha's older suburbs. Here RDP houses and backyard shacks were packed closely together, and ringed by informal settlements. I was told there had been a vigi-lante murder in Ikwezi Park the week before, and that people were still seething from the rape and murder of 20-year-old Bongiwe Ninini. Her body had been found a week earlier dumped in a disused drain next to a Site C shopping centre. This imbizo was intended to discourage people from taking the law into their own hands.

I arrived as people hurried into the school. It appeared that the loudhailer hadn't been very specific about what was going to hap-pen. People expected to see pictures of beaten criminals or vigilantes who'd been arrested and put on display as a cautionary tale. When the true purpose of the event was revealed they slouched away, vocally disappointed. Yet others had no idea what the meeting was about but as it was a community meeting they felt it was import-ant to attend. People sat on the desks along the walls of an empty classroom, and when there was no space left on these, they unstacked chairs and filled the floor.

The panel at the front was composed of policemen and women from several stations, many of whom were members of the Vigilantism Sub-Forum, and four priests. After a hymn and sermon, Major-General Brand began his pitch. His presence was commanding and people listened attentively as he told them about two recent crimes – both robberies – where the police had successfully apprehended and charged the criminals responsible. His point was that traditional law enforcement was working, so there was no need to resort to vigilante methods. His colleague, Officer Phatekile, elaborated on this theme: 'If you kill and at the end he was not the guilty person, you cannot bring him back.' And if your children bring back expensive goods, he told the parents in the room, and you know they don't have jobs, those goods must be stolen. 'Someone might've died! Just so your son could have an iPad!'

Brand elaborated. The crime rate itself was down in Khayelitsha, due to a mix of intelligence and detection. His officers had been arresting whole groups of tsotsis, breaking down the networks that generated criminals and crime. He paused and fixed the audience with a stare. 'I'm begging you to trust us,' he said, the shaky timbre of his voice underlining his sincerity. 'To trust *me*.' He ended with an upbeat: 'Together we can make Khayelitsha a safer place. Thank you. *Nkosi*.'

Brand's speech seemed to have pleased the room, though not enough that they didn't also put forward a few complaints, dressed as questions. Most of the people who asked questions were earnest, softly spoken young men, or loud, impassioned older women. They told the police officers about all the tik dens they were happy to identify. They also said they'd made this information known to the police before. They asked when a satellite police station for Site C was coming, and they were told it wasn't. They complained that the community police forums, which the police were encouraging them to attend, were political party platforms, which the police denied.

Afterwards, as I wondered what to make of this, I considered the demonstration of accountability that Brand made. 'I'm going to give you my mobile phone number.' This was followed by murmurs of approval. 'Please don't call me about *nyatsis* [girlfriends]' – people laughed – 'call me about *crrrrime.*'

❖ ❖ ❖

A few days later I was at a similar event in a community hall near Bardale. This meeting, too, was an anti-vigilante imbizo that had been arranged by loudhailer. Chairs were set out in the middle of the indoor basketball court, in front of a desk for a few police officers. It was a sunny winter's day but cold in the hall, and the acoustics were bad, particularly when the wind blew, or when pigeons, periodically racing in loops around the building, settled down on the roof. People trickled in but it was 1 pm on a Wednesday and attendance didn't get above about 40 people. I sat at the back with Isaac. I could see Angy near the front.

I had missed the beginning of the meeting, but Isaac pointed out the Blue Downs station commander, Colonel Damoyi, a short man, bald with a thin moustache, and a vaguely froglike air. He wore what appeared to be an SAPS-issue black leather jacket. It seemed to me a dubious sartorial option for a police force trying to change a reputation for being the country's worst gangsters. I recognised several other faces: Colonel Redelinghuys, head of detectives, in a long grey coat, next to Damoyi; off to the side were two female police officers from VisPol, and one of them was Captain Kock, sporting a severe purple bob.

A man from the National Prosecuting Authority did much of the talking, explaining in English the formal procedures that followed arrest, dwelling on bail and its role. The policemen again gave out their personal cell-phone numbers, and encouraged people to call them directly.

The event became more interesting during question time. First a man in a grey bomber jacket asked them, 'Why the hell does it take so long to get an answer from a detective once we open a case? We're always being told "there's further investigation going on".'

A man in a brown jacket told them, 'You claim the satellite police station is open 24 hours a day, yet so often we go there and it's closed.' And that wasn't his only complaint. 'And the policemen you send into the community – are they drunk? Are they on tik? Because they are so aggressive to us, I can't explain it any other way, how they do their work so violently.' He got a loud round of applause.

A quiet woman made a suggestion: 'You say you don't know where the tik houses are, but why don't you just ask the skollies you pick up with drugs on them?' Several others made similar points about the drug trade. Just about everyone wanted to ask a question or make a statement of some kind. The police were being given a hard time, but the mood seemed jovial nonetheless.

Then, on the third round of questions, Angy, who was addressed by name by Damoyi, stood up and took out a notepad with a long list on it. Under his breath Isaac exclaimed, 'Eish!'

She went through her points numerically. The mood was instantly charged, both among the policemen and in the audience. During some of the other questions, people shuffled and talked, or they laughed at or with the speaker. Now people sat stiffly in their seats, as if they were holding their breath.

As she spoke, I saw the policemen knit their brows, their faces frozen, as the tension in the room rose. I wanted to look down, my head tugged by some force I gradually understood as a physical impulse to cower. In that instant I recognised it as an instinct to submit, and to submit purely because I was confronted by an authority I feared, however illegitimate I knew it to be. I also realised that this was an impulse Angy lacked. Faced with the policemen she believed had deliberately tried to imprison her, destroy her reputation, and orphan her children, she stood up and told them, once again, what she really thought. It sent a potent chemical potion through my blood: a mixture of admiration and frustration at her recklessness, inspiration and abject fear on her behalf.

Her tirade continued, each point addressed in imperious detail. When she was done there was loud applause, but it was staccato and brief.

'Well,' said Damoyi, in the tense silence that followed, 'I count about eight questions and 10 allegations. We are here to speak freely, but let's keep to the purpose of this meeting.'

Damoyi explained that IPID was there to deal with police over-sight, so her comment was moot. Then he said, 'I don't want to personalise this, but last week, Angy, you told us that we hadn't done our job and gotten back to a family in Bardale about a rape case, but when we phoned them they knew perfectly well what was happening with the case.'

Having dismissed her, he moved on to new questions and people started filing out.

❖ ❖ ❖

As I left the Mfuleni imbizo, I mulled over the repeated performance about cell-phone numbers. At first glance it was a potent symbol of a police force making themselves accountable, accessible to people who lived in their station's vicinity. 'Here's a direct line to the guy at the top. See how much we care!' But that it was the most senior local officials – cluster and station commanders – rattling off their ten digits, really revealed what theatre this was. They were giving people these hotlines because, as repeatedly raised in these imbizos, and as documented in the Khayelitsha Commission, the phones in the stations all too fre-quently rang unanswered. And when someone did pick up, often no one responded, or they responded hours too late. And, in a functional system, a cluster commander could sort this out. Or a station commander could demand the extra resources for this most basic, most essential, most simple station function. The cell-phone numbers were an admission that they couldn't fix the problem.

As I decided how harsh I should be about these charades, an answer presented itself in a news headline. The police had not bothered to respond to Zille's query about the confidentiality of Phiyega's response, so she had released the full text for public scrutiny.

Phiyega's response was a complete dismissal. Her starting point was that the commission 'should not have taken place at all', that it was 'an expensive and resource-hungry paper exercise' whose conclusions were 'biased and misdirected'. Paradoxically, she maintained that it had 'highlighted what was already known' and that its findings were not serious because the police already had measures in place to deal with them.

Each of the findings addressed to the police were dismissed or denied. They were 'fallacious', 'absurd' and 'premised on wrong fundamentals'. Or she deflected the blame to another department or, with obvious relish, the provincial government. In most cases she simply rattled off the existing systems, protocols and guidelines. These were the very systems, protocols and guidelines the commission had found were not working. She dwelt at length on streetlights and CCTV cameras and roads in order to make the point that both the city and the province had neglected informal settlements and that the commission had 'missed a golden opportunity to dwell on this'.

She conceded nothing. To read her letter was to be dropped into an alternative reality where policing in the townships was perfectly adequate, where the issues raised were things the police had been 'talking about and dealing with all along' and where their existing measures just needed to be given time to work.

301

Her response to Recommendation Fifteen ('System to ensure public can reliably contact SAPS units'), in particular, caught my eye: 'All police stations have reliable telephone systems that are accessible to the community. There is no need for additional systems. Telephone numbers of police stations are listed in telephone directories printed and electronically and is tested on a regular basis.'

As I read this I recalled seeing footage of Phiyega testifying at the Farlam Commission, which probed police culpability for the massacre of 34 miners at Marikana. In one clip, pushing her to answer a point she was evading, an evidence leader asked her repeatedly to answer the question. Phiyega's reaction was to snap: 'I have answered many questions.' And though her face was a mask, her tone was a snarl.

The concluding paragraphs of her letter communicated the same emotion: total contempt. And it was not just a petty political contempt for a premier from an opposition party, but a colder, measured contempt for anyone who should call her and her own to account.

Judge Henney had appealed to the seriousness of the police force, to the fact that senior men had been watching and, in the words of Redelinghuys, 'no one would risk their career like that'. Yet by the time the trial concluded Provincial Commissioner Lamoer had been removed for corruption (and would eventually be sentenced to eight years in jail). A few months later National Commissioner Phiyega was removed for serious misconduct related to the Marikana massacre, and Mdludli, the head of Crime Intelligence, was suspended and under criminal investigation for murder. Even as I wrote those sentences, Phiyega's replacement, Acting National Commissioner Khomotso Phahlane, the man many criminal justice pundits had pinned their hopes on because finally someone with real police experience had the top job, was under investigation for serious corruption and looked likely to get the axe, making him the fourth national commissioner in a row to leave in a state of disgrace.

❖ ❖ ❖

Initially, I've said, I wasn't sure I wanted to write about Angy, as it seemed too hard to avoid my own bias to believe her. We had been introduced through trusted friends, and because I had far more access to her side of the story, and because I am disposed, on the whole, to like bold and 'difficult' women, I worried about an innate prejudice. Then as things went on, I faced another problem: my strong impulses in the other direction. In truth I often would have been relieved to believe Angy Peter was guilty. I was afraid of the implications for my family, if they lived in a city where such malevolence could come from the police and it was unstoppable. Who do you turn to, if the police turn on you?

Another, perhaps even more compelling, reason was that I wanted some justice in this story. If Angy were guilty, that would be justice for Rowan, at least. And if there was no justice, I wanted at least for there to be truth. I did not want to be left only with the intellectual's consolation prize – meaning, what you scrape from the gaps where justice and truth should be. Yet I failed to find out who was behind Angy's arrests, and even to really understand why these events unfolded the way they did. Did it have anything to do party politics, or was it contained within the police? Was it conducted only within Blue Downs station and merely given cover – or a blind eye – from higher up? Did Tshicila, fearing jail, have more strings to pull in Crime Intelligence than we could ever have guessed or seen? Or was it as petty as the consequence of a grudge held by a few policemen who didn't like being dressed down in public by a woman? I felt at times as if I was surrounded by a huge mystery in which I could move closer to the centre, or drift further to the edge, but which I could never completely step out of and examine in its entirety.

Chapter Twenty-Three

In September 2016, I drove again to Bardale, to check in with Angy and Isaac. Cape Town, watered by winter rains, was looking lush. Arum lilies grew wild beside the rivers; in protected reserves, long-tongued flies and monkey beetles were busy pollinating the fynbos. On the degraded land of the townships, the weed Paterson's Curse had taken hold of any ditch or sandy shoulder, and its bright purple flowers carpeted the Cape Flats. Closer to Mfuleni, wild oat, beard and bristle grass rippled in the wind, and cattle grazed by the highway, horn high in yellow mustard bloom.

Though Isaac had warned me Bardale had undergone a 'facelift', I almost didn't recognise the area. Most of the shacks were gone, replaced by two-bedroom state-subsidy homes painted in alternating pastel greens, blues, pinks and oranges, as had been promised six years earlier. Residents had been able to pick from two or three plans offered by different contractors, so their designs varied in small ways and people were adding gates, walls and backyard shacks to their plots. For a more personal touch, an enterprising resident had sold his skills as an artist and painted floral decorations next to the house numbers, which ran into the thousands.

The construction companies that had won the city's tender had in turn subcontracted construction to small teams of bricklayers and labourers, many of them Bardale residents. Angy herself had become involved in the construction business. I found her in a cinderblock building site in the next extension, wearing a pair of cement-splattered overalls, and joking with the men on her construction team. After being granted bail she was re-hired by Mandla Majola at the TAC. But then the TAC had a funding crisis and eventually they jettisoned her position. She immediately tried to replace her income through the housing project. Like others in Bardale, she had begged and borrowed the necessary equipment and people to lead a team for the Limpopo contractors. They gave her a house to build, approved of the work once two layers of bricks were laid and contracted her for a second, then a third, then a fourth. Eventually she'd built about nine houses in the neighbourhood, including her neighbour's home. And the contractors said they might be able to give her 50 in the next construction phase.

Angy enjoyed the work, enjoyed most of all doing what was considered men's work. If only she could get a bakkie, she'd be able to really expand, maybe even build for people outside the townships. She told me she wasn't missing the life of the activist, and was trying harder to keep herself out of contentious matters in Bardale. It wasn't easy. People showed up at her door. For example, there were the neighbours of the woman whose shack had burnt down, with her children locked inside it. There were rape accusations that were mishandled by the Family Violence unit, and there were abandoned children who needed a place to sleep. One night she helped organise a search party for a missing child and as the hours went by and their search yielded no results she grew more and more afraid, remembering affidavits she'd taken from mothers in Khayelitsha whose children hadn't been found alive. Angy began turning people away. There were many things she didn't want to be reminded of. Her tattoo had changed. She had asked an ex-con to do it, and his work was impressive. The wording 'Wrong Fully Acused' had been so artfully obscured by the face of a lion, you would never have assumed it had been anything else.

She shrugged when I raised the matter of the appeal. They

hadn't heard anything in a long time. Their lawyers had pulled out and they'd been handed to legal aid. King said he would come back when they got a court date, and the case had to be argued. Another highly respected silk had offered to argue with him, pro bono. But no one knew when the Appeal Court would hear it, and Angy believed it would remain in limbo forever. She and Isaac had long since stopped signing in for bail, and the police had done nothing about it. Isaac even went to the station to ask for his phone back – the one they were keeping as evidence – and, instead, they'd handed him Angy's passport. She took that as a message.

Other things had happened, and Angy and Isaac argued about how much to read into them. Policemen at the Blue Downs station had made ambiguous comments to people in the neighbourhood, using Angy's case as a warning not to be a trouble maker. Their house had been broken into again, almost four years to the day since the last burglary. The TV was stolen but nothing else was taken. They saw that as a threat, a warning. But what choice did they have but to live in uneasy proximity to the police?

The only person Angy was in active conflict with was Nomawethu, who had nominated herself for the position of 'Community Liaison Officer' for the housing project. Angy reckoned that Nomawethu hadn't realised it would disqualify her from being awarded building work. When she'd seen how well Angy was doing she'd become bitter and had spread a rumour that Angy had work because she'd slept with the contractor. (Nomawethu, for her part, mentioned no such problems when I spoke to her.) 'The last time I saw her,' Angy said, 'I told her "you don't bath, you smell and I hate you. Never talk to me again. And not for temporary, for permanent".'

Angy was diffident about the houses too. Some houses lacked ventilation vents, and in Angy's own house the plumbing had been so poorly installed that waste water from the toilet sometimes flowed through the kitchen sink.

Angy had contractors fix her plumbing and install a vent, but their home was not quite finished yet. They had repainted the internal rooms and laid tiles on the bare floor. The day I arrived, Isaac showed me the white border he'd painted around their door and the pattern of diamond tiles with which he was decorating their external walls. He retained his sense of humour. When I told him Advocate Ndlovu was moving up in the ranks and had been assigned as an assessor in a high-profile case at the High Court, he already knew. 'In fact,' he said, 'I thought the role would draw on one of his greatest strengths.'

'What's that?'

He broke into a mischievous smile: 'Silence.'

Before I left, Isaac and I stood at their gate looking at the field and the dramatic sky, azure blue patterned with thin clouds, as if it had been tie-dyed. This field was the one Isaac walked across after asking Angy to be his girlfriend. At the time she'd said, 'I'm going to pretend this never happened.' Those words left him burning with embarrassment, wishing he had an excuse never to return. This was the field where the man who stole the generator was almost beaten to death before being rescued by the police. A field of public shaming, private regret, and possible redemption. It was a field scattered with lone boots, with the glistering intestines of cassette tapes tangled in low bushes, and the glitter of sweet wrappers.

It was also looking different. A construction company from Limpopo had set up temporary offices at one end, a fenced-off area with stacked terracotta tiles inside and a mound of building waste outside. Isaac explained that there had been a huge battle over the field in the last few weeks – a series of land occupations, expulsions and counter-occupations, which were relatively contained within the neighbourhood until an Economic Freedom Fighters branch had caught wind of it. They encouraged their supporters to build shacks and the city had sent in armed eviction units. Once the field was cleared, a well-known Bardale man, seemingly in a bid to oust the local ANC councillor so he could take his job, led a small deputation to the community hall and, to everyone's dismay, threw a petrol bomb inside. (The hall was gutted and unusable.) In the aftermath, the construction company tentatively sought permission to erect their offices on the *hlabeni*, and after a long search for the responsible authority, had found out who owned it and its intended purpose. It was one island of land in a chain of *hlabenis* slated to become the long-awaited, almost mythical, railway line that would finally link Mfuleni to Cape Town. This was Bardale in a nutshell: houses gained, hall lost, integration with the city endlessly promised and always elusive.

I asked Isaac what it was like to live in a neighbourhood with Rara and Asavela, the only state witnesses who still lived in Bardale. He said they avoided each other. Asavela did anything she could not to make eye contact, looked into the distance, played on her phone. They didn't greet each other if they passed on the street.

'Don't you hate her?' I asked.

He was silent for a while, and then said, 'She wasn't an adult then. They were both still children. And she probably didn't really understand what she was agreeing to.'

Isaac had not yet found the lesson he wanted to learn from the case; it was not a good story to tell. He had been unemployed since leaving the SJC, and although he applied for jobs they all ended at the point where prospective employers did a background check. How could he explain away a murder conviction? Who would believe his story? He spent his days at home with nothing to do. Despite his friendliness, there was a palpable weariness about him, a sense of day-by-day diminishment. And it was not entirely surprising, when a few months later, I heard that he and Angy had separated. According to her, he'd started drinking and she'd kicked him out. 'He says to me that I should give him another chance,' Angy said, 'that it is because of the case and everything that happened because of it. But I also went through a trial, and I don't use those excuses.'

She and I met in the canteen of the new Isivivana building in Khayelitsha, where both the TAC and the SJC had offices. The SJC had refocused its safety campaign on discreet issues: litigation over the way communities were allocated police resources, and campaigning for street lighting for informal settlements. Working once again at the TAC offices, Angy passed many of her former colleagues in the corridors. She still had grudging respect for the TAC, but she made it clear she would have preferred to keep on building houses. Her construction career had hit a wall: when she'd explained her situation to the contractors they'd said they couldn't risk giving her a big consignment if she might go to jail at any point. So she'd returned to activism.

While she might not have claimed any 'excuses', friends said they saw the case take its toll in other ways. 'She's really crumbled at times, even though she's unbelievably resilient,' said Liat Davis, her colleague at the JSC. 'She's become very dark. She's way more pessimistic about what can be done. She used to be so committed. She used to have these ideas. And that's subsided to a large extent. She feels like this is the fight she was born into and now she has to suffer.' Angy herself told me her children complained that she'd become harsher. 'They tell me: "Don't talk to us like we're your Pollsmoor friends. This isn't prison."' And they, too, showed evidence of strain. One day Angy and Isaac were called in to see the school principal, because Hope had become hysterical and insisted, despite her elder sister's embarrassed denials, that her mother was dead.

When I asked Angy how she had changed, she said she had lost her passion. She didn't care about her job at the TAC. She did it as well as she could but it was just a job, a way to pay her bills. She would find a different job, a better-paying one, if she could, but with her criminal record the TAC were probably the only people who would employ her. And she avoided learning about problems in Khayelitsha, she turned away from anyone who asked her to help them in Mfuleni. As she said these things, she began, for the first time in our many conversations about everything that had happened since she was arrested, to cry. 'I'm not Angy any more,' she said.

ENDNOTES

Chapter Two

1. Much of the history and present day dynamics of Mfuleni were explained to me by an urban planner who had sent several years working on urban regeneration projects there for the City of Cape Town, which had involved years of community engagement and negotiation. A study conducted for this project – *Mfuleni Urban Node: Heritage Impact Assessment*, prepared for the Spatial Planning and Urban Design Department, City of Cape Town, October 2013 – provided details and historical overview.

2. It was also possible that their concerns were not just spiritual. The records of the Truth and Reconciliation Commission showed that in the late 1980s and early 1990s some policeman made a habit of shooting children in Khayelitsha, often in the back, often when they were not even involved in a protest but merely in the vicinity. See for example, the testimony of Sisana Mary Maphalane about the death of her son Lennox, Case Number CT00706.

Chapter Three

3. I was introduced to Rowan's aunt, Veronica by Nomawethu Mbewu. Veronica hadn't been a witness in the trial and hadn't been in Cape Town at the time of Rowan's murder. She granted me one interview about her family history and their dynamics, which I tried to connect with the court transcript, and a scant documentary record to recreate Rowan's background. It should be noted that Veronica was old and her memory was fallible. Nonetheless, I thought it better to include a personal account of Rowan's upbringing, even if it was not entirely reliable, rather than letting him be represented by his criminal record, and death, alone.

4. John Ndevu's thoughts, as related in this section, are drawn from my interview with his daughter Veronica.

5. There is a record in the national archives documenting a marriage between a John Ndevu and an Adelaide Ngqola that matches the timeline provided by Veronica, but I could not verify this.

6. Before South Africa became a republic in 1961, it was the Union of South Africa. The Union government was established in May 1910 by uniting four previously separate British colonies (the Cape, Natal, Transvaal and Orange River Sovereignty). The Transvaal and the Orange River Sovereignty had been the former Boer republics (the Orange Free State and South African Republic), until they were annexed by the British in 1902 after the Anglo Boer War. The Union government implemented the first apartheid laws, many of which

evolved from laws and practices already in place in the British colonies and Boer Republics.

7. This period of history is documented in Mabangalala: the rise of right-wing vigilantes in South Africa, Volume 10 of Occasional papers, University of the Witwatersrand, Centre for Applied Legal Studies by Nicholas Haysom.

Chapter Four

8. Another 50 000 people fled into Zimbabwe and Mozambique to escape the violence.

9. Mandla's affidavit can be found in the court papers for Case 21600/12 (pages 1522-1582). This was the first court claim lodged by SAPS to stop the commission. These are available on the commission's website.

10. Four men were arrested for her rape and murder. One of the suspects was Yanga Janet, a suspected gang-member, who had also shot another TAC member in the back that night. He was eventually acquitted. After Janet was acquitted from Nandipha's case, he and his cronies not only followed and threatened TAC members who were connected with the case, but stabbed one and broke into another's home. The police did not take this intimidation seriously, and the TAC had to apply for a court indict against Janet, and eventually used taxi drivers to help them arrest him themselves. The attempted murder docket against Janet – for the attempted murder of Makeke's friend – disappeared for three years, and when it miraculously re-appeared – minus important medical records – no charges were laid.

11. The last person to be formally executed by the South African criminal justice system was Solomon Ngobeni, in 1989. The death penalty was abolished in 1995, a move lauded as a symbol of South Africa's transition to democracy. There remains a popular desire to have it re-instated.

12. The *shoot-to-kill* voice is a reference to the many statements made by high-ranking police officials at public police events over the last 20 years that have exhorted police staff to use extreme violence to reduce crime. The first high-profile example of this is a speech by then Deputy Minister of Safety and Security, Susan Shabangu on 9 April 2008 where she told police officers not to worry about the consequences or regulations and 'shoot the bastards'.

13. Gavin Silber remembered that this discussion of strategy was always explicitly about the broader conditions of life in the townships: 'We knew that it had to focus on policing but it couldn't *just* focus on policing'. The campaign would ideally address the urban environment, too, as so many safety issues stemmed from the inadequacies of public transport, of street lighting, sanitation, and the difficulties emergency vehicles faced getting into informal settlements. They also, said Silber, wanted to get inaccessible information out of the police

force to produce a detailed understanding of what drove insecurity and poor policing.

14. These were the TAC, Equal Education, Free Gender, the Triangle Project, and Ndifuna Ukwazi. Many of them were started by, and staffed by at different times, a small set of people, principally including Zackie Achmat.

15. This affidavit has been edited more heavily than the others for length, and structure.

Chapter Seven

16. The other details of her life – her parents' religiosity, the politics, her family dynamics – I am confident are reasonably true. They are at the least plausible from the accounts of other people who lived in Khutsong at that time. Both of Angy's parents were dead and she did not keep in touch with the rest of her family, with whom, she said, there was some bad blood over the death of her twin brother.

Chapter Eight

17. The ANC held all the provinces between 2004 and 2009, after edging out the Inkhata Freedom Party in KwaZulu-Natal. This was read by some as a natural ascent to hegemony for the ruling party, and the defeat of identity-based political forces. The loss of the Western Cape upset this trajectory. It was also, probably, seen as a crushing symbolic loss because of the assets of the province: the Western Cape was also the country's second-most economically productive province, and Cape Town was and is the seat of parliament.

18. For more details see Pauw, Jacques, *The President's Keepers: Those Keeping Zuma in Power and out of Prison*, 2017, Cape Town: Tafelberg Publishers.

19. The murder rate is considered the most reliable indicator of overall levels of serious crime, as it is less sensitive to reporting errors than, for example, sexual assault or aggravated robbery.

20. This is still among the highest in the world, and many times the global average.

21. For an expert analysis and explanation of crime statistics in South Africa, see *A Citizen's Guide to Crime Trends in South Africa* by Kriegler, Anine and Shaw, Mark, 2016, Johannesburg: Jonathan Ball Publishers.

22. In 2017, the murder rate stabilised again. Criminologist Mark Shaw attributed the sudden rise to the expansion of drug markets in Cape Town, as well as an influx of guns into the city, which were sold from the police armoury by a corrupt policeman.

23. Aside from the dispute over the Khayelitsha Commission, you can trace this de-velopment through the conflict over the Western Cape Community Safety Bill.

24. The organisations had asked the premier to use a little-known power granted

by the Constitution to rope in other parts of the criminal justice system – the National Prosecuting Authority, the Department of Justice and Constitutional Development, the Department of Correctional Services, and the Department of Community Safety.

25. Gobodo-Madikizela, Pumla, *A Human Being Died That Night: A South African Story of Forgiveness*, 2004, Cape Town: New Africa Books.

26. This quote has been edited for concision.

27. It should be noted that the commission also documented several vigilante events that were not spontaneous and were carried out by small numbers of people in a premeditated fashion. But it is fair to say the large majority of vigilante murders have mob dynamics.

28. This survey was commissioned from a professional survey firm by the commission.

29. Herbst, CI, Tiemensa, M and Wadee, SA. 2015. 'A 10-year review of fatal community assault cases at a regional forensic pathology facility in Cape Town, South Africa'. South African Medical Journal, Vol 105, No 10, pp848-852.

30. Herbst provided some background to this study over the phone: she followed the determination of the cause of death that had been made by the original pathologist. This would have been made based on the injuries, as well the history relayed by the police to the forensic officer. In Herbst's case she was selecting those cases where the police had evidence or intelligence that the murder had been a vigilante attack. She might, she thought, have missed some cases, where bodies were found abandoned by roadsides, with multiple injuries, but there were no witness accounts to retrace events. But overall she believed she had a comprehensive picture of the murder victims coming into Tygerberg Hospital.

31. The police's own 'Bundu Courts' study contradicted this: only a handful, less than 3%, were linked to gangs. This study was prepared by the SAPS for the commission and was titled 'Bundu Courts Report'.

Chapter Nine

32. Of the accused, only Isaac was fully fluent in English, Afrikaans and Xhosa. Angy was lost in Afrikaans, and so were Azola and Chris, who were also not proficient enough in English to fully follow proceedings in that language.

33. His first statement claimed he saw Angy at the crèche, beating Rowan, but didn't mention Isaac, though the statement implicates Isaac, Azola and Chris in the assault at a different location. The statement also said he took Desiree to the scene of the assault, which he denied in court. There are also some omissions. The first statement does not mention that he witnessed the kidnapping – this was added into the second statement. So, too, was his sighting of the taxi

later that night, outside Angy's and then Azola's houses.

34. While Ndevu could not explain how he knew where the taxi drivers lived at the time he made his statement, Desiree said she remembered very clearly. She had gone with Roger and Rara to look at the house, and told her father about it.

Chapter Ten

35. The commission's analysis of the 171 complaints in their evidence revealed this. A small minority of the complaints were about police assault or brutality. A more significant minority complained about the police not responding to calls for help, but a greater number of these complaints were about the response people received once the police opened a case: lack of investigation, failure to keep families and victims updated, and police dockets not showing up at court.

Chapter Eleven

36. Its criteria, in full, were as follows: (i) the nature of the proceedings; (ii) the nature of the evidence; (iii) the purpose for which the evidence is tendered; (iv) the probative value of the evidence; (v) the reason why the evidence is not given by the person upon whose credibility the probative value of such evidence depends; (vi) any prejudice to a party which the admission of such evidence might entail; and (vii) any other factor which should in the opinion of the court be taken into account.

37. A few years later, however, there were some high-profile ones, all of them people in law enforcement who themselves who had tried to tackle corrupt figures in President Zuma's patronage network: Johan Booysen, Anwa Dramat, Robert McBride, and Johann van Loggerenberg.

38. As told by Antony Altbeker in *Fruit of a Poisoned Tree*, 2010, Johannesburg: Jonathan Ball Publishers.

39. As described in Jacob Dlamini's searing book, *Askari: A Story of Collaboration and Betrayal*, 2014, Johannesburg: Jacana.

Chapter Thirteen

40. It was Mohammed Abdullah, the paramedic, who narrated most of the story inside the ambulance.

41. It did not form part of either the defence's or the state's argument but Moller did also comment on whether the other injuries on his body – which appeared to be from an assault prior to the necklacing – could have been caused by a golf club wielded with the force one of the witnesses had demonstrated Isaac using. Moller said the marks on the head were not consistent with the marks a golf club would make, and if it had been used lower down on the body she would've expected to find evidence of bruising in the muscle layer.

42. This is the *Oxford Handbook of Trauma for Southern Africa*, by Andrew Nicol and Elmin Steyn, 2004, Oxford: Oxford University Press.

43. Steyn's full assessment was: 'If one assesses the eye opening, in this case the eyes could not open so therefore the patient scores one out of four. As far as the verbal response is concerned, [the best it can be scored] would be five and that would be for somebody who is well orientated and giving logical lucid speech. But in this case I would give three or a two or a four, depending when one assesses it, because three is for "inappropriate speech", two is for "incomprehensible" (so that is when somebody is groaning) and four is somebody who is "confused" (in other words there is some speech but it is not necessarily appropriate). So at the time when the paramedics were assessing this patient I would score verbal a three because there was speech but it wasn't always appropriate. And then for motor response it is a score out of six. The best, six, is for somebody who would move limbs or act on command. And in this case he withdrew, or made a purposeful movement in response to pain, and one would give him a five for that. So strictly speaking it would be 9 out of 15, or 10 at best, which is a reflection of significant, depressed level of consciousness. [...] To assess the motor parts of the Glasgow Coma Scale the person has to respond on command. So if he is told don't remove the mask, then he should not remove the mask or if he is told lift up your arm, he should lift up his arm.'

44. Steyn conceded that he must have been awake to pull the needle out, 'but when a person actually grabs a needle and pulls it out, it is a reflection of confusion... So in fact what he is saying here he is actually proving this patient was *not* of a normal level of consciousness by the fact that he pulled the needle out...a person who is fully awake shall say "Eina" or he may even swear. But he won't pull out the medical drip that he needs, he won't pull it out.' Rowan would also not necessarily have perceived the prick as painful: his nerve endings had been burnt away. And even if it was painful, 'we all know that a needle causes pain and yet we wilfully subject ourselves to treatment when it involves a needle. It is only when we are drunk, confused, head injured or a child that one would pull out that needle.'

45. The diagnosis of shock is not entirely straightforward as there are several compounding or mitigating variables, including age. The most reliable test is a blood gas lactate test, but this was not done and was not mentioned in testimony.

Chapter Fourteen

46. Specialised units such as the Organised Crime Unit were considered by many to be highly effective, allowing the police to concentrate skills and expertise and focus on complex investigations, so when National Commissioner, Jackie Selebi,

disbanded them in 2006, many people within and outside the SAPS reacted with dismay. Redelinghuys was out already by then.

47. Crime Intelligence has been perhaps the most abused function of the police, whose resources have frequently been turned towards factional battles. For more on this trend see Jonny Steinberg: 'Policing, state power, and the transition from apartheid to democracy: A new perspective', *African Affairs*, Volume 113, Issue 451, 1 April 2014. The use of Crime Intelligence to fight factional battles has also given corrupt police the cover to run 'side gigs' in organised criminal worlds. Police Commission Jackie Selebi claimed Glen Agliotti, a middleman to gangsters, as his informant in order to excuse their frequent meetings and communications. Gauteng Head of Crime Intelligence, Joey Mabasa, had made the same claim about Radovan Krejcir, a Czech mafioso, who had allegedly bribed him in exchange for extensive police protection. This was an old story stretching back even further into the past. For instance, the history of the relationship between Western Cape gangs and the police force is a history of gang leaders recruited to inform on the liberation movement, and of an enmeshment between source and operative, that had time and time again, raised questions of who was running whom. Often 'informant' has served as a fig leaf to mask a corrupt relationship.

48. Standing Order 101 is the policy that enables members of the public to submit complaints that police officers have failed to provide the services they are mandated to (as opposed to complaints to IPID, where the complainant alleges that police officers have broken the law).

49. A South African police docket is divided into three sections: Section A contains statements of witnesses, expert reports and documentary evidence, Section B contains internal reports, memoranda and correspondence, and Section C is the investigation diary.

50. From the *Mail and Guardian*, 'Khayelitsha violence: State mum over activists' arrest', 26 Oct 2012.

51. Here, as at several points in the trial, Henney, reluctantly, conceded that if no police witness could explain it, he'd have to admit they had been doctored.

52. Mrs Nobunto Sifuba, who represented the residents of Strand when they were moved from their informal settlement, had recorded the allocation of all their plots in Bardale. She was later called to confirm that the address in the hearsay statements was the incorrect one, and to establish how important the numbers were. As some of the streets were unnamed, and the houses didn't have conventional numbers, these erf numbers were what residents regularly used as their address when they bought a SIM card, registered for a government service, or took out an account in a store.

53. This is contained in Crime Intelligence Protection Services disciplinary case 16/2012 number 7010430-1, Sergeant AP Tshicila. Tshicila told the court he'd never seen this letter, even though it came from the man acting as his representative.

54. Personal correspondence with the SJC.

Chapter Fifteen

55. Common Purpose is a controversial but often-employed piece of legal machinery adopted from English law, which attributes joint responsibility for the consequences of a crime to everybody who has been involved, no matter what their role. Under Common Purpose, the getaway driver could be held guilty for the murder of a bank teller by one of his fellow robbers, even if he had no idea that the robber's gun was loaded or that he intended to use it. In South Africa it has a particularly colourful history as a tactic of the apartheid state to send protestors to the gallows, as in the case of the Sharpeville Six. Since the end of apartheid it has still enjoyed a robust career in ordinary criminal trials, and in one of the more bizarre and depressing applications, in 2012 the state made a bid (subsequently abandoned) to charge 259 striking miners at Marikana for the murder of 34 of their colleagues – at the hands of the police. Common purpose can be justified on two grounds: prior agreement and active association. The first wasn't open to the state as they didn't have evidence that the attack on Rowan was planned. Cell-phone records, when they were finally obtained, showed that Angy had regularly been in touch with Azola – they were friends and colleagues – but not on the day of the murder. And the accounts of the eyewitnesses made it seem as if the assault occurred spontaneously. But the second route granted more leeway. The state would only have to argue that given that they were involved in the assault and also seen leaving in the taxi, and given that necklacing is a foreseeable conclusion to a vigilante attack, then they knew what would happen to Rowan, even if it couldn't be proven that they were there. They would then be 'actively associated' with his murder.

Chapter Sixteen

56. Azola and Chris also gave testimony on their arrests. Both had been arrested at home by two policemen, one black and one white, who had told them to leave their belts and shoelaces at home. They were taken straight to the station and neither took part in an identity parade. Their versions differed in small, but perhaps important, respects from those of John Ndevu and Desiree (whose versions also contradicted each other). Ndevu and Desiree both claimed they had been inside the houses of the accused at different points, and that while there they had heard Azola (Ndevu's account) or Chris (Desiree's account) say 'Hayi Roy!' when the police officer woke Azola/Chris. This was presented as an incriminating utterance. Both Azola and Chris denied either of them were

there. Instead they had both seen a female in a pink gown there, but in Azola's case this was 'a small child' standing on the opposite corner from the van; for Chris it was a woman, perhaps in her 30s or 40s, who was not Desiree Jack, hiding behind the van.

Chapter Eighteen

57. The other trademarks of Ndevu's honesty are that he did not try to hide Rowan's criminal activities, and that, according to Isaac, he did not 'take sides' when Rowan was confronted about the theft of the television. He also hadn't tried to 'adapt or turn his version so that it could coincide with that of Desiree. This he could have done very easily.' But Ndevu had testified first, and Desiree's evidence had shifted substantially towards corroborating his version – now including a murder weapon – than her statement before then had indicated.

58. Henney was adamant that Desiree 'did not influence' Asavela: 'Although this was highly irregular and inexcusable behaviour on the part of Muthien, there is no indication that Asavela's evidence was influenced by her or the other way around.'

59. In this case: 'He also could have embellished or found support for his evidence without being caught out when he said he only became aware of Desiree again after the deceased was placed in the taxi, by saying that Desiree was with him to back up his version.'

60. As when, for example, Henney said: 'When the prosecutor then asked her why did she not just go to the police with this suspicion, she answered that Accused 2 already called the police. She answered this while she knew that he did not contact or call the police because he suspected the deceased.' Yet Isaac had called and tried to open a case – this was clearly part of his evidence, but the police had refused to open it because he didn't have the serial number of the TV. He also argued that she did not dispute that she called Redelinghuys to complain about Rowan's release – but she had. She in fact said she had called Damoyi instead, in part to complain about Redelinghuys. But without referring to the details, Henney said her account was 'not convincing'.

Chapter Nineteen

61. The Number is over a hundred years old, and was begun by Nongoloza, a bandit who commanded a gang of thieves called the Ninevites. The gang terrorised the workers who flocked to Johannesburg during the gold-rush years. Nongoloza was eventually arrested and spent decades as a prisoner. His life became mythologised and underpins the secret traditions and symbols of the Number. This prison gang split into three 'lines': 26s, 27s, and 28s, each with a strict and complex hierarchy. The 26 gang is associated with money, smuggling in prison and accruing as much wealth as possible. The 28s are

the warrior line, and must fight on behalf of all the groups. The 27s are the guardians of the gang law. Historically, induction into the gangs required a profound indoctrination into its history, and a highly stylised performance of its rituals. But in the last twenty years there had been a pollution' of the Number through an integration with the street gangs of the Cape Flats. These street gangs became highly lucrative commercial entities in the same period and were able to buy influence, rather than earn it, inside prison.

62. 'The line distinguishing men from women, the active from the passive partner, is drawn repeatedly, obsessively,' writes Jonny Steinberg in *The Number: One Man's Search for Identity in the Cape Underworld and Prison Gangs*, 2004, Johannesburg: Jonathan Ball Publishers . 'To be the active partner one must be an *ndota*. In other words, one has to stab, one has to be beaten to a pulp without crying out, one has to sit in a dank cell for weeks and eat a saltless diet, one has to emerge from *agter die berge* strong. To be a woman, one must be nothing: a being who can never join the Number, who must walk barefoot and never leave the cell without permission, who must not conduct business in the public world of the prison.'

63. These female gangs fight each other, and in 2012 a group of Vatos Babes and Vuros Babes committed a spate of robberies. Increasingly women in street gangs are involved in robberies and shootings. A new body of research highlights the role played by female assassins in Cape Town's deadly gang wars: see Mark Shaw's *Hitmen for Hire: Exposing South Africa's Underworld*, 2017, Johannesburg: Jonathan Ball Publishers.

Chapter Twenty-One

64. A mitigation is supposed to inform the highly subjective process by which a judge arrives at the sentence for a crime. Henney's career had spanned both the imposition of minimum sentencing and its removal – minimum sentences are now more like 'guidelines' so he would have had more discretion over whether to be lenient or harsh. Mitigation hearings typically present evidence about disability, illness and family conditions that could move a judge to impose a lighter sentence or recommend that special arrangements be made for a prisoner. Social workers visit the offender's family, and speak to the victim or victim's family about their wishes, eventually compiling reports that are presented to court. The defence can also call people to testify about the characters of the guilty parties. One social worker, Astrid Klaase, was assigned to both Angy and Isaac and another, Judy Radloff, to Azola and Chris.

65. Nomwethu Marawu, Azola's mother, first cleared up the social worker's report: Azola was not an errant father, he had supported four children from two marriages, and they had all lived in Dunoon until his arrest and trial, when his first wife had gone back to the Eastern Cape to be supported by her family. The mother of his youngest two children, to whom he was not married, was

working and studying part time, and so the children lived with Nomwethu, her husband and her mentally unstable elderly father. They all had to get by on her meagre income of about R700 a week, which she gained by selling clothes and food on the side of the road.

66. They had nonetheless, Zackie Achmat pointed out, continued to support her. A few days before sentencing the SJC had held a fundraiser where they raised R50 000. Joel had also submitted another bid to Amnesty. They put forward another R350 000, which settled the arrears for the main trial. King then agreed that he'd argue an appeal pro bono. The RAITH Foundation also undertook to raise fees for a possible appeal. Since the fraud incident, Achmat had refused to be personally involved in any future fundraising nor did he want the TAC involved, but wouldn't discourage people from making donations.

67. Henney had later come to believe that evidence – a note by a policeman – wasn't drawn from Rowan's own words, but drew on the story presented by Angy and Mzinyathi, the man who'd called Ta Ager on speakerphone. It was not, then, really a confession.

Index

Acknowledgements

I give great thanks to the Miles Morland Foundation, whose support was indispensable to writing this book. To Ester Levinrad at Jonathan Ball, who believed in this book even when it was a hot mess, and my editor, Mike Nicol, who guided me with implacable calm through the revisions that have brought it to its current form.

To readers of parts or the whole of this manuscript, Sam Beckbessinger, Bongani Kona, Paul McNally, and Lesley Lawson, who provided invaluable advice. To Brenda Goldblatt, for strengthening my nerve. Max and Cormac, without whose love, support and advice this book would never have been finished, and probably never begun. To Kim, my love, for being there, remarkably, right from the start, and still at the end.